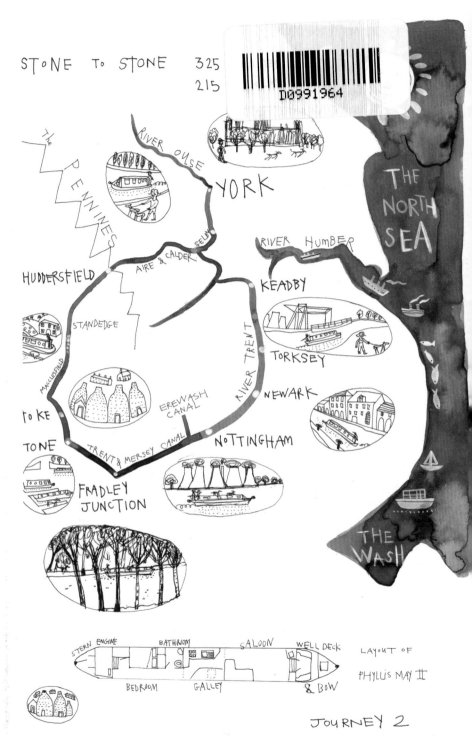

STONE TO STONE  325
215

THE PENNINES

RIVER OUSE

YORK

THE NORTH SEA

AIRE & CALDER

SELBY

RIVER HUMBER

HUDDERSFIELD

KEADBY

STANDEDGE

RIVER TRENT

TORKSEY

MACCLESFIELD

EREWASH CANAL

NEWARK

STOKE

STONE

TRENT & MERSEY CANAL

NOTTINGHAM

FRADLEY JUNCTION

THE WASH

STERN  ENGINE  BATHROOM  SALOON  WELL DECK

LAYOUT OF

PHYLLIS MAY II

BEDROOM  GALLEY  & BOW

JOURNEY 2

# NARROW DOG TO WIGAN PIER

www.transworldbooks.co.uk

# Narrow Dog to Wigan Pier

Terry Darlington

BANTAM PRESS

LONDON · TORONTO · SYDNEY · AUCKLAND · JOHANNESBURG

TRANSWORLD PUBLISHERS
61–63 Uxbridge Road, London W5 5SA
A Random House Group Company
www.transworldbooks.co.uk

First published in Great Britain
in 2012 by Bantam Press
an imprint of Transworld Publishers

Many thanks to the editor of the *Western Telegraph* for permission to
quote from Vernon Scott's book *Inferno 1940*.

Many thanks to City Lights Books for permission to include the poem 'It was a face
which darkness could kill' by Lawrence Ferlinghetti, from the collection *Pictures of the
Gone World*, included in *A Coney Island of the Mind* in 1958.

A CIP catalogue record for this book
is available from the British Library.

ISBNs 9780593067673 (hb)
9780593067680 (tpb)

This book is a work of non-fiction based on the life, experiences and recollections of
the author. In some limited cases names of people, places, dates, sequences or
the details of events have been changed to protect the privacy of others. The author
has stated to the publishers that, except in such minor respects, the contents of this
book are true.

Addresses for Random House Group Ltd companies outside the UK
can be found at: www.randomhouse.co.uk
The Random House Group Ltd Reg. No. 954009

The Random House Group Limited supports the Forest Stewardship Council (FSC®),
the leading international forest-certification organization. Our books carrying the
FSC label are printed on FSC®-certified paper. FSC is the only forest-certification
scheme endorsed by the leading environmental organizations, including Greenpeace. Our
paper procurement policy can be found at www.randomhouse.co.uk/environment.

Typeset in 13/15pt Bembo by
Falcon Oast Graphic Art Ltd.

Printed in the UK by
CPI Group (UK) Ltd, Croydon, CR0 4YY

2 4 6 8 10 9 7 5 3 1

To our grandchildren

Bethan, Rhiannon, Max, Leila, Cicely, Greg, Felix

Special thanks to our agent David Smith of Annette Green
Authors' Agency, who suggested I write this book

*. . . love does not consist in gazing at each other
but in looking together in the same direction.*

Antoine de Saint-Exupéry

# CONTENTS

# CHAPTER ONE

# STONE

## *The Grimpen Mire*

*What did it feel like when you
watched your boat burn up?*

*Jim Francis is dead – Two whippets are a conspiracy – Jesus Christ would want me to go to Europe – The Loch Ness Monster – Peter Scott was quite sure there was something there – You are probably clinically insane – The Creature from the Black Lagoon – Time to hand in our chips – The* Phyllis May *began to roar like a Bunsen burner – Our poor buckled* Phyllis May

*Jim Francis is dead*
*You know Jim*
*Jim Francis*
*Well he's dead*

*Arnott told me*
*On the towpath*
*How is Jim I said*
*Dad is dead he said*

*I mean it's ridiculous*
*Jim gone*
*He had so much power in him*
*He leaves so much space*

*When I was in trouble*
*Jim said Come here*
*And he took an envelope and a pencil*
*And worked it out in a minute*

*You can't just cancel someone like Jim Francis*
*He was too big too clever too kind*
*But Jim Francis is dead*
*It's ridiculous*

Just look down the running club, I said to Monica – Haddon and Vernon and Jack and Doctor Ian – all gone. My coach told me in seventy-two that no one who had run a marathon had ever died. Now all my mates are dead, or they have got palpitations, or strokes, or third sets of hips. Our generation thought we had got it all worked out, with our marathoning and our communes, and our home brew and our rock and roll and our poetry.

Every generation thinks it has got it all worked out, said Monica. Now let me concentrate on this bloody dog.

Jim and his new friend can have little puppies, I had said to the Lady Who Knows about Whippets. Little maggots, all wriggly. Little darlings.

You are a very foolish person, said the Lady Who Knows about Whippets. Breeding whippets requires knowledge and intelligence, neither of which you possess. Whippets are driven by forces beyond our understanding and an entire male and a female whippet in a household would lead to destruction and despair. In any case your Jim is ten – too old. He won't know what to do because he has never done it. He will fail and all will be sadness and pain.

Jim, fail? He's a man's dog – a manly dog – a proper dog – no problemo in that department. Jim fail? Never.

He will fail, said the Lady. But we have available a spayed rescue bitch that no one has managed to keep – an excellent dog. Just because she can jump a seven-foot wall from a standing start she has sometimes been a difficulty. But you are retired and have got nothing to do and can give her the attention she needs. If you can't manage her you can give her back – it will be her fourth home and she isn't two yet.

Jess is a red brindle with a white flash on her chest and a white muzzle and a white tip to her tail and white socks. She is a shade taller than Jim, and thinner. No potter could catch her brindling in his glaze, no sculptor her grace. Beside her the beautiful Jim, the pedigree Jim, looks like Edward Heath.

When I was a little boy I had an encyclopaedia which explained that a candle fired at a plank would go straight through. There was a photograph to prove it. I remember it every time Jess runs towards me at forty miles an hour.

Jess has no concept of going for a walk – she just runs away. In fact she is half wild, and leads Jim on, forming a pack to raise hell against every dog, cat, rabbit or squirrel that thinks it might share the earth with them. One whippet is a liability – two are a conspiracy.

We got Jess mainly to be a friend for Jim. They would

not grieve so much in kennels if they were two. But for Jim it was yet another betrayal and he would lie and stare at us accusingly and leave the room if Jess appeared.

It was a year before Jess realized that she had a home and her face opened and her brown eyes softened and she began to look straight at us. It was not an easy year but Monica and I had fallen in love with her and Jim was beginning to realize she was not going away.

This dog, said Monica, has demonstrated every bad habit a dog can possess. She has been shut up in a small garden all her life and never made any proper relationships or been given any intelligent training. Some fool has taught her not to accept a pork scratching until you say the word.

Say the word, I said.

I don't know the word, said Monica.

Pieces of eight! I said, Shazam! Open Sesame! Jumping Jack Flash! Edward Heath! European Monetary Union! A piece of cheese for old Ben! New custom-blended Blue Sunoco! Elementary, my dear Watson! Give me the moonlight, give me the girl. . .

Shut up, said Monica.

Monica and Jess looked at each other in despair.

I am now an established WRITOR, I said to Monica later – the oldest young writer in Britain. I have written two bestsellers. People stop me in the street and shout to me across the cut. They call me Terry and want to be my friend. They write from all over the world. Only yesterday a chap in New Zealand emailed to tell me that his father read *Narrow Dog to Carcassonne* before he died. A lady wrote to say she read a little of *Indian River* every night and then went to sleep. Then there was the girl who wet herself on the train laughing at Jim. People say they have read my books many times and ask Where is the next one? I must follow my destiny and produce another work. I owe it to society. We'll have an expedition – another impossible dream, like crossing the Channel or sailing down to the Gulf of Mexico. Perhaps Holland or Germany. I shall picture the colourful characters and the waterside cities and address the main historical issues of the twentieth century and Jim will get up to mischief and so will Jess and I will tell funny stories and it will be the Narrow Dog Trilogy.

If you are looking for someone to climb up and down the lock ladders of Northern Europe with a rope between her teeth, said Monica, then I suggest you try the lonely hearts section of the *New York Review of Books*. Some mad old Harvard professor might give you a try. Some ill-favoured skinny Boston babe. Me, I had enough of it when we went to Carcassonne. What's the point of spending fifty grand to wear ourselves out and risk our lives and our health and not even be sure to get the money back? Why don't you write books at home like everyone else? It's because you can't get it up unless you are fighting the current in some desolate sound, pursued by carnivorous reptiles. Why don't we stop all this and live out our days in peace? God knows there are few enough days left.

I am an arteest, Monica. Without my art I will wither away. What do I say to the fan who read a bit of my book every day and it cheered him up when he had cancer? What do I say to the young people who send me pictures of their whippets and say More Jim please? I know I am seventy-five and there is not much time but all the more reason. It's like Jesus Christ said about the talents – if you've got it, use it. You can't argue with Jesus Christ. I bet Jesus Christ would want me to go to Europe.

Write a novel, said Monica. Write a novel like everyone else. You said you were going to do something about the Loch Ness Monster. Go to Inverness and do some research – you can get there in a day. Then sit at home and write a novel.

No one ever spotted the Loch Ness Monster quicker than me. I had just arrived on the shore of the loch and she rolled out, her eye glinting inside a wave, her back oily black. Twenty yards away her tail brushed the surface from underneath, then she turned on her side and was gone. Whether it was really Nessie or a wave reflected from a far shore I never found out, because I did not see her again, but I thought it was a sign, and my novel *Narrow Dog and the Loch Ness Monster* would be the best thing I ever did.

The story had begun to come to me when our friends Pauline and Ray on their narrowboat *Lady Rose* told us how they had spotted a corpse in the fens. The shoulders first, which stuck out like a sort of bag, then the hair. OmiGod the hair.

The police questioned them for three days. How long had they known the deceased? How did they know the body was there? Why did they not report it sooner?

Why did they make these mistakes on this form? Why are their navigation lights not working? Pauline and Ray decided never to report anything to the police ever again, even if they came upon a bus full of Girl Guides upside down under a bridge. *Horseman, pass by* – that's our motto now, said Ray.

But what a story, I said, what a story. And I went away and a plot grew in my mind, starting with the discovery of poor Ben McFee in Loch Ness.

*They bumped alongside and Grandad prodded the bag with the boathook and it was soft but something underneath it was heavy. He shoved and hooked but the bag would not turn over. Ginger took up the other boathook and they heaved and tugged and the bag partly turned then it slipped back and Grandad swore but then they got it firm and turned it over and held it.*

*Oh My God, said Grandad.*

*The thin beard was red as life, but the skin on the face was china white, and the eyes bulged and stared, and the lips were drawn back from the teeth in a terrible smile.*

*Oh My God, said Grandad. It's Ben McFee!*

My studio is up in the roof but I could have been anywhere. I could have been on a plinth in Trafalgar Square. I was possessed. Time meant nothing. My novel had me in its jaws and raced away down the labyrinthine ways of mine own plot. The heroine on the brink of womanhood, the fearless Ginger her friend, the *Phyllis May* banging through a storm on Loch Ness, the villainous Russians, Jim, the mega-yacht, the Monster. I was having a lovely time. I even got the Red Arrows into it.

I used to be married to an adventurer sort of fellow, said Monica. We went away a lot and did expeditions and I had to dodge alligators and shiver in cathedral locks, but at least I used to see him quite often. Now he goes up into his studio and comes down late at night gibbering about temperature gradients and plesiosauruses and food stocks and shoals of fish called bleak and how Peter Scott was quite sure there was something there, and Sonic Drogues and Monsters dancing in the moonlight. I know I complained about the adventures but this is as bad. Any more of this and I shall start to give some encouragement to my little friend down the bridge club who brings me runner beans.

You are a miserable little woman, I said, ancient person of my heart. But have no fear. It is finished. *Consummatum est.* I am sending it to my editor and my agent – they will be delighted. They will be astonished. Best thing I have ever done. Now I can carry on writing bestsellers and stay at home – no more dicing with death, no more impossible sea crossings, no more paperwork to be organized by poor Mon with brutish foreigners. I am not a travel hack now – I am a literary Figgar, pushing the omelette of the human imagination and painting the subtlest colours of the heart. In my hands I hold three hundred and fifty pages of deathless prose. Pass the stamps and the bubble envelopes – like Chaucer said, whom I so much resemble – *go, litel bok.*

It did not take long for my editor and my agent to come back.

They both said the novel was bollocks.

For three months of the year the sun does not rise in Stone Staffordshire. It grudges a cold glow behind a fog that hangs at a hundred feet, and in the middle of the afternoon it goes somewhere else.

After Christmas the pubs are empty and everyone has a cold – the one where someone is standing on your face. All you can do is wait for the spring – it's worth it, but it is a long wait and many go mad. It's worse if you have lost your job.

I am old and I've been around and have lots of memories. I have been much blessed but like most of us I have made a lot of mistakes, suffered my share of humiliations, caused unfair grief to the innocent, and generally ballsed up any amount of stuff. Now it was all coming back.

Sometimes you are moored on the side of the cut and you have no fenders because they came off at the last lock. When a boat comes by you swing against the side, but not with a thud – with a hard knock that runs up your whole body. That is how the memories were returning – my mental fenders had gone and I was crashing against the follies of my past.

Othello's occupation's gone, I said. A week ago I was famous and now I'm just another writer who can't get published. I am a wreck upon the sand. There's only one thing worse in the universe. People who see me cross the street. And no one is answering my letters.

In the publishing industry it is accepted that a communication can be ignored if a reply requires any thought or commitment. By comparison the brutish worlds of international manufacturing and consultancy operate with oriental courtesy. Across the years I had fought and won some ground but now my letters and emails were again being diverted to Father Christmas, who had better things to do than write back to a chap who didn't believe in him.

I saw rudeness and snubs all round. I got caught up in a correspondence with some Good Ole Girl who decided I had insulted the state of North Carolina because I said it made me think of how the earth looked at the dawn of creation. The worst thing was I was *caring* about all this.

I knew I was losing contact with reality and tried to look into my own mind. I was an arteest, and I knew arteests were keen to be loved and admired because they had been deprived of attention and approval when young. I had a damaged personality, but this was part of being a writer, and I must accept it and enjoy the good bits. There were few better bits than looking at a page and knowing it was good and you had made something that no one else had ever made, no one else could ever make, that had not been there before.

We have had two thousand letters, said Monica, and two have been hostile. The fans are lovely, and they are thrilled when we reply to them. You are depressed. We both worked too hard on the voyage down the Intracoastal Waterway and now you have exhausted yourself with your Loch Ness Monster. You are suffering a reactive depression. In fact you are probably clinically insane. Why don't you go for a walk with the dogs?

Walking is very good for depression. There won't be any mud on the towpath – it's too cold. Look at dear little Jess, how she loves you, and your Jim. Look at their little faces. Let me put their coats on. Here, take these pork scratchings with you.

The towpath was covered with ice and Jim and Jess pulled me along, skidding. I commanded them to come to heel and they took no notice.

Oh well there is a good hedge here. Should be safe enough – what is the point of a whippet if it can't run? Young hearts, run free.

Jess is faster than Jim and was well ahead as the dogs took off south from Aston Lock at forty miles an hour. Aston Lock which looks out over all the world. *What spires, what farms, are those?* Aston Lock where all our adventures have begun.

I tried not to think about my latest letters to Santa, about the fools wasting my time with a proposed film project, about the bastards who had tried to steal my ideas and my staff from my business in the eighties, about that job applicant I was rude to in Uttoxeter forty years ago, about the literary festival down south that didn't know if they wanted me because I was not really important, and the fog in the sky pressed down on me and I had a sore throat.

A blizzard of barking.

I ran towards the noise. The dogs had broken through the hedge. I could just see over the snowy branches – Jess was chasing a sheep, and Jim was hard behind. As I watched, the sheep fell off the bank on to the ice of a large pond and Jess leapt after her. They faced each other and Jim stood on the bank raising hell.

The sheep fell over and Jess grabbed her by the neck and began to shake her. Wool began to fly about. Jim jumped down on to the ice and both dogs began to threaten the sheep. The sheep called for help at the top of her voice. The noise was terrible.

I had a whistle and blew and blew and shouted and shouted. I was only ten yards away but the bank was steep. Jim came to me reluctantly and I tied him to a bush, where he barked like a fool and began to gnaw at his lead.

The sheep was spinning slowly on her side as Jess plucked her like a turkey. Jess would pull out some wool then fall over and scramble back up and come in again. There was blood on the sheep's neck.

A dark presence at my shoulder – a big chap. This was private land and he had to be the farmer. He probably had a gun and was going to kill us all. Hello, he said.

OmiGod, I said. Is that your sheep?

Yes, he said.

Shoot the dog, I said. It's your right. Give me the gun and I'll shoot her myself. OmiGod. This is not acceptable. It's all my fault – I have an untrained dog. I am so ashamed. OmiGod. What can I do? I'll give you money.

Whippets are not supposed to bark much but Jim sounded like a hound of hell. Jess was barking too and skidding around and the sheep was getting more bald.

The light was going out behind the clouds. The snow was blowing off the bushes. The dogs, the sheep and I were steaming.

The farmer went away and came back with a pole about twelve feet long. It just reached the sheep. I poked the sheep and it spun away. I tried to reach Jess but couldn't. I was shouting and shouting and whistling and whistling and waving a pork scratching and the dogs barked and barked and Jess fell over and got back up and went for the sheep again. It was almost dark.

I'm going in, I said.

Careful, Gaffer, said the farmer.

The bank was steep but the snow cushioned me as I slid down, kicking at the ice to break it, and sank up to my chest. I was so relieved to be doing something to end this standoff from hell that I did not notice the cold. I did notice the mud – it was like standing in two feet of rotting treacle. I swept with the pole across the top of the ice and pushed the sheep nearer the side, then against the bank and the farmer grabbed it and put it on the bank and it ran off and the farmer caught Jess.

I stood armpit-deep in the stinking mud and water and ice. It'll die, I called up to the farmer – the shock, the bleeding. OmiGod it's all my fault – I haven't trained my dogs. You'll have to tell the police and they will come and kill them both.

Bit of blue, she'll be fine, Gaffer. Whippets, eh? Used to have a greyhound cross – the one they call the long dog. Lovely nature.

I wriggled up out of the pond like a marine dinosaur that had decided to evolve as a land animal but was not sure it was all going to work out. Perhaps I had used up all my blood sugar in grief or perhaps the bank under the ice was impossibly slippery but it must have taken five minutes. The farmer pulled me up the last foot of ice and slime. You are a gentleman, I said.

I got to Jim just as he snapped his lead. You get home, Gaffer, said the farmer.

It was four o'clock in the afternoon and night had fallen. The ice cracked on my clothes. The dogs shivered and whined and stumbled, frost on their muzzles and ice on their coats. When we came up against anyone I hid like a spy. We worked our way from corner to corner. I smelt like the Grimpen Mire.

It is not unknown for me to drop in at the Star or Langtry's on the way home with the dogs so Monica had not been worrying, but her eyes widened as I stood at the kitchen door.

Black mud up to my thighs, with a few highlights of dead vegetation. I was cased in ice, and my Breton sailor's cap was topped with snow like a birthday cake. The dogs looked like monstrous rats made of sugar with bright eyes staring. Jess had blood on her muzzle. Both were trembling and whining.

You look like the Creature from the Black Lagoon! You smell terrible! And the dogs – why are they covered with ice? Poor Jim looks exhausted and Jess looks half dead. What have you been doing? How can you do this to poor innocent creatures? Have you had an accident? Got into a fight in the Red Lion? I can't trust you even to go for a walk. You went mad and tried to drown them!

You must be patient, Mon, I said. Things are not going well for me just now. In fact I think it is time to consider our position on a number of matters.

I think it is time you got out of my kitchen, said Monica. Go into the garden and dump those clothes and get the dogs' coats off. Poor little devils. Trying to drown the dogs!

Let me have a shower and I'll tell you what happened, I said, and this evening we will have a serious talk.

I'm not coping, Mon – our lovely dogs, and I get them into dreadful life-threatening and humiliating situations. I can't get a book published. I am not at all sure I want to go off on damn silly expeditions any more. We'll sell the *Phyllis May*. I'm bored with boating. I'm bored with writing. I'm bored with everything. I was stuck in a swamp and that is just how I feel – stuck in the bloody Grimpen Mire like Sherlock Holmes in *The Hound of the Baskervilles*.

You are not happy unless you are writing, and Sherlock Holmes did not get stuck in the Grimpen Mire – he had more sense.

But what can I write? I don't want to write and no one wants my new book anyway.

*They fle from me that sometyme did me seke*
*With naked fote stalking in my chambre.*
*I have sene them gentill, tame, and meke*
*That nowe are wyld and do not remembre*
*That sometyme they put theimself in daunger*
*To take bred at my hand*

But what have we got to prove, Mon? We have three lovely kids and lots of grandchildren. We made a success of our business and have written two bestsellers and run fifty marathons and know how to make elderberry wine. We are seventy-five for God's sake. What's the point? We've been there, done that, and are wearing life's T-shirt. Time to hand our chips in over the green baize and pocket our winnings and drain our glasses and push back our chairs and walk off down the street between the flashing neon lights, skipping over the puddles, never to be seen again. To everything there is a season – a time to cast away stones and a time to gather stones together. A time to be born and a time to die. To die, to sleep . . .

What do you mean, *to die*? Go to Switzerland and commit suicide? But we are not ill! We can sell the *Phyllis May* but I don't want to commit suicide – bugger that.

But there is nothing left remarkable beneath the visiting moon.

I've got my bridge and the church.

And I've got nothing.

There is something dreamy about the way fireflies move – in slow arcs and as you focus on them the dark hedges blur behind them. Those camping holidays in France, and then of course the glow-worms in the hedge on the steep hill up to Cosheston in the war. But the glow-worms were a green light and the fireflies in Brittany purest white, not like these, which are the colour of blood. And they are speeding up now and whirling round and the door of the *Phyllis May* exploded and she began to roar like a Bunsen burner and it was no good thinking of childhood or holidays – here we were down at Canal Cruising boatyard and the *Phyllis May* was in flames and it was a winter night and the boat next door was going down and there must have been twenty firemen in yellow jackets and why the hell weren't they trying to save something, instead of standing back and hosing water up and over and on to the roof and shouting?

An electrical fire – the dolt in the next boat had gone to London leaving his boat unsafe. His boat had gone, of course, and a third boat which was the home and held all the possessions of a chap who lived in the boatyard.

Are you insured? I asked.

No.

Next morning we came down again and I held Monica close. The shell of the *Phyllis May* was buckled and in the bottom there was a foot of charcoal. The smell of oil and paint and smoke.

> *All her bright golden hair*
> *Tarnished with rust,*
> *She that was young and fair*
> *Fallen to dust.*

What did you feel like when you watched your boat burn up? asked a journalist. I thought it was the silliest question anyone had ever asked me, apart from the lady in North Carolina who wanted to know if the world looked very broad after a day in a narrowboat crossing Pamlico Sound.

There were a lot of journalists and TV cameras. My son Clifford had emailed from Boston Massachusetts to say we were the second item on the BBC world news website. I guess it was a quiet day.

Monica was crying. People have been telling us for ten years we would lose her and they were right – we lost her while we sat at home watching television. Lost our lovely *Phyllis May*.

People walking across and sympathizing – the police wanting to know if I had upset anyone recently. I'm always upsetting people, I said.

Then they came back for two more interviews because they didn't believe I was joking and thought they might have solved the crime of the century. *Horseman, pass by*.

Can we do the interview now? asked the TV lady.

Yes, I said, but give me a decent plug for my books. Might as well get something from the wreckage.

The insurers were prompt and gentlemanly, and explained that the hulk of the *Phyllis May* would probably be sold to people without much money who would fit it out and live in it. So she would have a good end. But the moving finger had written – nor all our piety and wit would lure it back to cancel half a line, nor all Monica's tears wash out a word of it.

The foot of charcoal was the quilt my Canadian friends gave us when we left Toronto. It was the painting of the shrimp boats that I bought in Beaufort South Carolina for Monica's seventieth birthday. It was Frank Collis's painting of the poplars near Hoo Mill. It was our hi-fi with the Mordaunt Short speakers. (Sir Mordaunt the Short was one of Arthur's knights, our son Clifford would say, and then we would laugh – he always said it and we always laughed.) It was the little printer. The William Morris curtains. My Ricard sign from the Left Bank, the long thin poster of sport fish from the Gulf of Mexico, the Gullah painting from *Gone with the Wind* country. The log-box with *Phyllis May* on the front side and *Kiss Me Again* on the backside.

But most of all the very body of the most elegant steel shell on the cut – the Jonathan Wilson design that Mike Partridge, the boat painter for whom the boat was built, had adjusted by half-inches to give the flow from front to back, the low bow, the rise at the stern, the tumble-home, the look that was proper for the Queen of the Waterways.

Our poor buckled *Phyllis May* had crossed the Channel, banged across the Étang de Thau on the Camargue in a storm, braved the Albemarle Sound and the Pamlico Sound on the Atlantic coast, crossed Lake Okeechobee in Florida in fog, and driven out on to the Mediterranean and on to the Gulf of Mexico. She had stayed strong and dry and tracked like a darling and her engine had never missed a beat.

You know, said Monica, I am not happy for things to finish like this.

Fuck no, I said.

# CHAPTER TWO

# THE MERSEY AND LIVERPOOL

## Paradise Street

*A strange and beautiful country it seems*

*They're not going anywhere – A serious boat owned by proper canal people – The northerners will think I am a sissy – Tonk tonk tonk went the Russell Newberys – The wind blew us across the lock – Swallowing noises under our hull – I was born into a disintegrating world – Rivers of flame running down the hills – What arsehole adjusts the carburettors of bombers? – You came down the Mersey on your own? – The whippets shivered as I let them slip – Paradise Street – The smoking room in the* Titanic *– Sunshine through the golden chain*

Lines on the Loss of the Narrowboat *Phyllis May* by Fire in the Yard of Canal Cruising, Stone, Staffordshire – by Jim, Ship's Whippet.

> *I never loved the* Phyllis May
> *She rolled, a drunk in pain*
> *Day after day, day after day*
> *Across the leaping main*
>
> *When she went up like a flare*
> *I bounced and barked with glee*

*They're not going anywhere*
*And they're not taking me*

*But I haven't seen a lucky day*
*Since I left my dear mother*
*Just when I thought I was OK*
*The buggers bought another*

In twenty years narrowboat design has developed in a number of ways, few of them important, but together the advances make a more comfortable boat. Of course nothing can be done about the absurdity of a craft that is only seven feet wide, but do you want to go through the locks or not?

The *Phyllis May* was sixty feet long, the most common length in the eighties, but the modern boat tends to be two feet shorter so she can sail on the northern waterways of the UK, where for reasons not revealed to me the locks are not as long as everywhere else.

The modern engine room is more compact, so the two feet lost in the length is not noticed inside the boat. And the machinery is much more accessible. In the *Phyllis May* if I wanted to clear the prop or do any maintenance I had to strip naked, grease myself all over and crawl on my belly like a snake. In the *PM2* I lift the floor and please myself.

Two people can now stand on the back counter, and walk straight over the top of the engine to the bedroom cabin (the cosiest place on earth) then to the bathroom with a toilet that whizzes and gurgles and does not smell. The shower would be big enough if I could lose a couple of stone. The galley leads without interruption into the twenty-five-foot saloon. As on the *Phyllis May*, no dinette or cupboards split up and cramp the interior.

The old fit-out was teak and oak. The *PM2* is ash – a light-coloured wood too hard to take a nail. The graining is subdued at floor level but when it reaches the ceiling it has flowered in arches and flourishes that would grace a chapel. There is plenty of light because of the colour of the ash and the wide windows, and more again because of the Houdini hatch in the roof. This is a window that opens upwards for a quick getaway. We could have done with that for our journey across the Channel.

Out through the front door and you are in the bow area, where there are lockers to sit on. And alas there is a cratch. A cratch is an absurd canvas thing like a black tent that fits over the bow and makes it very difficult to get in and out. It is meant to be a faint echo of the old tarpaulins on the haulage barges, and is a bloody stupid idea. Monica loves it and I am trying to think of a way to destroy it.

Overall the *PM2* is very similar to our dear dead darling. The Longport boatyard where she was built is where Jonathan Wilson, who built the *Phyllis May*, learned to shape his steel shells. The gunwales and the bow are low and the tumblehome (the slope on the sides) is emphatic, giving her a businesslike and marine air. Slow curves add interest to the hull. The engine is marinized from a two-litre forty-three-horse Kubota cylinder block – so was the engine on the *Phyllis May*.

But the ambience of this craft is different – the *Phyllis May* was light grey with a white roof to defend against the tropical sun and two pots on top and a brass tunnel light and roses and castles on her back doors – she was all flowers and fairies. The *PM2* is a sad green, a dark old canal green, with a rust-red roof. She has very little decoration. This is a serious boat owned by proper canal people, not a pair of mad old geezers desperate for glory.

And everything works – a cruise in the *Phyllis May*, particularly in the early days, was a travelling catastrophe, and it took eight years and a new engine to bring her up for long journeys and sea crossings.

I would never have a boat built specially – I have heard too many nightmare stories of delays and failures. But the *PM2* had been built into stock, by a yard of good repute, and lay waiting for her prince to come.

We found her four days after the fire and bought her on the spot.

We'll go round the north, said Monica – the *PM2* will go round the north. The *Phyllis May* wouldn't go round the north. And you'll write a book about it.

But I don't want to write a book about the north, I said. I've not been to the north since the fifties. I'm Welsh, naturalized Midlander – different cultures. The Welsh love to talk and tell you all about their feelings. The people from the Potteries want to be your friends and take you to the football and buy you drinks and tell you jokes. The northerners are not the same at all – they are trained from birth to say as little as possible and not give anyone any money. They might not like me. They will probably think I am a sissy because of how I speak. They are strong-minded and not always very polite. The only northerner I know is my old running coach Fred Wrigley, and think of the awful things Fred said to me when I wouldn't train. And it's not big enough – the north I mean. I am a semi-global adventurer, used to traversing continents and vast countries, not just a piece of a small country without many canals anyway.

We'll start with Liverpool, said Monica – you like Liverpool. You went to read your poetry there with Adrian Henri. We'll go from Stoke-on-Trent through the Harecastle Tunnel and along the Wirral to Liverpool. And I will organize a crossing of the Mersey.

You can't cross the Mersey – there are forty-foot tides, there is something called the Devil's Bank, and there is no canal link.

There is a link now, Terry. From the Wirral you can sneak into the Manchester Ship Canal and then out into the Mersey and run down with the tide and lock into Liverpool right in the centre. It will be a good start for your book.

What can I ever find to write about? There is no book for me in the north – unless I tell the story of my life as well, and no one would be interested in that.

Your agent David has been on about you writing your memoirs for years.

Tonk tonk tonk went the Russell Newberys. Tonk tonk tonk. I love the old boats with the tarpaulins and the old engines. You have got to love the noise they make – it is like the past coming along the cut to say Come back, come back, it is all still here, tonk tonk.

But it wasn't much fun really for the old transport boaters and the modern love of vintage engineering can decay into rivet-counting, bowler hats, waistcoats and canal snobbery. I am not much good at history, having been taught by Minnie Morris at Whitchurch Grammar School, Cardiff, and have no interest in freight carrying long ago. One more account of the Jam 'Ole Run in your otherwise excellent canal magazine, dear editor, and I shall cancel my subscription forthwith.

The waterways pioneers Tom Rolt and Robert Aickman fought near to the death over whether their Inland Waterways Association should concentrate on the past heritage of the canals or their leisure potential. I think Aickman was right, and let's keep putting our money on the future – there is plenty to be done. Have you ever tried to find a toilet pumpout in Chester, or a pub in Little Venice, or navigate from Reading to Devizes?

But Tonk tonk tonk went the Russell Newberys. There were twenty-eight of them in the canal basin at Ellesmere Port. Colourful boats smart for the rally, with their grey-haired owners chatting and waiting to go through the lock and turn right on to the Manchester Ship Canal.

The *PM2* was not turning right – she was turning left towards the Mersey, where she would tackle the four-mile crossing to Liverpool. Monica had timed our departure to catch the tide. The only trouble was there were twenty-eight Russell Newberys in our way

Tonk tonk tonk. It had to be the only moment of the year when the Ellesmere Port lock was impassable.

It was three years since we crossed a great water and the experience of fear had not changed. It makes you feel you are falling apart from the inside. It builds up and builds up and then vanishes as you begin your adventure. This would be at Eastham Lock three miles west, where you lock out on to the Mersey and head towards the Liverpool docks on the other side. I knew that there were sandbanks – one was called the Devil's Bank – and there were currents and if I got to Liverpool and tried to bring our fifty-eight feet into the narrow entrance to the docks the current could rip me away and out to sea. Waiting for the Newberys, knowing that we could miss our tide, made us extra nervous. Tonk bloody tonk – come on, come on.

But the Newberys cleared five minutes before our deadline and we set out into the basin of Ellesmere Port, long purged of all gear and detail – just a pond, and I leaned on the throttle and made for the corner where the canal heads to Eastham Lock.

This was no twenty-foot cut – this was the Manchester Ship Canal, fifty yards across, as wide as any man-made canal we had sailed in the USA, the water black and the banks heavy with greenery. It was high summer and noon but cold and dark with a wind. We moved slowly, the dogs quiet below.

Monica's little hand-held radio squawked and fizzed – our proper marine radio on the *Phyllis May* with its roof aerial had burned – and Monica asked it what it wanted.

There is a ship, she said to me. Eastham Lock wants us to slow down and hug the shore.

And coming out of the haze towards us a ship, a small ship but a ship, and I swung in to the side and it came near and it passed and it was full of people and we waved furiously and they waved back, looking rather surprised. The Manchester Ship Canal, the great ship canal, artery of trade, had come to this — one ship full of gongoozlers to shiver the black mirror of the cut, and a narrowboat the size of a Players Number Six to wave at because there was nothing worthwhile to do on the Manchester Ship Canal any more but gongoozle.

We pushed on, and in the way things do at sea the distant lock unveiled its detail reluctantly through the darkness at noon.

A mess of sheds and gear right across the canal, then a light on a pole, and then two red lights one above the other. Now we knew which gap to head for. We dallied outside the lock and the lights changed to green and we entered. There seemed to be no one at home and the wind blew us across the lock, which was sixty feet wide, and wedged us under a wall.

The lock-keepers came out of their little huts. These were not chatty British Waterways staff — these were sea-men — sweatered and sou'westered and taciturn and What is this tiny painted bugger doing here?

They shouted and pointed and somehow I levered the *PM2* off the wall and on to the correct side and they took our bow and stern ropes.

Over the lock wall I could see the estuary, the long yellow Devil's Bank, the fogged outline of the shore three miles away, and the waves running before the wind, shining black, and we waited in the lock a long time, and I was afraid.

A hundred yards behind us the gates of the lock were closing and we sank three feet, taking our time. Then the gates on to the Mersey opened and I turned to wave to the lock-keepers but they had gone back into their sheds so Sod them and down with the throttle and we were out of the lock and into the flood which swung and thumped and made swallowing noises under our hull.

We were being pulled about – the currents outside the lock were conflicted and I could not set a straight course. The tide was still running up the river and the wind was hard from the north-east. Wind over tide – a choppy, disorganized sea. An hour of this is not going to be very nice, I thought – I wonder if any water is coming in at the front.

Monica was beside me holding her chart down on the roof. It cracked and flapped but Look, there it is – the green buoy.

And there ahead was a green buoy and beyond it a red buoy and further again the tiny ghost of another green buoy – just like the navigation buoys we had learned to follow on the Atlantic Intracoastal Waterway.

The *PM2* settled as we came into the main current and bridged the short waves as a narrowboat will and I pushed down the throttle and began to reel in the buoys, one by one.

Just pop down and check there is nothing coming in

at the bow, I said. She still has those little inland scuppers smaller than letterboxes so she won't drain very quickly. And I hope the dogs are OK.

The scuppers are all right. And the tranquillizers are working, said Monica. A bit of moaning, that's all.

May there be no moaning of the bar, I said, when I put out to sea, and I pushed the revs up to two thousand and it was all coming back – this is Tits Magee, conqueror of the Atlantic coast, to whom fear is a stranger; Tits Magee who circumnavigated the globe in red satin, accompanied only by a newt in a jar. Bring on the white horses!

But the tide had passed the flood and begun to run out and the wind was following and there was no more choppiness, no more confusion. I can see on the Liver Building the Liver Birds grow from fleas to cutty wrens to sparrows to Liver Birds – whatever Liver Birds may be – and watch the sharp and shapely buildings rise around them, and this is the red buoy where I turn right across the stream.

I am heading for the lights of the lock though not getting any nearer – that's how it is at sea – and suddenly you are there and the current sweeps you away downstream past the entrance and you half turn and claw back and it gets you again and swings you away and somehow you avoid hitting the wall and you are in the throat of the lock and the red light has gone green and the gates are open and you are in the North Countree, in a new world, on your way to Wigan Pier, and a strange and beautiful country it seems as you look through the docks to the city centre skyline.

★  ★  ★

Drowsed with the fume of aviation fuel I was born into a disintegrating world.

My father was a sergeant instructor at Cranwell, Lincolnshire. Both my parents delighted in me as a baby, though my mother had chosen to call me Carol Ann, and when I arrived had no name for me so called me after her doctor. Laughing over this story with the principal and the English tutor at my interview (you are Irish, Mr Darlington?) got me into Oxford seventeen years later. It's a funny old world.

Despite my mother's best efforts, including photographing me in drag – I looked really pretty – I grew up a boy and in due course an enthusiastic heterosexual like my fathers before me.

Mum and Dad had met at Sunday school in Pembroke Dock, a military town in a forgotten corner of Wales, a corner so beautiful that I will not tell you where it is. Dad's father was a chimney sweep and Mum's father a night-watchman. Willy-nilly grew they, divinely formed and fair. They were more beautiful than Douglas Fairbanks and Mary Pickford – their features were more regular. I did not inherit their looks – I was an ugly little bugger with an overbite and a residual chin, though I looked good for a short time when I was nineteen.

When the war began my father was posted away and my mother and I went to Pembroke Dock to live with my grandfather. His terrace house looked out on Pennar Gut, a shining inlet three miles long running into Milford Haven. At one end Pembroke Castle and at the other a brood of elephantine fuel oil tanks on the side of a hill.

My grandfather was kindly and distant, like the king of a far country who had come to Pembroke Dock to die. He was big and handsome and had one eye. Most of the time he sat by the fire in a striped shirt with no collar and a waistcoat with his friend Fred who came round every day to sit on the other side of the fire.

Sometimes Grandpa called on God's wounds like an Elizabethan – 'Zounds 'oman' he would say to my mother, innocent of what he was saying.

He had three stories to tell, from his boyhood in his home town of Landshipping up the river and from the dockyard, and he told them over and over. The stories were family possessions, to be brought out and enjoyed, and that is what you did in the evenings before the radio arrived on its wire from the little hut on the hill.

One of the stories was The Flying Man of Landshipping—

*One day Grandad was drinking in the Stanley Arms Landshipping and the evening was going well. Then one of the men at his table pushed back his chair.*

*Boys, he shouted, I am going to fly!*

*He climbed up on to the table and raised his arms.*

*Yes boys, I am going to fly, and heaven knows where I might land!*

*He launched from the table and fell on to the floor and broke his leg.*

It's how you tell them, of course. The secret with this

one is to emphasize the phrase *heaven knows* and in particular *knows*, which should be pronounced sonorously and in the Welsh manner, sounding rather like *Norse*.

Grandad had written a poem about Landshipping. I remember a verse –

> *The cattle that graze on those pastures green*
> *Compete with the finest ever seen*
> *And pigs and goats and chickens roam*
> *A credit to their farmyard home*

All the family and the neighbours were proud to have in their midst one who was a poet, who had been touched by the fire.

Some evenings he would say to my mother I'm going up to post a letter, but I never saw him with a pen in his hand, except once when I gave him a fountain pen to hold and he looked at it as if it were an incendiary bomb, because it was a technology from a new world.

There was a bucket in a shed at the top of the garden. I was washed every week on the kitchen table but underwear was not provided. I was hungry a lot of the time, and unhappy. Perhaps I asked too much when others were enduring more, but in school I was bored and bullied and in the night people would try to kill me.

Pembroke Dock was the most important Coastal Command base in Britain. The Sunderland flying boats, the ones that looked like white double-decker buses, would draw a line of chalk in the Haven half a mile long before heaving themselves into the air. Turning to swans, they banked west, off to hunt U-boats in the Western Approaches and over the Atlantic until their tanks were empty and their crews exhausted.

Hitler did not think Pembroke Dock was a good idea at all, and when he had captured the French airfields he reckoned he could do something about it.

Monday 19 August 1940 – three o'clock on a quiet sunny afternoon. I was playing in the road when there was a great noise, and three dark shapes tore hard and low along shining Pennar Gut; just over there, a hundred feet up, swifter than anything I had seen in my four years of life, left to right, from creamy grey Pembroke Castle towards Llanreath where the great oil tanks slept on the hill. As I was pulled into the doorway of number nine there was cracking and huffing and blasting and then it was quiet for a moment and then people started getting themselves together and pushing me back into number four.

The Junkers 88 and the two Messerchmitt 109s were gone, leaving the fire to foul the afternoon.

Within minutes the smoke was a thousand feet in the air and the tanks were bursting and the smoke was bursting and the flames roared inside the smoke and you could see it pump and reach and spill and rivers of flame were running down the hills and into the sea and the sirens had started and we were looking at the biggest blaze in the UK since the Fire of London.

Not a shot had been fired in defence.

Soon there rained a ghastly dew. The washing was black on the lines, the sheep were black in the fields, the earth was black, the air was black. We did not see the sun for a fortnight.

Over the next three weeks the great tanks burst one by one until eleven of the seventeen were destroyed – thirty-eight million gallons of oil, needed to send our merchant ships to America for food and supplies and power the destroyers to protect them.

Near the site the heat was terrible. The six hundred and fifty firemen received a thousand injuries. In the town the women would bathe their eyes. A tank exploded and swept five firemen into the flames.

Vernon Scott of the *Western Telegraph* interviewed Mrs Addie John for his book *Inferno 1940*.

*I saw a fireman, covered in oil from head to foot, coming up Llanreath hill from the beach. He was swaying all over the road like a drunken man. I offered him a cup of tea which he gladly accepted and with great difficulty he pulled off his boots and removed his oilskins. I gave him rags and paraffin to clean up the worst and then, on the doorstep, he washed himself thoroughly with warm water and soap. I gave him his tea but he broke down and wept. I told him he could rest and gave him an old trousers and jacket. He slept on my bed and when I woke him later he told me he came from Tenby. He never did mention his name.*

The Luftwaffe returned to drop more bombs around the target and machine-gun the firemen.

For three weeks the battle of good against evil wore on. A fireman was interviewed by Vernon Scott:

*We saw a mouse crawl out over the top of the moat. It was coated with oil and seemed to be blind. But we thought Good luck to you you little blighter, you've survived so far, and we took it to some grass and left it there.*

The night of 12 May 1941. What pervert puts a whistle in bombs? What arsehole adjusts the carburettors of bombers so they roar in and out? Isn't it enough to kill people – do they have to feel terror too?

We were under the stairs. My mother held me close. My grandfather was there in his striped shirt and braces. I can still smell the gas from the meter.

Uncle Clifford tumbling down from his bedroom, crowding in, his shirt tails flapping. Go back – put some trousers on, said my mother – have you no decency?

That night thirty-two people were killed and two thousand houses damaged. The military installations were untouched.

The next raid was the Fire Blitz – thousands of incendiary bombs. As the town burned we were lying in the fields and on the beaches. Four were killed that night. We had a dud incendiary through the roof next door – chubby little chap with fins. Phosphorus – if you put water on them it only encouraged them.

Uncle Clifford firing his Home Guard rifle from the doorstep did not bring the bombers down. Even little Cocky Roblin could not scare the hell-birds away. Cocky was the air raid warden who patrolled the blackout. He made my mother laugh so much – Oh,

Mrs Darlington, Mrs Darlington, I'm shaking like a leaf!

Cattle machine-gunned in the fields. Houses taken out like teeth. Jigsaws in the rubble. Shrapnel on the mantelpiece.

Strange images of death.

It needed my father to rescue us and take us to paradise.

★　★　★

Liverpool looks at the Mersey over a line of dock basins, each the size of several football fields, two abreast the length of the city and beyond. But the marine traffic moved to container terminals thirty years ago and along the old docks the elder tree grew in the cracks and hung its snow along the wharfs and vandals smashed the warehouses and offices.

Coming into town from the south the *PM2* passed through Brunswick Dock and Queens Dock and Wapping Dock, and switched off in Salthouse Dock, which lies in the centre of the city inland of Albert Dock. A lot of empty water and empty sites on this short passage but no dereliction now and in Queens Dock there were yachts and cruisers and here in Salthouse Dock a line of new pontoons and thirty narrowboats, covered with bunting.

It does not take boaters long to recognize us, maybe because we have our book covers in the window.

It's you, isn't it?

No, I am an imposter, and this is my narrow dog Jim, who is also an imposter. And this is my other narrow dog, Jess, who is not to be trusted either.

Come and drink with us tonight, here on the quay. We have whisky. We are all going out on to the Mersey tomorrow, up to Eastham Lock, and need to steady our nerves. We want to be among the first to try the new link. You came down from Eastham Lock – on your own? What was it like?

Went right over three times, but they come back up of course. Jim saved us. He is a devil with a baler.

Are you Tits Magee?

At your service, madam.

Have you got your shorts on the right way round?

The Albert Dock, between our Salthouse Dock harbour and the Mersey, was the first dock to be saved from destruction by developers and vandals. This happened in the seventies. Now the magnificent basin, with warehouses around, pillared and cloistered, is a Tate Gallery, shops, museums, bars and restaurants. The interiors of the bars and restaurants are modern, black and chrome and dreadful American beers are offered there, but you can eat royally and what is to stop you having a pint first on the waterfront a few yards away, or at the Baltic Fleet, a pub not too far upstream? Development has not yet reached the Baltic Fleet, which brews its own beers and serves scouse on the days you are not there, but I reached the Baltic Fleet and I wasn't sorry. (We have scouse in Stoke-on-Trent and Stone, but we call it lobby – it is meat and vegetable stew and is very nice. In Liverpool scouse without meat is called blind scouse – bet you didn't know that.)

Monica and Jim and Jess and I walked down from the Albert Dock past the Echo Arena and the Revenue Building to the lock where I had manhandled the *PM2* into the city. Apartment developments, some new houses, empty sites, and on our right the light and space of the Mersey. The tide was out – a soft wind and the heavy smell of yellow mud.

It was a long walk and Jim was getting tired. Monica keeps saying he is getting old, but how can my Jim be old? How can my puppy be old, that chased me round the garden and rolled over on his back and chewed my fingers and went to sleep on my chest? Perhaps that was how my mother felt about me – that would explain why in my sixties I was still her Carol Ann.

We'll let them off the lead. Let them stretch their little legs. It's cruel to have them on the lead all the time. Here, this is the place – now we are back on the pontoons – there is no way they can get on to the streets from here. We'll let them go and they can race each other to the boat. They are very clever creatures with memories like steel traps. They will know the boat and jump into it and wait for us. Little loves.

The two whippets knew a game was on and shivered as I let them slip. Their claws scratched the boardwalk as they accelerated, Jess ahead and Jim after her. They slowed as they came to the narrowboats and leapt aboard the first green boat they met, right into the boat, scaring the poor boaters, who threw themselves on their Persian cats, which were staring death in the face.

Those guys were lovely, I said, letting us off without a

caution. I don't think they knew what Jess can do to a squirrel. We should not have let them slip, taken that chance. The fool dogs didn't know their own boat.

They would have known the *Phyllis May,* said Monica. Her voice broke.

When you think of heaven do you think of snowy peaks? Too cold, too far away. Sand and surf? No, this is not a package holiday. Valleys perhaps – and what do you see there? Buttercups and lady's smocks and grass and streams which are very clear with lots of fish and jewelled with marsh marigolds.

But a rural heaven would not be enough for a chap who has spent too long in Hong Kong and caught the breeze in Carcassonne and loitered in London and tarried in Taipei and pissed about in Paris. I would get impatient with the bluebirds.

To design my own paradise I would start underfoot – just like the people who are remaking Liverpool. Round the docks and the Liverpool One area are granite, marble, brick, cobbles, flags – surfaces always changing and guiding you – now smooth, now rough – this way a bit – here, over here. The ground changes key every ten yards, and you are engaged, refreshed, delighted.

Then a street. The name is always a problem – Excellent Avenue – Perfection Parade – Beautiful Boulevard – Celestial Crescent – how boring – why not just Paradise Street? That's better – let's all know what is going on.

You need a variety of levels – walkways up interesting steps where you can sit and drink beer from cans and watch the people passing and chat with Jim Francis and Doctor Ian and the others.

There would be a lawn, but not too big, and many restaurants, including a Thai restaurant that makes that green curry with coconut. And a French one that does mussels and muscadet, and a pub round the corner that does Timothy Taylor's Landlord's Bitter.

Many shops, with marine polos, and T-shirts with really interesting slogans like I'M THE BIGGEST BITCH ON THE BEACH and SALE NOW ON and SORRY I'M TAKEN and trainers and shorts so everyone can look like a fourteen-year-old junkie.

There would be street stalls, but not many, and the fruit stall would sell sweet grapes and cherries. There would be light and space and colour.

Just over the road from Salthouse Dock is one of the world's biggest retail developments, just completed on forty acres around Paradise Street. It has everything I have mentioned, except Jim Francis and Doctor Ian.

★   ★   ★

Fifty years ago I was an executive with Lever Brothers, and I would travel to Port Sunlight to argue with chemists and engineers. Just an ordinary executive, but in the Adelphi I was a prince.

The Adelphi Hotel, Liverpool, was built in 1826 and refurbished in 1912 to coincide with the launch of the *Titanic*. She is titanic indeed, taking up the whole of a

Liverpool block. From her elevation in the centre of the city her pillared and majestic proportions look towards the Mersey, back a hundred years before it all went to hell.

I would wander her halls and swim in her marble pool. The Sefton Suite with its wonderful chandelier is a replica of the smoking room in the *Titanic*. I was startled by the Masonic meeting room as big as a Congregational chapel that held the corner looking out over Lewis's store. Masonic devices in the plaster of the breakfast room under the ceiling puzzled me as I addressed my kipper. Behind the main ground-floor concourse, room after room, some well lit from high windows, some internal and dark with coloured pillars six feet thick like an Egyptian tomb.

But most of all I enjoyed my marble bath with the gold-coloured taps, and the hot water pouring and gurgling. I am a big chap but I could stretch out and float. I never found another bath where I could stretch out and float, and I have tried quite a few.

Thirty-five years later Monica and I went to Liverpool to a concert and were surprised that we could not find the Adelphi in a book of hotels but we managed to ring and book a room with a spa bath. It didn't cost very much. The room was dismal and the spa bath was plastic with holes in the side and didn't work. The hotel was still titanic, but

*Over the mirrors meant*
*To glass the opulent*
*The sea-worm crawls – grotesque, slimed, dumb, indifferent.*

*Jewels in joy designed*
*To ravish the sensuous mind*
*Lie lightless, all their sparkles bleared and black and blind.*

*Dim moon-eyed fishes near*
*Gaze at the gilded gear*
*And query 'What does this vaingloriousness down here?'*

We had made friends with a Liverpool antiques dealer. What happened to the marble baths in the rooms?

Torn out – they skipped the lot.

★　★　★

It was after the six o'clock news when we heard an aero engine. It clattered and popped and ran to a stop. My father and Uncle Jerry hurried out into the dark and the rain and after a while came back with a man wearing a big coat. He looked pale and he didn't want to talk to us kids. Dad and Jerry took him into the morning room and there was a lot of muttering. Tea was brought in.

After an hour or so the man left and we heard the engine start up again. Dad and Jerry went out and watched the plane take off. Through our tall windows we just saw its shape because it had no lights.

Dad and Jerry came back in. Hush-hush, said my dad, looking very pleased.

My father was at Melksham in Wiltshire teaching mechanics how to service instruments on war planes. He was a warrant officer now, with badges on his

47

uniform, and he lived like a country gentleman. In fact we all lived like a country gentleman, including his pal Jerry, who was another warrant officer, his wife and their two boys.

Fearful of the bombs in Pembroke Dock and my mother's exhaustion in the besieged town my father and Jerry had rented a house called Westfields, just outside Trowbridge, Wiltshire. Westfields was up a drive a hundred yards long with horse chestnuts blazing with candles or rich with conkers. It had tennis courts, a paddock, stables, a woodpile eight feet high, chickens that laid warm eggs, an orchard, a loft full of apples spread out on the floor not touching each other, a roof where you could walk about, and thirty rooms. There were bathrooms and lavatories.

The sun would shine through the arch of golden chain. At breakfast there was marmalade – I don't think marmalade had reached Pembroke Dock. Vera Lynn would sing 'Yours' and 'There'll be bluebirds over the white cliffs of Dover'. In the newspaper there was a pretty lady called Jane who took off her clothes for her dachshund Fritz, and put them back on for her boyfriend called Georgie Porgie. This did not strike me as strange at the time. In my comics were Big Eggo and Corky the Cat, both fully committed to making Hitler look even more ridiculous than he was. I thought the Red Army was Red Indians. At weekends my father would organize schemes like picking the apples or the peaches or gassing the rats in the compost heap and us kids would hunt caterpillars and beetles and tadpoles. After dinner on Sunday Dad would wrestle with me on the floor.

At school I was with the red team and wore the sash with pride. We leaned over the fence in the playground and waved to the trains and the engine-drivers and the people on the train waved back. I still dream about the waving back and I always wave to little children from the boat even when they don't care. I made a friend called Roger because I told him he had forgotten his gas mask and he told me back I had forgotten mine and we laughed. Some of the gas masks had Mickey Mouse noses but mine was black and went flubba dubba dubba when you breathed out. A bomb fell in our field and made a big hole, but it didn't frighten me because it didn't whistle and when it went Bang we were still alive.

One morning a letter came with my mother's call-up papers to join the British army. My father said this must be Hitler's last desperate move.

Nobody laughed at the next letter – Daddy has been posted to Whitehall, to the Air Ministry. He has to go to London and we have to go back to Pembroke Dock.

*They looking back, all the eastern side beheld*
*Of paradise, so late their happy seat.*

# CHAPTER THREE

# LIVERPOOL AND THE RUFFORD BRANCH

## The Kingdom of the Mad

*Fierce bees coming over the fields*

*Mr Morse hit Mr David on the chin – Come here he said and drew a knife – We do not mention the python – Captain Johnny with his sloops and corvettes – Blood on the leaves and blood at the root – Where was his guardian angel? – That chap can play the clarinet – The very earth was alive and flowing – You can fly with gulls and eagles – Magic texts – My God you are English! – Under the control of an alien presence – A slimy little bastard everyone knew as Slug – I was born on a boat! – In comes Adolf with the hypodermic – I balanced on the edge of clouds*

Everyone who is brought up in Pembroke Dock loves it always. It is not too big, it has hills and views, and it is near wondrous beaches. But like anywhere else, it is best if the right people are there with you.

When my father came home from Whitehall he was an officer and had more badges but I didn't care about that because he never came for long and the first thing he did was hug and kiss my mother a lot and I felt funny and sad because they didn't notice me though I was hanging on to his legs and then when he left it broke my heart. Most of my friends had no father too.

One day my mother came home with two young men in RAF uniform. They talked and drank tea and ate biscuits. The young men went away quite soon. All the time you knew that they wanted their girls or their wives and Mum wanted Dad and people you met down Pennar Gut were not as good.

My school was called the Coronation School. My father had gone there and all my uncles. It smelt of boiled cabbage and there were dirty drawings on the lavatory walls. Nobody bullied me but at night I would pray that Mr Morse and Mr David would not teach us, as they frightened me so much. Mr Morse was hairy white and very aggressive. He caned the other boys a lot but not me because I was quiet and my mother had visited the school when I arrived and she was beautiful. Mr David was bald and not quite as bad. After some months I found I was getting used to Mr Morse and Mr David. In fact Mr David gave me a penny once for knowing that 'harbinger' meant 'herald'.

Just as I was getting used to Mr Morse and Mr David, Mr Morse hit Mr David on the chin and broke his jaw and we did not see Mr Morse after that.

Miss Davies was nice. We had slates to write on with slate pencils. Some of the slates had squares on them already to help you but the slate pencils scratched. Miss Davies showed us charts with the shapes of aeroplanes on them in colour so we could tell if it was a Junkers or a Messerschmitt or something else, but by the time the charts came the planes had stopped coming.

I knew that Stalingrad was important and felt that we were bound to win now.

We had two books in 4 Albany Street, Pembroke Dock – one was *The Fifth Round* by Sapper. That was great, about Bulldog Drummond. The other book was about Trinity House, which is responsible for light-houses and light vessels. It was really old and full of blotchy black and white pictures. I read it right through. I cannot remember if it included the South Goodwin Light Vessel, which shadowed us across the Channel, but I bet it was there.

I was in the St Patrick's choir and went to two services and Sunday school – the Sunday school where Dad passed Mum his notes. I loved the music and the words from the Bible and once a year we had a special outing. The minister was the Reverend J. Iorwerth Thomas. He was handsome and very nice – the nearest thing I had to a father.

American soldiers in the streets – Got any gum chum?

We were not begging – it was a sort of greeting. What is a little boy supposed to say to an American soldier – ask him if it rains a lot in the Bronx?

The American soldiers understood what society required of them and put their hands in their pockets and chucked us some gum. The gum was little pink rectangles flavoured with cinnamon. There were no sweets in the war and this was rare stuff indeed. You can find gum like it in British shops nowadays if you are lucky and I always buy some because when I chew it I am on Milton Terrace and there is Milford Haven below me and the GI in the jeep and his smile and God Bless America.

At the end of our street Italian men – each evening a hundred of them walking down the lane. They must have been prisoners of war coming back from work. Each evening they walked by and we would shout Hello and they would say *Buona sera, buona sera*, and they would help us repeat it until we could say it too.

They lived in a circle of Nissen huts down the lane. One day I walked into the camp. An Italian asked me into one of the huts.

Come here, he said, and drew a knife.

Then he took a patch of leather, about three inches square, and fastened it to the table with a steel pin. He took his knife and cut a notch in the side of the patch and pulled the patch round as he cut it and it began to turn into a leather bootlace. I watched astonished and he finished the lace and then he gave it to me.

*Miss Thrale, did you see his shoes?*

*His shoes, Dr Morelle?*

*Gentlemen don't wear brogues with rubber soles.*

*I must say he looked a bit like the murderer in the case of the Shepherd's Bush Python.*

*Miss Thrale, we do not mention the Python.*

Post-war radio – dear dead days beyond recall. It came in by wire from the little Rediffusion hut on the hill, swooping over our terrace houses and into my grandfather's dark kitchen, into our little speaker, delivering a clear signal – the signal that had brought news from the war.

*Children's Hour* – *Toytown* with Larry the Lamb, played by Uncle Mac, with Dennis the villainous dachshund, and Mr Growser – *Somebody ought to be ashamed of himself. Breakfast with Braden – Me, I'm going back to bed.* Valentine Dyall and his *Appointment with Fear.* I was frightened to listen to it myself so my friends would tell me the stories in school the next day. And *Dick Barton*, radio's first serial. I never found out what happened when that woman turned round and picked up the knife from the table, because they cut it out of the omnibus edition.

But that wasn't as bad as when I was listening to a natural history programme –

*The frog advances on its prey, getting nearer and nearer, and then just as the fly is beginning to feel his presence, faster than the eye can follow –*

And then faster than the eye can follow Rediffusion pulled the plug on the frog and switched over to a programme in Welsh. I guess the chap who cheated the poor frog of his dinner is long dead, but if you are not, sir, here is a seven-year-old boy telling you that you are an idiot.

No programme more comfortable than *Monday Night at Eight*, because it was on every week for ages and had lots of good things and best of all Ernest Dudley's detective Dr Morelle and his Miss Thrale. They always got their man and there was a little twist that sorted everything out and Miss Thrale had a lovely voice and a lovely name and I imagined her as beautiful and sexy though I could not have known what sexy meant.

Despite my rich diet of radio, and reading many of the books in the town library, I nearly didn't get into Pembroke Dock Grammar School because I never learned my tables. They had dropped down the crack between Trowbridge and Pembroke Dock and I do not know them to this day. But I did get in as a Grade Two pass or something and then we moved to Cardiff and the family was back together.

My parents quarrelled a lot in Cardiff and it wasn't the same for me with my dad. I had found it hard when he kept leaving me – it was like having bits of your inside torn out and they didn't grow back.

★ ★ ★

Six narrowboats sailed out of Salthouse Dock, across Albert Dock, and into Canning Dock, and across the front of the Liver Building. A new canal with bridges and tunnels had been built along the waterfront, and we passed in royal procession through the sculpted concrete channel. Two young British Waterways chaps would shepherd us through the locks out of the north of the city, where we would head inland.

In Canning Dock there was the South Goodwin Light Vessel. We had passed it in the Channel on the *Phyllis May* seven years ago. It had taken an hour and a half to reach and an hour and a half to get away from. I thought it would never go. It was like a bad memory, an old enemy waiting for me to die. It had followed me to Paris and waited for me on the Seine and now here it was again – grown bigger – waxed fat on the new mistakes I had made, the new things I wanted to forget.

We passed the statue of Captain Johnny Walker, the winner of four DSOs. In the Second World War we had to have supplies from the USA to survive and Hitler and Admiral Doenitz with their U-Boats had their hands on our throat.

Churchill said everything depended on the Battle of the Atlantic, and of all the battles in the Second World War this was the one that made him most fearful. But we had Captain Johnny with his sloops and corvettes that were hunter-killers as well as escorts and we had the Sunderlands in Pembroke Dock and we had the civilian merchant seamen who never stopped sailing to the USA and back, though their losses were terrible.

In the Coastal Command Control Room in Rumford Street Liverpool the little wooden ships were pushed around on big maps.

> 'Tis all a Chequerboard of Nights and Days
> Where Destiny with Men for Pieces plays;
> Hither and thither moves, and mates, and slays,
> And one by one back in the Closet lays.

There was a viewing room where the top brass could overlook the patterns of pursuit and death and there were beds where they might sleep. The battle lasted the whole of the war.

In June 1944 Captain Johnny moved his forces to the

D-day landings. Not one U-boat got past him. In July he died of exhaustion. He was forty-seven.

Also on the wharf, not far away, was the statue of Billy Fury, who died young as well, though he is better known.

Monica brought me up a cup of cocoa. John Lennon was out yesterday morning, I said, when I went to buy a paper. There he was, standing in a corner, bronzed and quiet, opposite the Cavern Club. Hi John, I said, loved 'Woman'.

Your rat, he said.

And last night I got up for a pee and looked out through the window and they had lit up the Echo Wheel on Salthouse Dock. It is a bit smaller than the London Eye but it was doubled in the basin.

> *I saw Eternity the other night,*
> *Like a great Ring of pure and endless light*

A cold day and the narrowboats churned on – now the new channel and old wharfs decayed to sad basins, now and then a lock.

Ahead something monstrous, out of scale, not of our planet or time, grew until it occupied earth and heaven.

When the tobacco warehouse on Stanley Dock was built in 1901 it was the largest building in the world. It is a rectangular brick building fourteen tall storeys high, beautifully detailed. It covers twenty-six acres. It was still in use in the eighties. The *PM2* ran alongside it and we marvelled at something so right in its proportions, so handsome, even when someone had got the decimal point in the wrong place.

Liverpool was a centre of the tobacco trade, and once the biggest slave port in the world.

*Blood on the leaves, and blood at the root.*

We rose through more locks into Litherland.

★   ★   ★

A long way away I heard a voice singing –

> *O how amiable are thy dwellings*
> *Thou Lord of Hosts, Thou Lord of Hosts!*
> *My soul hath a desire*
> *And longing to enter:*
> *To enter into*
> *The courts of the Lord.*
> *My heart and my flesh rejoice*
> *In the living God.*

The voice came nearer and I realized it was my voice. My mother was holding my hand. There was pain. My father was there too. You have been singing for half an hour – how do you feel?

I was in Cardiff Royal Infirmary. I had been playing bows and arrows and an arrow had hit me in the eye.

Where was his guardian angel? my mother asked.

Losing the sight of an eye was a dreadful thing but it is hard to assess the effect it had on my life. It certainly weakened me emotionally. It made me less physically attractive, and I was no looker already, but to my surprise girls don't care how many eyes you have got. I have never really worked out what girls look for but I have known some crackers and married a beauty queen. When I find out how this can be I will let you know.

I had to give up my plans to be England's main spin bowler. The sports I could play could not be ball games, as my judgement of distance was now compromised, nor physical contact sports, because I was a coward, nor games involving agility, because I was clumsy. That left rowing and running, which I pursued with enthusiasm for much of my life.

I didn't appreciate my hair as a teenager. It was thick and black and wavy. I greased it and tried to make it look fashionable but as I didn't know what fashionable was all I did was spoil it. Anyway the grooming process was probably what mattered, getting prepared in order to go and find a mate.

Then I cleaned my shoes and put on my suit and picked up my clarinet case. Ian George (my middle names) and his Band were all set to enslave the audiences of the UK and beyond.

The core of the band was three people – Roger, who was a fine musician and pianist; Tony, who did his best with a drum kit I had bought for ten pounds; and me. A guitar would also join us, and a trumpet. We played New Orleans style, inasmuch as we could claim any style at all, but we were really a little dance band. It was tremendous fun.

I would hustle for gigs at youth club dances and harvest festivals and at our zenith we could play in tune for two hours without repeating ourselves.

My idol was Sid Phillips – five years later his band played at a Jesus College Commemoration Ball. I get paid for doing what I enjoy most, said Sid.

I still love his records – he had a fluent clarinet style, perfect pitch, and time has been kind to his music, as it is to the best.

One evening the sound system failed at an Oxford dance and I got up on stage with half a dozen guys and played. The college Captain of Boats was there and went back to college and asked Why has this chap not been accepted in one of the eights? What do you mean he is no good at games? That chap can play the clarinet for Chrissake!

After our practice in Roger's house we would head out to catch a bus, because every Saturday night we would go to a dance. The City Hall was grand, though a touch municipal. The Marina on the pier at Penarth was more louche and there was a pub opposite and it had a better band and you could go out on the balcony and snog. I was never lucky at either venue, despite years of faithful attendance. Girls were pleasant to me but not interested in moving on to the next stage, whatever that might be.

Many years later I realized why. These girls had been brought up with males who had not gone to grammar school. Grammar school boys seemed like sexless creatures, and might even be the enemy, with their posh voices and posh ways.

There was one girl who liked me – she was called Anne Poole – Hi Anne – but she lived in Newport and it might as well have been Alpha Centauri.

★   ★   ★

Coming out of Liverpool the water is clear, so you can better see the extravagant mix of objects that the loyal citizens of Litherland throw into the canal. The colours of their food containers rival the very kingfisher, and their plastic bags mock the soft hues of the canal bank flowers, though not the water lilies, which shine yellower than yellow among their pads, or the marsh marigolds, which shine yellower again; flakes from the heart of the sun.

Among the lilies coots coots coots, bald, black and bustling, with little coots that were nothing like as smartly turned out and here were even more coots and families of ducks, the colours of the yukkers a downy echo of the mother duck. And there were herons, and families of swans, the new ones grey and untidy and going cheep cheep like laptops. The rubbish thinned and ceased and the weeds under the surface shifted and pulled.

We lifted the whippets on to the roof. Jim went to sleep in his bed in the sun, and Jess walked up and down wondering how you are supposed to kill a rabbit from up here.

Round the corner our first northern lock, which would take boats of fifty-eight feet, like the *PM2*. The *Phyllis May* would never have got through, for she had been on the long side of sixty. The lock was wide, with heavy gates and heavy gear, and a little white cruiser was waiting for a partner to share the passage. The gentleman was slim and grey, and the lady was plump and grey with bulging blue eyes. I drew alongside.

Watch out, she said. That couple coming towards us. We met them last year. The man is bad-tempered and violent.

Watch that couple, I said to Monica – they are bad-tempered and violent.

I just spoke to him, said Monica, seemed OK.

She and the gentleman closed the lock without exchanging a single blow.

Different couple, said the lady – looked the same – very deceiving. Now be careful – just down there, on your side. There is a wide shelf under the water. If you stay too far back your stern will hang up as the lock empties, and your bow will drop and – boat sunk, you in bottom of lock. So many deaths like that.

I moved the boat forward – watch out, shouted Monica, you will get your fender caught in the front gate.

In Staffordshire we have seventy feet of lock – ten feet to play with. But in a sixty-foot lock I am dealing with inches. Back a bit – there just wasn't enough room. I centred the boat as best I could. There was enough room and there was no shelf.

There is no shelf, I said.

The lady said something incoherent.

No shelf, I said.

I didn't want to let it go but I let it go.

On we went – a call from a passing boat – Watch out at the next lock. There is a fierce breeze coming over the fields.

The lady addressed a crew coming up the other way. Be careful – there are fierce bees coming over the fields.

Once you have paired with another boat to go through a passage of locks you are stuck with them for as long as you both want to move along. Sometimes relationships are formed that last until death.

You have got to stop, said Monica. That wretched woman is too much for me. She told me you can tell when the lock is empty by the feel of the gates slackening – I have been boating for fifteen years and someone is telling me when a lock is empty.

We're stopping here, I called to our partners. Have to do something to the boat (like getting it the hell away from you, I thought).

Look at the grass in the big field, said the lady. It looks like waves.

I looked and could see nothing, then kept looking and I began to see how the wind was stroking the grass into water and pushing it across the field. The very earth was alive and flowing, as in a Van Gogh painting. I realized I had never known how to look at a field.

It takes the mad to show us how to see, said Monica.

★  ★  ★

Poetry comes to get you – a fire in the brain, a need, a desire that offers its own satisfaction.

*Lord send me some comfort,*
*For here it is hard to find*
*Send me a sign or heal me Lord I pray*
*And fondly ask and hear a word in my mind*
*Sing sing it seems to say*

If you can sing, what else matters, what else can compare? You can describe heaven and hell, you can win love and honour. You can see through conspiracies and destroy enemies. You can walk in the clouds, fly with gulls and eagles –

*Gulls' wings, deep driven into the shoulders*
*Feather spread on muscle, bound on bone*
*Climb away from me white in the sun*
*Tight into the wind*

I was sixteen and poetry had come to get me.

*I hang from a rope of light*
*Oh Lord switch off the light*
*Let me fall*

It had come to warn me too.

Some of the books of poetry I found in libraries or borrowed from teachers were printed on rough yellowish paper and the pages were not the same sizes and the books were small. These books often had the best poetry in them. It was as if they were magic texts. T. S. Eliot's 'The Love Song of J. Alfred Prufrock' was like that, where in a strong start he compares an evening sky to a patient etherized upon a table.

Another poem in a little shabby book from France was Louis Aragon's 'Ballad of the Man Who Sings under Torture'.

*And if it had to be*
*I'd tread this path again*
*A voice speaks low to me*
*Of days that will remain*

Poems of the Resistance, the struggle against the invader. Yes, these were magic texts.

I translated Aragon's ballad for our French *assistante*. I was quite good at translating, perhaps because I would without hesitation change the sense of a verse to fit in with my rhymes. There are a lot more rhymes in French so I don't know what they are complaining about.

Do you have a pen friend? asked our *assistante*.

Sainghin-en-Weppes is a small red-brick town of gripping ugliness near the Belgian border not far from Lille. There I was privileged to be a temporary member of the family of Alexandre Barrez, a hugely fat butter merchant. Alexandre worked hard in his factory next to his house and was a rich man. His son, my friend, was called Louis.

Ten years earlier Alexandre had been in a Resistance cell and one of the members had been captured by the Gestapo. *Il n'a pas parlé*, explained Louis – he didn't talk. I often think about how Alexandre felt going about his business that day, waiting for the black Citroën to pull up outside.

Louis and I got on well, and I ran with the pack of French boys that he led and I learned to speak French.

Butter was rationed in England, but here I could eat my fill. And the crispy bacon, and the omelettes they make in the north by chucking a lot of butter in a pan and eggs and bacon on top of it. I can taste them now, and the chips, the chips.

You are English – you must like chips! All the Tommies liked *les frites*!

There was no talk of Vichy in Sainghin-en-Weppes – there were the allies, and there were Les Boches.

Around the town the poppies bloomed, to mark bodies never found, like my dear uncles, paratrooper Douglas Godfrey, and stretcher-bearer Roy Darlington.

In the busy kitchen was one record, a twelve-inch disc with 'Moonlight Serenade' on the front side and 'American Patrol' on the backside. We played it all the time.

Louis and his gang came to England. One summer we were in pursuit of a group of French girls who had turned up in Roath Park, Cardiff, and I was on a bench pressing my attentions upon a rather nice young lady with short dark hair when she said – My God, you are English – I thought you were French!

I don't know for how long my French was that good, but I love to speak French and it became a part of my academic success and then important to our business. I could use French in northern Italy, and in Canada, and in countries where I did not have the language people seemed comforted by the fact that I was not just another ignorant Brit – I did have another language though not theirs.

The night I met Monica I chatted about French poetry and the language became essential in our voyage to Carcassonne and our book.

I owe a lot to Louis and miss him. He married the daughter of a local wine merchant and in his middle years they bought a chateau in Normandy and he worked for the European Commission. When my firm did research for the Commission we saw each other but Louis did not much want to carry on being friends.

He had failed his baccalaureate and I had won a scholarship and got into Oxford and Louis was the leader of the pack.

I saw an American TV programme the other day about a school – *Roswell High*. The proposition was that this school was under the control of an alien presence so vicious that only the highest courage and intelligence could frustrate its shameful purposes.

I recognized Whitchurch Grammar School at once.

In the fifties people didn't want to think. People didn't want to go forward – let's settle on what we saved from the inferno – let's enjoy it. No, no questions, no change. Follow the rules – it worked in the war – do as you are told – it worked in the war.

South Wales had its own forces of reaction. The shameful thirties with the Means Test had made you an angry socialist, and centuries of English domination had made you a Welsh nationalist. My problem was I was neither, and having been brought up without a father I was not much good at following rules.

My father decided that he did not like the look of most of the socialist nationalization programmes because they would lead to waste. I agreed with him, and having carried out as an adult many studies of public sector activity, I still do. They don't speak Welsh in South Pembrokeshire and at the time of the birth of the United Nations Welsh nationalism seemed a move the wrong way.

School life was highly politicized through debates and arguments and talks and not to go with the tide was a bit like announcing in an English public school that you had your doubts about fair play as a concept, were not too sure about God and telling the truth, and any chance Matron is up for a shag?

The central annual event in a Welsh school is the eisteddfod, which is a series of competitive turns, mainly musical, and literary competitions. I was entered for the Impromptu Speech. I was fourteen. The theme, revealed just before the speech, was 'The Welsh Language and Culture'.

They might as well have given me a hand grenade.

Welsh, I explained to my audience, four hundred people having a slow day, was a language rich in proverbs. I offered a proverb in Welsh – as I don't speak Welsh I just made a series of Welsh sounds. As you are all aware, I went on, this proverb means *Never fly your kite near high-tension electric cables*. The house went up with a roar. I won.

Next day the headmaster called me in. He had received complaints from the governors about my making fun of the Welsh language. He wanted me to know people had been upset and I had let him down and let the school down. I felt pretty let down myself and my father went round twice to his house to sort him out but fortunately he was not in.

I was told much later that the headmaster was a place-man – a political appointee, who had gained his job by hanging round the local Labour Party. (Welsh local politics was not known for its purity.) He was proud of his position, but edgy, humourless and out of his depth. He didn't like me at all. When I won a State Scholarship he called me in to say he had been told that these scholarships were awarded for promise not achievement but had not realized what that meant until now. He sounded as if he had rehearsed saying that.

I said I wanted to try for Oxford. He lent me a book about Oxford and wrote me a decent enough reference listing what I had done for the school and since no one else was interested I wrote my own syllabus and tutored myself.

The English master was a slimy little bastard everyone knew as Slug. He had a sallow face and a small moustache, and was just over thirty. He was clever, with a first from Cardiff, and a follower of Professor Leavis from Cambridge, the daring new literary critic. He had a record of violence in the classroom.

Slug taught me to use the concrete not the abstract, the Germanic word not the Romance, the active not the passive, and he had good judgement though he was hard on Tennyson and Milton. He cast me in heavy roles in the school plays, and introduced me to BBC Wales where I acted in radio programmes. (My Pembrokeshire accent – *Durrlington* – did fine for the boy who threatened Heidi.) Slug stayed close to me, took an interest in me, was jealous of me and bullied me. I am not sure my being a foot taller than him helped our relationship. Once he struck me across the face in the classroom and I went to the headmaster and handed in my prefect's badge, which was not accepted.

My school career came to an end after a row in the corridor with Slug. The headmaster suggested that having got into Oxford I did not have any reason to be at school and because I was an unpopular and disruptive element I should hand in my prefect's badge again and this time he would keep it and I could go home.

I guess I was a problem student and a right arrogant little bugger and towards the end I am not sure I was in my right mind, but these were mature professionals and I was unimpressed with them at the time and am un-impressed still.

The headmaster died shortly after. He was in his fifties. They said it was cardiac asthma but I reckon it was all too much for him. Slug went full term and died recently. Some people liked him, or at least appreciated his good taste. I saw him once after I left school. He came up to speak to me in the street and I walked past him.

★   ★   ★

Ahead the crews of three narrowboats, all shouting.

You can't wash your boat at a water station when people are waiting!

Yes I can – you have no right to speak to me like that – I was born on a boat! I have come across the Ribble and I can't have salt water on my boat!

There is a queue for water and you are washing your boat. That's selfish!

If you looked after your own boat better it would not look such a mess!

We took our place in the queue for the water station and as it unwound the people from the shouting boats came along crew by crew to tell us what bastards the others were.

When we arrived at Tarleton we went for a walk to look at the Douglas River. Tomorrow we would sail down it for an hour and come out into the mighty Ribble and sail that for an hour and then squeeze along Savick Brook and then break free on to the Lancaster Canal. This river passage is called the Millennium Link. It opened in 2002 and until then the Lancaster Canal was cut off from the UK system. You book your passage months ahead and only six boats are allowed at one time. The tides in the Irish Sea reach forty feet so the moon has to be in the seventh quarter and it is not a bad idea to fit in a bit of prayer and fasting the night before. A line of six boats was moored waiting for the crossing.

A hundred yards ahead a big bloke in a blue T-shirt was standing in the middle of the lane looking at us. He stood there until we were upon him then he slipped to one side. He rematerialized on the bank of the river, looking at us. As we went back to the boat he looked after us all the way.

This north country is a funny place, said Monica. Mad women and canal rage and stalkers. Perhaps they are all mad up here – perhaps it is because of the emissions from the power stations, or perhaps the money for the health service doesn't reach this far.

A chap standing on the bank watching the river go by – look at that current, he said. My engine is only twenty-eight horse. I've never been on a river and we'll be swept away and I have been married six weeks. Snuffed out after six weeks – am I being fair to my lovely wife?

He was about sixty. He wore a tweed jacket and a camel waistcoat and dark corduroy trousers and a hat with a rather wide brim and a leather belt with loops for his windlass. He wore a green paisley cravat. His greying beard was shaved five centimetres from his face and not one hair was longer than any other. He was what a narrowboater would look like in the pages of *Vogue*. He was beautiful. He had spent a long time on his dress and toilette, as if expecting to die.

Think about it, I said – your boat is forty-five feet and you have a twenty-eight-horsepower engine. We went to the Gulf of Mexico with a sixty-foot boat and a forty-three-horse engine. Do the sums – your power:weight ratio is better than mine was.

It was the first time I had ever used the term power:weight ratio, and I felt pretty good about it.

Look down there, he said. Were the currents in the Gulf of Mexico moving as fast as the Douglas River?

No, I said.

Were they moving anything like as fast anywhere along the way?

No, I said.

★   ★   ★

*When I go mad*
*Upon my record sheet*
*Set down this rhyme*
*And then some black*
*Or whey-faced quack*
*Upon my fate*
*May meditate*

Shite, said Colin.

Arsehole, I said.

Fat shite – you've got four stone of fat on you after the deep insulin. Go home and get it off. You don't belong here – wasting my time and the resources of the health service.

You look like Adolf Hitler, I said, with your pasty face and your cowlick. You are frightening the patients. There they are – poor mad buggers lying there and in comes Adolf with the hypodermic.

I can see Colin now. He'll be dead I suppose – he was in his thirties. I loved Colin. We spent a lot of time insulting each other – I don't know why – we just made each other laugh. Mr Pugh was nice too – he ran the ward – he was a big chap, which could be useful in his job. And his number two – Sorry I don't remember your name but I still think of you and I can see your face and sorry I didn't say hello when we stood together in the urinal at the Park Hotel in 1954 – I was still a bit forgetful of things what with the electro-convulsive therapy but it came back and you were such a nice guy.

Whitchurch Mental Hospital was next to Whitchurch Grammar School, and there is no doubt which institution was the more sane. And you can forget *One Flew Over the Cuckoo's Nest* and Jack Nicholson and Nurse Ratched as far as I am concerned – as I relaxed on my bed enjoying one of Colin's cigarettes, the storms in my mind had blown out and Whitchurch Mental Hospital was a grand place to be.

I suppose I had better tell you how I got there.

When I went home from school I took a job up the road in the Income Tax Offices, playing my small part in the conspiracy to delay the repaying of Post-War Credits to the public. It was very boring and the files were covered in dust. And I couldn't sleep. I would lie awake for hours listening to the night cars coming one by one down the Caerphilly Road. I tried sleeping on the floor and that helped a bit. I tried long walks and that helped too, but one day when I went for a walk I became convinced I was a gull – the one in my poem – and that hallucination lasted for half an hour and scared me. I was very unhappy nearly all the time. In fact I was heading for a nervous breakdown. In fact I was going mad.

There were enough reasons for this. There was my programme of study for Oxford. I had no experience of writing a study schedule so I covered everything that had ever come up in the entrance papers. Each day there was a reading target – the overload would have sent Professor Leavis bonkers. Then there were my experiences in the war, and there was the accident to my eye. And I fell in love with the girl next door and wanted to marry her but she was not interested. That bit was really bad. Then the tension at school. And of course I am a loony.

I went down to Cardiff Royal Infirmary and saw a psychiatrist. I told him I felt terrible and he gave me a cigarette and a cup of tea and said You are very ill and must come to hospital right away.

Thank God, I said, and wept, and let go. By the time I got to the hospital I was raving.

In the foyer were plants in pots and behind them were black servants whose job was to serve the matron's obscene desires. I was taken to a small panelled room and there was a bed and as I lay there I balanced on the edge of clouds, I stood in the middle of Dalí deserts wider than the Sahara, I climbed towards the sun, always frightened and falling. Back on earth at night the devil visited me in the form of a wasp. I put him in my ear and that meant I was a grown-up man now. My parents visited me and I could see they were frightened – Mr and Mrs Darlington you should prepare yourselves – he may not be able to communicate with other people very well in the future.

Deep insulin treatment involves a row of mattresses. Me and my six mad mates lay in a row and we were injected with insulin and passed out. After maybe an hour we were revived and drank pints of glucose in water and then we went back to the ward, nursing our sore arms. We had a lot of these sessions. Dr Capstick was very nice and spoke with me as if I was OK and we were two intelligent people discussing medical issues. I put on a lot of weight.

> *Between my teeth insert the rubber gag*
> *Electrodes on my head I see*
> *Here jerks a modern man*
> *Convulsively*

Electro-convulsive therapy was a funny one – a gag with holes in it to hold between your teeth, and then a blast of electricity and you pass out. It didn't hurt.

I was in Whitchurch Mental Hospital for months. We had dances in the main hall. They gave us two full-size cigarettes as we went in and I danced with Phyllis, who was small and pretty. She didn't say much but I guess she was mad as well. It must have been towards the end of my stay because we had a nice time though I didn't see her again. Then Mr Pugh's ward and Colin – My God, Colin, are you dead, you shite?

When we saw Terry leave and he was so well we felt it made our jobs worthwhile, said Mr Pugh to my parents.

They cashed in their Co-op dividend to buy me a coat and the day I left for Oxford I bought a copy of *Wide World* on the station. I was away – I was free – and the sun shone silver on the wider current.

# CHAPTER FOUR

# THE RIBBLE AND THE LANCASTER CANAL

## The Glittering Path

*My new girl, my special new girl*

*He tried to cool his engine by throwing buckets of water – The countryside sort of lies there – You are a hooligan and a show-off – The library, the river, the pub and a Staff Nurse – The Tombstone Shagger – The snorting laugh, the tortured vowels – They are scum – Skin like white porcelain – Cartwheels along the rim of the waves – It goeth neither up nor down – Kipper suprême – Change of husband if you don't watch out – A fly pressed like a flower – They were going down like ninepins in Lancaster – Permission to step on your gunwale, captain? – His face streaming with blood – Out on to the Gulf of Mexico*

The Ribble Link has rapidly become one of Britain's best-known waterways, opening up the lovely Lancaster Canal to anyone moored on the 'main system'. It has especially made a difference to those moored on the Lancaster and their compatriots on the Leeds and Liverpool Canal.

It has, however, also made a difference to the local RNLI stations at Lytham St Annes! In the last two months, there have been five launches to narrowboats using the link. Luckily, all have been resolved without serious injury or loss of life.

The latest incident was typical of the call-outs that we, as

*RNLI volunteers, have been increasingly facing. The owner, on his own in the boat, found that his diesel engine started to overheat while navigating the River Ribble on his way to Tarleton Lock. He tried to cool his engine by throwing buckets of water over it, but this failed and the boat foundered on a mudbank.*

*Lifeboatman Pete Whalley, report in*
Waterways World *magazine*

No, I had seen nothing like the River Douglas as it rushed up itself with the tide, and as we came out of the lock I had to hang on and push the throttle down to keep control, and the six narrowboats left the junkyard of abandoned craft at Tarleton to fester in peace as we fought downstream. Downstream was upstream in a way, because the tide-stream was against us, but I am sure you get my meaning.

The river wasn't very wide, and ran between muddy banks topped with grasses and plants that don't mind salt. Apart from the grasses and plants there is not much scenery on the Douglas, because there are no hills or trees. The countryside sort of lies there, limp and green and damp, intermittently covered with brine, not making much of a statement, no trouble to anyone.

The Douglas bent around on itself and got broader and the tide rose under us and we saw a little more of the flat Douglas country, and there were two fishermen and some swans, which did little to populate the scene. The river had settled towards high tide and was broad and glittering silver, and with such a royal path and carpets of green at the side going on for ever and five miles away to the left the clouds layered in grey and silver and cream over the Irish Sea, we did not lack for beauty.

Our problem was one of manners. We were the second boat out of the lock and the narrowboaters on this crossing were following each other, uneasy in these new waters.

I was catching number one rather quickly – do I pass him? Will that be considered rude? I settled a hundred yards back and thought He must know what he is doing, let him lead the flotilla in.

But he slowed and then I slowed and then he slowed some more and I said to myself, Sod it I can't control the boat at this speed, I'll go ahead.

Overtaking on water is like everything else on water – it takes seven times as long. We drew alongside and pulled ahead in inches, then moved across and took over the lead, exchanging a manly maritime wave.

When we had been sailing for an hour we came to the great T-junction with the River Ribble. Here you turn right with the tide towards Savick Brook another hour upstream. Although there are acres of clear water it is important not to cut the corner as much of the junction is inches deep. You have to go left down the Ribble and then turn back on yourself in the middle of the stream round the Asland Lamp or it's a night on the mud for you and the cover of your favourite waterways magazine. One chap chose the wrong date to get stuck and had to leave his boat on the bank for two months, waiting for the next equinoctial tide.

The Asland Lamp is a great skeletal tripod and on top of the lamp is a cormorant, or should be.

We rounded the lamp and looked back from the Ribble and saw our companions passing across the mark, at ninety degrees to our course, their windows looking like the pattern on the side of a caterpillar. All the boats were running steady, except for one, which wasn't running at all because it had broken down on the Douglas and crawled back into the lock. It is always a good idea before a major crossing to check if you have any oil in the engine, and I will try to remember that myself.

The countryside remained the same, that is to say there wasn't any, and the river did a bit of splashing and glittering but narrowboats don't mind a bit of splashing and glittering – in fact they love a bit of action, as long as there is no swell and not too much going on of a sideways nature.

On the *PM2* there is room on the stern for two people. Have a look at the temperature gauge, Mon, I said – I can't see it from here – I'll watch the revs.

I took us to 2000 revolutions a minute. In the dear old *Phyllis May* the engine would be screaming and jumping off its mounts and the boat would be fighting to get away. But the *PM2* felt good. *Come on, sailor – bring it on – think I can't take it?* I went to 2500, and the *PM2* still felt good. Seventy Fahrenheit, said Monica, and rising fast.

I pushed the throttle handle right down – 3000 revolutions a minute. Our bow wave was creaming out and there was a maelstrom behind us but the *PM2* was holding steady.

Slow down, said Monica, you are on ninety degrees – you'll boil her – and you've left everyone behind – look, the rest of the boats are nearly out of sight. Slow down, you fool, slow down.

We turned left into Savick Brook, which looked like a drain for a rather small field, and waited under the sea lock to rise to the Lancaster Canal. Our companions arrived one by one, and did not appear to have taken offence. I suppose they had no more idea of the etiquette of such occasions than we had. New engine, I said to the helmsman nearest to me. Trying the engine. Important to understand the engine – safety, you know. Always comes first.

I would have thought at your age it had stopped mattering who was fastest away at the lights, said Monica. Is it offers of sex you are looking for, from one of the boating ladies not too far into her seventies, or to command the bar at the next pub? You could have blown up the engine and involved others in a nasty and dangerous shipwreck. You are a hooligan and a show-off – the oldest boy racer out of jail. The waterways should be protected from people like you.

Tell you what, I said, we've got a hell of an engine here. A-wop-bop-a-loo-bop-a-wop-bam-boom!

★ ★ ★

I crossed my eyes horribly and tried to dribble. *I could not get the ring without the finger*, I shouted – *har har har, har har har*. I rose from my chair and lurched around the room.

Thank you very much, said Patrick Garland, and Anthony Page caught me as I fell over a chair. *I coupled with your mate at barley-break*, I bellowed.

I didn't get the part of the ugly and murderous De Flores in the Oxford University production of *The Changeling*, despite having one eye and playing the boy who bullied Heidi to a national radio audience. So I took up rowing instead.

My Oxford life fell into a pattern, with my three years divided between the library, the river, the public house, and the arms of a Staff Nurse from the Radcliffe Infirmary.

There never was a more boring undergraduate than me. I was not a pale-faced nerd who did nothing but work – I made lots of friends, and belonged to more than one of the elitist college societies, God forgive me. In fact I did almost everything you should do, to an unremarkable level.

But a top second was easier than a first, the second eight was very fast, and the college magazine was easier to edit than *Isis*. And the lady undergraduates were not half as pretty as my Staff Nurse. If they were they went out with lords, not terrace-house Welshmen.

My first impression of my college was the pile of trunks in the entrance. *Trunks?* Here were people who owned *trunks*, in which they put belongings when they *went away* – to *public school*. I didn't know anything about public schools, but the trunks looked pretty important.

My room, with two small bedrooms attached, was on the second floor in the second quadrangle. My eye had disqualified me from national service but my room-mate had served two years as an able seaman.

The culture of the able seaman was largely to do with rum and women. The seamen did not like women, but accepted their need for them. My room-mate was proud of his nickname – 'The Tombstone Shagger' – a title won in the graveyard of some distant port.

Good afternoon, sir, I'm Bill.

Bill looked after the half-dozen rooms on our stair-case. He would wake us with a cup of tea in the morning and clean our room and make our beds. He was called a scout.

Jesus College had its famous alumni – the poet Henry Vaughan, Lawrence of Arabia. In the hall there was a portrait of the founder, Elizabeth I.

A small college, an old college, a Welsh college, a college with three small quadrangles, in one of which I would live for two years, and a chapel where I would marry Monica.

The dominant culture was tribal Welsh. There were several undergraduates to whom English was a second language, and a few could hardly speak English at all. Dylan Thomas was the great father in the sky, and rugby was the sport and the drinking and singing rarely ceased. Jesus College was doing well – a Jesus College undergraduate won the university Newdigate Prize for his poem 'Death of a Clown', and another the national Hawthornden Prize for his first book of poems. The eights were gaining places on the river and the college was a force in university theatre.

The mix of public school and tribal Welsh worked

fine. The public school boys were not always very bright, but always confident and cheerful. A lot of the time they would talk to you almost as if you were one of them. Many of them went to single-sex schools and were not much good with girls. I decided the upper classes reproduced themselves vegetatively, like rhododendrons.

Our literature tutor was a war hero – a proud and mannered man who seemed to have read less than I had. We were taught in pairs – none of the famous one-to-one Oxbridge tutoring. Our other teacher was the world's greatest expert on etymology, and so good that I almost began to care about how words changed over time.

Professor Tolkien lecturing on the topic of dragons – I could see the dragon on the floor in front of the podium. I could hear its claws scratch, feel the heat of its breath.

Allen Ginsberg reading 'Howl' to the Henry Vaughan Society. Thirty undergraduates in Harris tweed sports jackets sitting on the floor, struck dumb. Don't you ever feel like you want to fuck the stars? he asked.

The wrinkles of W. H. Auden went deep. Had he fallen over he would have shattered into pieces like a chocolate orange. Later I came to love his poetry, but that evening I understood only three words in a half-hour reading. The words were *cold rewarding soup*. Don't ask me the context.

And the mist on the river and the smell of smoke in the autumn and the crumbling black stones of the colleges (they had not been cleaned yet) and the wisteria outside my window and the swing of the current on the Isis and the crack as your blade hits the water and the beer and the jokes and the friends and the songs.

Was Oxford worth the sweat, the breakdown? Yes, it was great — I loved it. I worked hard and trained hard and the study and the sport toughened my mind and body. My father, the chimney sweep's son who would never become a senior officer, may have been held back by a conspiracy of the upper orders — but now I was part of the conspiracy.

And yet, and yet, and yet . . .

In the fifties nearly half the Oxford undergraduates came from private education and today the proportion is the same. The class system, defined by the secondary school you attend, is here set in concrete, though Oxford is supposed to serve the whole country.

And I bought the proposition that my friends and I were little marvels, better than all the rest. To compound this delusion, like everybody else at Oxford from the lower orders I tried to take up the accent that no one could get right unless they had been to public school — the snorting laugh, the tortured vowels, *actually, yah*. I bought the élitism and the snobbery and became ashamed when I realized it was all bollocks.

The glittering path led to the past.

But perhaps Oxford had made me a gentleman? To be a gentleman was considered a very good thing. My father, from the humblest of backgrounds, was without doubt a gentleman. In fact an officer and a gentleman. He spoke softly without an accent, and moved quietly as if looking for a way to make things easier for you. He asked the family if they minded when he smoked at the table. In the war he knocked someone's hat off in the Grand Cinema in Pembroke Dock because they did not take it off for 'God Save The King'. I understand that is the sort of thing a gentleman would do. He kept his promises and paid his debts. He lied to me once in my life – when I was on the way to hospital with my destroyed eye I asked him if I was going to have an operation. I didn't want an operation because I knew they hurt. No, he said, you will not have to have an operation.

But it wasn't really a lie because he didn't know, did he?

I was not a natural gentleman like my father. I did not have his military grace. Some would have put me into the class defined by Somerset Maugham in the *Sunday Times* the year I went to Oxford –

*I am told that today rather more than 60 percent of the men who go to Universities go on a government grant. This is a new class that has entered onto the scene . . . they are scum.*

One day Bill our scout took me aside – Mr Darlington – the young man who had your room before you would go out every night with his friends. When he came back he would go into the Common Room and tear the curtains down and roll himself up in them and go to sleep on the floor. Ah, Mr Darlington, he was a real gentleman.

This *is* Henry Hall speaking, said Jinny Fisher. He's here for a fortnight.

We opened the door from the kitchen and could just hear the soft voice.

Jinny Fisher was our boss, the owner of the hotel on the shingle beach. She was small and fat and fierce. My friend from Oxford and I were at her hotel for the summer. To stay solvent as a student I had been a gardener, an ice-cream bike man, a tutor, an income tax clerk and an agricultural labourer, and now I was a waiter.

I have never understood how The Waves prospered. It was not luxurious, the owners were not very nice, the beach was stones, and the staff were students who were often disaffected and did not know what they were doing. The Waves must have found a tiny niche before the jet planes came – a niche for rich people to enjoy a seaside holiday right on the gravel beach in a Sussex village. Perhaps they had never seen a proper beach – for sure they had never been to Pembrokeshire.

I put seven plates up my arm and forged out into the dining room. The best thing about the dining room was Anne Rogers, Henry Hall's daughter-in-law. She was here with her husband, Mike Hall. Anne Rogers was twenty-two, dark-haired, with skin like white porcelain, and was playing the lead in *The Boy Friend* in London. She looked very like Monica, but I had not met Monica yet.

Henry Hall spoke to me as if I was a human being and he was an ordinary bloke, not a world-famous bandleader. I did not take the opportunity to have a chat with him about running a band. I mean it must be different anyway if you have thirty musicians and are on the BBC.

The Waves operated a system of tipping whereby the guests offered their gratuities to something called the *tronc*. This evil entity was in the hands of the management who doled out the money to all the staff at the end of the week. The trouble was that I knew damn well that all the money did not get doled out, and I resented accepting as a gift from management the money I had already been given by my customers.

More guests are arriving in the dining room – the captain who comes to dinner in his uniform, the self-made builder surrounded by his family (set a little out of the way so he did not disturb the class hierarchy), the head of the Suncrush soft drinks empire, the couple who are uneasy all the time because they can't afford it here, the au pair with whom my mate spent last night grappling on the sofa.

Time to fetch Clemence Dane her beer. She was in bed upstairs – huge and not well favoured, her grey hair drawn back over each ear. She made me feel like Red Riding Hood – What big bosoms you've got, Grandma!

Clemence Dane was a famous author but to this day I have not read any of her books. She thanked me and perhaps decided to give something to the *tronc* later.

Off to the dance on the pier tonight.

★

My mate found a blonde girl – so many more blonde people down here than in Wales or Oxford.

I made friends with a Swiss gym mistress some years older than me. I kept her picture for years – she looked sweet in her fifties tailored suit but Monica found her and tore her up.

Before arriving at The Waves I had attended a selection course and been chosen as a Unilever senior management trainee. Now I had to go to London to attend an interview to place me somewhere in the organization, so that I could take root and grow. The night before I went for a swim with my gym mistress under the pier in Eastbourne. It was a night to remember, particularly her cartwheels along the rim of the waves with no clothes on.

At the interview in Unilever House I was not at my most alert and was placed in Transport Division, where they wanted people to look after fleets of bloody lorries all their life, and it took me a month to sort that out.

My Eastbourne story should end with me marrying Anne Rogers, but remember she had a husband already. Mike Hall came to Lever Brothers as a consultant on public speaking and the poor chap had to tutor me when I was a rather senior executive. Anne Rogers appeared in the news recently. She had been upset because she wondered if the profession fully appreciated she had played the lead in *The Boy Friend* sixty years ago. Monica seems to be better tempered than Anne Rogers – she doesn't get upset like that even when there is no water in the pounds and the boat gets stuck.

Clemence Dane is long dead and Henry Hall and

the Fishers. The Waves is a pub. It was so long ago.

But if we went to the beach at night in the fifties and picked up a handful of gravel and threw it hard down it made sparks and I bet it still would.

★　★　★

The Lancaster Canal is over two hundred years old. It has no locks, because it goeth neither up nor down, but followeth a contour for forty-two miles between the Irish Sea and the foothills of the Pennines. It begins at Preston, leaves Blackpool and Fleetwood away to the west and closes on the Irish Sea at Glasson, then goes to Lancaster, Morecambe, Carnforth. It stops at Tewitfield, and further north you cannot go on an English canal.

I have always said that the Trent and Mersey from Stone south to Fradley is the most beautiful canal I have seen, and I have found people who agree with me. There is of course the Gloucester and Sharpness, the ship canal, with its broad towpaths hanging with wild fruit and the walks by the Severn. Then there is the Shropshire Union north of Norbury Junction, which looks over the Shropshire plains, and the Monmouth and Brecon clinging to the hills among the oaks and then of course the Caledonian through Loch Ness and elsewhere there is the Camargue and North Carolina – what the hell – can you count the ways?

The Lancaster Canal reminds me of the Trent and Mersey, with its reeds, and green slopes, and its views. But it turns more, the water is clearer and there is more wildlife. Moorhen chicks like tin toys hopping along. A nest of grey swan youngsters with their arms around each other asleep. Herons. Coots coots.

You might meet three boats in a day. On the side of the cut, cruisers and narrowboats, bought for folly or vanity and left to decay. But not so many that the canal is spoiled.

Infinite riches of lilies. On the towpaths and in the fields elder, the glorious weed. So much sweetness will be wasted in the autumn, because Monica will not be here to make her elderberry wine. Once when I was running with Stone Marathoners after the rain I ran alongside an elder bush and knocked it – a perfumed shower, free of charge.

Because of the clear water you can see the fish. First you see through a glass, darkly, but then face to face. Roach – silver with fiery fins. Bream – deep-chested as whippets. Tench – green and black and gold. You will see single spies, and then battalions. You will see the shoals sweep and curve as if they shared one mind, and you will feel the twist of an ancient lust and be a hunter again.

The sea is on your left – there is an extra layer of clouds and the wind is always coming from there and the rain which is a Pembrokeshire spindrift or drizzle and the wild gulls crying.

When we returned from the Gulf of Mexico Monica and I decided to stay at the Ritz Hotel in London for a few days to celebrate.

The dining room in the Ritz is perhaps the most beautiful in the world – huge and high and so well proportioned and the paintings up the walls delicate in yellow and rust and green.

Although we were staying at the hotel they did not want to serve us tea because they were booked up with tourists and I ate one of their prawn cocktails in our room and was in bed for a fortnight. See what happens when you venture above your station in life.

Breakfast at the Ritz, I had thought, I bet that's something. If you can improve on a classic English breakfast I bet they can do it here. I bet they have things that I have never heard of; things which taste even better than black pudding. I know, I'll have a kipper! Kipper at the Ritz – what joy – it will be the fattest, richest, most beautifully cooked kipper that the world has known. It will come on a silver platter, with little shellfish around it, a slip of seaweed, and breads specially chosen to match the taste of the kipper. It will be Kipper Royale, Kipper Suprême, Killer Kipper!

My kipper came on a plate – little slabs of smoky-smelling something that was no longer a fish. It was a dark varnished colour. This boneless wonder looked as if it had been boiled in a bag last Friday and tasted of salt and grease.

I would have been better advised to turn left off the Lancaster Canal not long before I reached the University City. Here you step down, lock by lock, to the sea. There is such room on these green treads that your dogs may run free and the grass at the lockside is mown and all ahead you can see the mist over the sea and the little port of Glasson.

There are on this earth, in this valley of sorrow, places

that take you away, magic places, where things make sense and there is room and time and soft winds and rings to tie up to and pubs and boats bobbing and a smokehouse where you can get kippers as kippers should be.

Kippers hairy with bones, kippers that curl up off the plate as if greeting you, kippers that are light-coloured and fine-fleshed, kippers that offer forksful and then crumble in your mouth. A thousand generations in our sceptred isle have smoked the herring over a wood fire, and metabolized its richness into muscle and brain and bone, and our bodies are telling us At last, the kipper, the kipper – that's the stuff!

Jim and Jess ran in safety along the shore and Monica and I walked behind them. The *PM2* knocked at its mooring and the light came from all sides at once, soft and white.

*If I could snare*
*Her beauty in my halting rhyme*
*Then words so fair*
*Would ravish time*
*Enchant the clock and still its chime*

*If I could break*
*And mould those words to match her grace*
*Then they would take*
*To them a face*
*No bronze or quiet stone could trace*

*And yet I own*
*No painted words for all my care*
*Will blend this tone*
*Eyes blue as air*
*The gold the gold that dusts her hair*

What's that? asked Monica over my shoulder.

Just a little thing I wrote for you at Oxford, I said. Thought it would go nicely in the book – change of pace and all that.

Change of husband if you don't watch out, said Monica. First of all you didn't know me when you were at Oxford, and secondly my eyes are green and thirdly my hair was dark.

What you don't understand, I said, is that I knew you long before we met. Every night when I went to bed there was a gap on my left-hand side exactly your shape. I hungered for my little Welsh darling. I knew you, I could smell you, I could hold you, talk to you, years before we met.

It was that bloody Staff Nurse, said Monica.

Most city basins have grown a crop of apartments. Often these are based on the elegant shells of warehouses, but in Lancaster they were designed by the mayor's cousin, who had read a book about post-modernism. They crowd on you, pompous and dark, and give you a small ache, just in the middle of your forehead.

On the evening of our arrival I popped up on to the bridge for a pint. No Jim, sorry – they wouldn't let you in, old dear, or Jess – omiGod the betrayed eyes.

The ground floor of the hotel had been stripped out and painted black – a weekend drinking factory. There was a line of twenty pumps.

What bitters do you do?

John Smith's.

I have nothing against John Smith's, which is a good beer for drinking, but I will have no truck with an organization that thinks lager is twenty times more important than bitter. I crossed the road to a pleasant-looking pub. Lots of tables – maybe eat here tonight.

I opened the menu and inside was a fly, pressed like a flower.

The next morning the whole crew of the *PM2* set out into the University City. From the canal you have to cross the road. Round here the towns are pushed up alongside the coast and the motorway is pushed up alongside the towns. Traffic tears up the motorway and when it comes off the motorway it keeps on tearing. Not just cars – container lorries and giant wagons up and down and round corners with one wheel on the pavement. It's a bit like the French traffic game of Kill the Pedestrian and His Dogs, but played with bigger pieces. The worst town is Tarleton, to the south, but Hest Bank and Lancaster run it close and run you close too if you walk their pavements, where there are any.

We stumbled on to the uneven pavings of the pedestrianized shopping street. It was low-rise, lightly populated with shoppers – ill-dressed, ill-favoured and undersized.

I do not doubt that most of the citizens of the

University City of Lancaster wear only the latest fashions, are beautiful, and indeed tall and well muscled, and I was unfortunate in my timing this Tuesday morning, but I have to tell as I found.

Watch out, steer to port – here is a big chap – a policeman or security man, technicolor tattooed with jaundice-yellow patches and threatening slogans. Monica and I are tattooed as well but we are arteests and adventurers and my tattoo is very discreet. I know Monica's isn't but Monica is not twenty stone with a shaved head and a baton.

I'll drop into Wilkinson's the ironmonger, get an Allen key, tighten up that handle.

Coming out of Liverpool the throttle handle had come off in my hand. You don't half feel a fool taking a narrowboat across a dock with your mate in a following boat and you realize your throttle bone is no longer connected to your engine bone.

Two minutes, I said.

Wilkinson's had been redesigned as a haunted house – one of those with corridors that keep turning back on themselves. It seemed to sell cheap things, like a discount store – dusters and rolls of paper and crisps. After twenty minutes I found someone who looked like she worked there and she told me to look upstairs. After another twenty minutes I found the stairs and near the top there was my Allen key – in fact a packet of six all different sizes with little rings to hang them up – only 95p the lot.

When I came out I pointed out the little rings to Monica and she was about to tell me what she thought of my little rings when a wheelchair came past and an old gent tipped out on to the pavement.

We picked him up and settled him and Monica was raising the topic of my little rings again as another gent, formally dressed in a black suit, fell headlong a few yards ahead on our left. They were going down like ninepins in Lancaster.

A bulky lad who looked like a farmer stopped us and spoke for some time. I'm sorry, I said, I don't understand – I come from another part of the country.

He explained again slowly that at home he had a dog of whom he was very fond – a long dog, which is a type of lurcher. He had spotted Jess and he had decided she would be a suitable mother for his dog's puppies, and he wondered if we all might enter into the necessary arrangements. I explained that alas Jess was no longer active in the reproduction department but how nice of him. It would have been lovely, he said, and Jim and Jess tried to climb up inside his jacket.

Back at the boat a short chap about fifty with a round face. Hello, I am Norman – that is my boat next door. Permission to step on your gunwale, captain? They tell me you are a writer.

Yes, I said.

This is my friend Arthur.

Permission to step on your gunwale, captain? asked Arthur. He was slim and tanned, about the same age as Norman, with no teeth. They both shook my hand. They smelt of drink.

We have a plan – what with you being a writer, said Norman.

Oh yes?

I will tell you our plan, in complete confidence of course. We have been working it out for some time.

He dropped his voice and they both leaned in towards me. Our plan is to fit my boat out to go to sea and go out from West Kirby. We expect to make a lot of money.

How?

Ah, that's what you tell us – you are the writer.

Monica and I sat down to lunch and there was shouting. Norman and Arthur were quarrelling on the towpath with three other men. They all began to exchange blows and Arthur fell down outside our galley window, crying out, his face streaming with blood. The group moved away down the towpath, Arthur complaining and the others arguing and trying to clean him up.

In the afternoon Norman's boat slipped away and a new neighbour arrived in a fifty-eight-footer.

At four o'clock the next morning our new neighbours began to shout at each other. We lay uneasy in the basin of the University City, under the glowering apartments, until the tumult had died.

By my troth, quoth Lancelot, this is a dreadful place.

★   ★   ★

*In a nook*
*That opened south,*
*You and I*
*Lay mouth to mouth.*

*A snowy gull*
*And sooty daw*
*Came and looked*
*With many a caw;*

*'Such,' I said*
*'Are I and you,*
*When you've kissed me*
*Black and blue!'*

I don't know if you are familiar with the place where the Ross Spur passes the Wye – the river in its green valley, going south for Monmouth and the Bristol Channel. On its bank our main characters in their youth – Terry, twenty-three, and Monica, twenty-two. Monica had just put on her swimming costume, managing to preserve her modesty while holding my interest without difficulty.

This girl was gorgeous – pale skin, green eyes, dark hair, brilliantly clever. This was the best girl ever. I had been so lucky to crash that Cardiff University hop just when her immature thirty-year-old boyfriend had decided he couldn't commit. Bastard, hurting my Mon. And she's coming up to London so I can see her there. Shall I explain some more about Charles Baudelaire or give her another kiss? Tough choice that one.

Tell you what, I said later. Let's take this mattress and sail on it down the river.

OK said Monica.

I pulled the inflatable down the bank through the soft grass and settled it in the shallows. My new girl, my special new girl, and I rolled on to it and it bumped away and put on some speed and we sailed laughing the length of a couple of cricket pitches, and on to London and Canada and Stone and Carcassonne and out on to the Gulf of Mexico.

# CHAPTER FIVE

# THE LANCASTER CANAL

## *Further North You Cannot Go*

*Ghosts on the sand, lying drenched and still*

*He was a real trainee – A loser all my life – A Bolton parson telephoned me recently – Now I'm engaged to Miss Monica Ann Gell – We would have to ask the Archbishop of Canterbury – Love before dinner – Fresh green and yellow summer skins – Do you do much ocean racing, Terry? – The tide was gathering speed – It looks like a cowpat – The jewel of the north-west coast – Like being at sea*

Decent chaps from Oxford went into the universities or the BBC or the law or medicine or the Civil Service. They did not make money from society – they served society. But I wanted experience of the real world so that when I became a famous poet I could offer more understanding of life. And I knew I had some growing up to do – perhaps business life would toughen me up.

Unilever sent me to Lever Brothers, which with the US firm Procter & Gamble dominated the UK market for soap.

Management studies had not yet arrived from the USA so Unilever management trainees hung around their betters in offices and factories, hoping to pick up something or other that would illuminate their later years. I spent a morning with a guy in Port Sunlight who explained the system they had developed for keeping track of ladders.

Trainees were tolerated rather than welcomed, because they did not stay long and one day they were going to get all the best jobs. They were exotics – there were very few university graduates around and fewer had been to Oxbridge – What do you *read*, Mr Darlington?

I did not meet the expectations of all who met me. The head secretary in the north-east office made her opinion known –

*Now that trainee we had before Mr Darlington – he wore tweed suits and had a lovely sports car and a really posh accent. One day he came into the office with a pheasant hanging out of his pocket. I would drop my drawers for him any time. He was a real trainee.*

The main rule for a trainee was not to get sent out on the road. The road meant the regional sales offices, small and inbred, where no one was promoted. It was vital to get back into head office, among the influence, the jobs, the money.

After three months it was time for my interview with the board. I was clear on my strategy.

I would like to go out on the road, I said. I want to feel the wind in my hair, the sand between my toes. My constituency is the common people. I will absorb the wisdom of the grocers our customers and win the trust of the humble sales representatives. The real Lever Brothers, its heart, is out there on the road. What are we, if we cannot give to ordinary people . . .

Just a minute, Mr Darlington, said the Chairman.

He looked around his colleagues.

Terry, we have never heard a trainee talk like this before. It's people like you we need in head office.

There was not much to eat or drink in the war and in the fifties the business community was jolly well going to make up for it. Well into the thirty-year post-war boom our time had come. Drunk at lunchtime, drunk after work, three-hour lunches, best restaurants, damn the expense. You could entertain practically anybody and charge it against tax. If you ate in, Levers had four levels of canteen, and at the higher levels the lunches got longer and drunker.

With two dominant firms in the soap industry it was easy to fix prices and with the high margins you could have dozens, hundreds, of people hanging around, circling each other.

*The smylere with the knyf under the cloke*

I would try to write my *Punch* articles on the train, when I was not too crushed or frozen and the railways were not on strike. The offices in Lever House were noisy as London rebuilt itself outside the window and the meetings were interminable. No one took any responsibility for anything.

*While meeting in the sales office this morning*
*To discuss the allocations of bargain packs in Scotland*
*It occurred to me*
*That the waves seethe along the rocks in Barafundle*
*And the sea lies in the bay's hand like a green stone*

But if I leave now I'm a loser, I said to Monica, and I'll be a loser all my life.

My first real management job was as a liaison manager with the Port Sunlight factory and the research establishments. This meant working with boffins – scientists and development engineers.

The perfumiers were the best.

These guys were arteests. They wore bow ties. They would work at an organ, yes an organ. They each had a big desk with hundreds of little bottles on it. On the left the little bottles contained the low notes, the heavy smells of musk and ambergris, and on the right the high notes – the light florals and so on. They would dip a little paper taper into a bottle and then another taper into another bottle and build up a perfume. A perfume had to have a bass, like music, and a middle range and high notes.

Then there were the development engineers. Tweed sports coats, serious expressions, like Michael Redgrave in *The Dam Busters*. They would stare at their new machine, which was usually called a Pilot Plant and never seemed to work, and hit it hard with the heel of the hand in the top right-hand corner. If this didn't work they would kick it with their left foot.

Sometimes this would do the trick, but often the machine would make a grinding noise and burst into flame –

*Gentlemen, the Board is most concerned that recently*
*Due to bad planning in the factory*
*A number of matters have been going awry*

*You may have read the harrowing obituary*
*Of the Foreman working late to ensure delivery*
*Who slipped and was boiled up in the soapery*

*In Foods Division because of some uncertainty*
*Blue baked beans were manufactured in huge quantity*
*And puzzled letters are still arriving hourly*

*A Bolton parson telephoned me recently*
*To remark that in a pack of Indian tea*
*His wife had found an operative's glass eye*

*A line of costly packaging machinery*
*Driven far beyond its nominal capacity*
*Broke out and packed three passers-by from Wallasey*

*I hope all management will now try seriously*
*To plan ahead and work efficiently*
*You can go now No smoking in the lavatory*

When I had finished my term in this job many of the scientists wrote nice letters and wished me luck and sent copies to my boss. They realized that I was really interested in their machines and tests and formulations. Their letters did much for my reputation and I was appointed Senior Brand Manager in charge of Lux, Unilever's biggest toilet soap.

Now don't forget – if it doesn't work, follow the professionals – hit it in the top right-hand corner with the heel of the hand.

It started with a badger.

Herbert from J. Walter Thompson was telling us about India in the war. It seems his colonel fell in love with an Indian boy. One night there was a great cry and the colonel rushed from his tent, gravely wounded in the personal department. The doctor was called for and the colonel explained that a badger had crept into his tent and bitten him.

It's not funny I know and we should be ashamed, but we laughed and laughed and tucked into the oriental food, which seemed to be mincemeat and spices in oil.

That night I awoke with a terrible pain in my stomach. I crawled out into the night and knocked up the doctor round the corner, who gave me two aspirins. I packed to go to hospital, but they sent me home from the outpatients.

The pain came and went over two months, and I lost two stone. The local doctors of Barons Court were unhelpful – Who is this guy in a posh suit? Finally I went home to Cardiff and saw the family doctor. He sent me to a surgeon who said I had a gall bladder that was giving me colic and I had better have it out.

I went to a small private hospital in Llandaff.

I woke up with a six-inch wound in my belly and had to get through the night in agony – the worst time I have ever had. It still hurts when I think of it. I rang for the nurse and a teenager gave me two aspirins. I read since of a doctor who had the same experience and devoted his life to promoting pain control. I hope he had every success.

I was blessed with many visitors. My father loved Monica, and brought her along, bending the rules on visitor numbers by explaining that she was my fiancée. She wore a hat and looked adorable.

My trouble was that I was finding it very difficult to commit. Monica was my best girl of course – she would be anybody's best girl – and I had cast aside all others, but I had been so much hurt by my first love for the girl next door that I just could not open my heart, if you will forgive the sentimental fifties way of putting it.

These days they take your gall bladder out through your earhole and you are better in a fortnight but I was home in Cardiff for three months. I had time to think. And I had been so knocked about by the pain in hospital it had changed me.

When I came back to London I went straight to Monica's flat and went down on my knee and now I'm engaged to Miss Joan Hunter Dunn, I mean Miss Monica Ann Gell.

You don't have to feel worried or ashamed by your feelings of sexual desire, said the chaplain. God put them there for a reason.

Oh good, I said.

The Jesus College chaplain looked very frail. I felt that any feelings of sexual desire would have shattered him into pieces. But he had three kids fair play so perhaps he was a bedroom athlete, who would leap out of his cassock and take up the merry chase before the chords of evensong had died away.

The college chapel is not licensed for marriage, continued the chaplain. We would have to ask the Archbishop of Canterbury for a special dispensation and he's expensive and takes some time. Your best plan is to get married in a register office and come along the next day and have a service here.

I don't know if this matters, Chaplain, but I am getting married in my own clothes.

In your own clothes? You are getting married in a lounge suit?

The chaplain looked as if I had insisted on wearing a gun-belt. Letting these lower-middle-class people into Oxford might be a good idea in principle but people like him had to sort out the problems that arose in the front line.

It's very unusual. I'm not sure . . . I'll tell you what – your wife can wear a short dress, and then it would probably be all right.

Looks like we are going to make it, I said to Monica before the big day. The bursar nearly turned nasty about the punchbowl but as long as the chaplain does not break his leg you and I are going to be joined in jolly matrimony on Saturday.

It was a vicious cold dark day. Nearly everyone made it

through the snow and Cousin Ken played upon the organ in the chapel. Monica looked enchanting in the short velvet dress that she had made herself and I was in my black Simpson's suit, looking striped and convincing and in my early fifties. As we kneeled we had an excellent view of the chaplain's broken leg, his plaster covered by a green sock.

In the hall we filled the college punchbowl with mulled wine, and when our guests had emptied it we fled into the West Country in a Mini, which handles pretty well in the snow.

Bath, Salisbury, Henley, exploring the potential of love before dinner. As we had been the last couple in Europe not to sleep together before we married this was extra good fun.

Our little flat was on a shopping parade in Chessington, Surrey. Monica was looking forward to returning to her job at Tiffin Girls' School – no longer little Miss Gell but married Mrs Darlington.

I don't know what got us interested in the idea of a canal holiday. There were few canals in South Wales and I couldn't remember visiting one, apart from the dykes in Lincolnshire in my babyhood. But it seemed a good idea to go on a canal holiday this year.

In the early sixties the only canal voyage known was Llangollen and back, and we went to Market Drayton to hire a boat. By the quay a few plastic cruisers swayed in the wind. One was green, and looked neater than the others. It had a little outboard engine.

The boat was small enough to do circles in the cut

and when Monica drove it did circles all the time. Also Monica was pregnant with our first baby and the locks were heavy. So we divided the work – I drove the boat and did the locks and Monica heated the baked beans on the gas ring.

The Shropshire Union Canal north of Market Drayton is ravishing. There were a few cruisers like ourselves. Every ten yards there would be a plop and a line of bubbles and a water vole would make his getaway.

One evening we sat in the boat and two grass snakes came swimming by in their fresh green and yellow summer skins, more beautiful than Cleopatra, more graceful than whippets.

Put a snake down on flat ground and he will bugger off as fast as he can. He throws a loop out to the left and one to the right and the loops travel down, with other loops following them, until his whole body is driving him ahead. Now imagine that movement in water, with the snake relaxed, the loops smooth and symmetrical running down his body – a swimmer on the surface comfortable and graceful, with no surly bonds of earth to break the harmonic of his path.

On the Llangollen Canal the country became hilly and it started to rain, as it does when you cross into Wales. But it was a fine day when we flew our cruiser two hundred feet into the sky on the cathedral legs of the Pontcysyllte Aqueduct, and tried not to look down too often because inches away was the void, then the stones in the bed of the Dee, and the green water tumbling.

On the way back we came across one of those

narrowboats moored by the cut – you know, the ones that look like sewer tubes and go on for ever and have flowers on the top and quaint people live in them. The old chap asked us in and his wife made us a cup of tea.

Incredibly they lived on this boat, moving round the canals mooring to mooring like the Flying Dutchman. They were sweet and grey and old and doddery and past it as you would expect at seventy, but happy and proud of their tube and its flowers on top and roses within. I thought of our lives over the shopping parade in Chessington and the filthy trains and the terrible people I worked with in Lever Brothers' head office and my heart ached.

Audlem is near Market Drayton, and I am pleased to report has a number of public houses to this day. On that day we went in at lunchtime. We found ourselves in someone's front room – sofa, table, carpet, ornaments.

The effect of the smell of a room on a townie who used to live in the country – the damp straw and plaster smell of his grandma's cottage – it reaches inside him and says Come back, for Christ's sake, come back.

Then someone put a tape in the player, just for us, and played a set of tunes they had put together themselves. They played it because we were welcome there. We did not have to push through a drunken crowd to reach a bar spilled with beer.

We went back down to the boat and the sun shone on the fields and on the cut and on that day unknown to my conscious mind I decided this was my country and I would live here.

★

In those days the soap companies were the biggest of all advertisers. Lux toilet soap spent the equivalent of twenty million pounds a year, but was struggling to hold its place at the top of the market. *Nine out of ten film stars use Lux* was the slogan and the advertising agency was J. Walter Thompson.

I never got on with JWT. I respected the creativity of the company but there were so many snobs and drunks. I didn't feel easy with them – they were always boasting, poncing about. *Do you do much ocean racing, Terry?* I wasn't sure they felt easy with themselves. One senior man I had known had just fallen from a high building.

*Life is for living, Terry*, one of the Lux account managers explained to me one evening, when I turned down the third gin and tonic. He spoke as a man of some experience would talk to a little child. He died quite soon afterwards, a victim of the third gin and tonic.

Anyway here I was, the new Senior Brand Manager in charge of Lux toilet soap. I asked to see the current commercials.

*Pamela Tiffin?* I said. Who the hell is Pamela Tiffin? Are we going to have the housewives of Britain rushing out to buy Lux because *Pamela Tiffin* says she uses no other? You must be joking. Is this the best you can do? I have never heard of Pamela Tiffin. Aren't you supposed to have a man in Hollywood who is friends with Princess Margaret and sleeps with all the big stars? Can't he get us a few people someone has heard of?

Pamela Tiffin is a very beautiful and talented lady, Terry, and unfortunately Robin Douglas-Home has killed himself.

Oh Lord. Poor chap. But look, let's start again – do some research. Ask a couple of hundred housewives who they think are the most beautiful women around and then go and sign them up. And no more commercials with unknowns pouting into a dressing-table mirror like tarts waiting for a John. I never saw such boring bloody stuff. This is the sixties – let's have some action. Let's make some noise.

You have to give it to JWT – they did just fine. Petula Clark on a *bateau mouche* in Paris, Kathy Kirby at the Palladium, Janette Scott on a white horse, Claudia Cardinale whizzing round the Colosseum.

I can quit now, I said to Monica. Lux toilet is the market leader again.

Terry, this letter says you have been selected to go to Canada for six months. You will have to tell them I am pregnant – will they pay for me and the baby?

★   ★   ★

Monica does our planning and had arranged the whole of our narrowboat trip up north when I was stuck in the Grimpen Mire of a Stone winter. So the river crossings and the lovely Lancaster Canal had been a surprise to me.

Two things I had expected were Morecambe Bay, because the canal would pass within a couple of hundred yards, and the Midland Hotel, where I knew I would fall in love.

We walked down from Hest Bank to Morecambe

Bay. We had to cross a main road and the railway line to Glasgow, and it took half an hour.

When we got to the beach the sky was darker and the bay was endless and empty and I was oppressed by ghosts. Ghosts on the sand, lying drenched and still, or erect and turning in the mist. Their faces were pale and I knew they were shivering and I could hear their cries for help. It happened just there, over there.

No one had protected them, the twenty-three young people who were drowning, and no one would come to save them now. The forty-foot tide in the huge flat bay was like a galloping horse and the February wind was like a knife.

*The incident highlights the need to ensure sensible health and safety arrangements are in place for all workers in Britain.*
*Justin McCracken, Head of Operations for the*
*Health and Safety Executive*

But aren't you and your mates the chaps who are supposed to ensure sensible health and safety arrangements, Justin? Why did you not challenge the gangmasters? Because Morecambe Bay is a public cockling ground? Because they were illegals, because they were Chinese? Because, like so many government regulatory agencies, you did not do your bloody job?

Monica had gone ahead over the dun and black platforms of mud covered with yellow grass. Between the platforms were run-offs and channels filled with mud. Jim and Jess strained and whined – we were going to play The Game.

A dismal shore – rocky, muddy, broken, ugly. Out towards the sea, mud, mud and a grey horizon – Grange-over-Sands breaking the line to the north – and to the south the Midland Hotel a tiny white blur.

Monica was almost out of sight and the dogs were screaming. I let them slip and Jess went ahead, dodging and swerving to follow the grassy knolls, flying where no ground was beneath her. As she crossed a dark background her brindled coat vanished and there she was again, her white socks flailing. Jim swerved and raced after her but halfway he stopped – I'm an old guy now and what the hell?

When they went to look for the Chinese cockle-pickers they found twenty-one corpses spread around the whole bay. Most had left the vehicle but a few remained with it to die. Two were never found.

It was dusk and the air was cold and four miles out the tide was gathering speed.

We reached Tewitfield, which wasn't very much, just a turning point, near a main road, but green and pleasant with services. We had reached the northernmost northern point of the English canal system. There was a bloke already moored there. Ho ho – we know who he is, he said.

The bloke was in what I can only call a wide narrowboat. That is a narrowboat which is twice as wide as a narrowboat. As the locks are broad or none round here, wide narrowboats are quite common. A narrow narrowboat has barely room to stay alive but is slim and elegant. A broad narrowboat has bags of room and looks like a cowpat.

Yes, it is him.

And you are you.

Indeed.

And that is Monica?

No question, and this is Jess.

Read both your books – got them on board. Will you sign them?

To get a signature people will mail us their copies at home, bang on our roof from the towpath, chase us along the cut. It is much nicer than being ignored.

The Midland Hotel Morecambe is on the south side of Morecambe Bay. Nothing is out of reach of ghosts, but their influence is scarce felt here, just a quiver of cold now and then, a shape darkly on the far sands. The Midland Hotel Morecambe has its own powerful ambience.

One of the few defences we have against time is to make something very beautiful. The Midland Hotel Morecambe is small – forty-four bedrooms – well enough placed on a sandy and pleasant part of the great bay, but not on a towering headland, not even isolated from other buildings. The Midland Hotel makes its own space, its own rules.

How simple it all is – this is just right, this adds up. Energy is mass times the square on the speed of light. The building is not complicated, not brutal and stupid and blundering like the apartments on Lancaster canal basin. How simple, how easy it all is.

Start with a colour – white of course. Then a shape – a rectangle naturally. Convex to the sea and concave to the railway station that serves it. Glaze it and take care that the window fittings are simple and flush. That's right, plenty of glass. Get the window proportions right – height and breadth must balance, and echo the building as a whole. A large atrium – space, space, and some genius artworks, carpet, sculpture – Eric Gill, who else? A circular staircase swinging up the four storeys. A terrace at ground level with a glass wall to the sea – that will do for the restaurant. Behind it a long bar looking through the terrace. Round the corner a little circular bar. Here you haven't much room and every detail must be right – the stools, the counter, the taps, plenty of height. Freedom is what we are after, light and freedom and more lightness and look at the sun on the sands and see how the sky is growing red. After dinner we will walk out on to the promenade into the bay and look out at the rising tide and back at the simplicity and truth of the jewel of the north-west coast.

Built in 1933 – an RAF hospital seven years later. They are not long, the days of wine and roses. But the Midland Hotel Morecambe has just been rescued and refurbished and God bless her.

Back across the Ribble tomorrow, Terry, back to the Rufford Branch. That is if the gales will let us. Those big trees are thrashing about – it will be like being at sea.

# CHAPTER SIX

# THE LEEDS AND LIVERPOOL
## Simon Rodia Funny Little Guy

*The swell was twenty, maybe thirty feet*

*Mid-Atlantic in the mad July gale – Outside the pub with her skirt pulled up – The Toronto Salute – The lights of Yonge Street bold as blood – A long way up for the hell of it – It begins with the creeping – The City Lights Bookshop – El Camino Real – Some gentle people there – A pheasant in a Christmas tree – Wigan Pier is among the most hopeless – You will not necessarily be attacked – A million times I was wake up all night*

I was swept up, then down. I hung on to the rail. The swell was twenty, maybe thirty feet. The gulls had all been blown away. Whoops, up she goes. I wasn't expecting this.

Down and a crash and a wallow and a bang. She's taking it quite well, and not skidding sideways. Just up up up down down down. Sometimes you are weightless as an astronaut, and then your knees cannot take your mass. There is a long fetch from Newfoundland to the mid-Atlantic, for the swell to build up.

Monica sat in a deck-chair in a blanket, looking pale, holding Lucy, who was grinning. Most of the passengers were in their cabins, throwing up. But the pills the doctor had given to help me make it through the night of Lever Brothers were excellent for seasickness as well.

The little Dutch liner *Ryndam* bashed on, butting mid-Atlantic in the mad July gale, taking the young executive and his family to Canada, to help him prepare for international command. But he just wanted to be a poet and live somewhere quiet – perhaps managing a waterworks – a quiet waterworks – a waterworks in the country – where there was plenty of water and not too many pumps or anything, and a staff who knew how it all worked and did everything you asked.

His second article for *Punch* was shortly appearing – 'Off-peak Off-beat', about people who lived on the edge of society and went against the tide. That was a much more important step in his career. But it was wonderful to go to Canada – very few English people crossed the Atlantic in the early sixties.

Each day stretched to twenty-five hours, with lectures and films and talking with the students and the old folk who gather round Lucy and ask to hold her, and drinking rum and Coke and watching the waves and the wake and waiting for the shore – and after a week there it is, far away on each side.

Not long ago the U-boats lay under the St Lawrence River like pike. They sank twenty-four ships, taking nearly four hundred lives. Just one U-boat was sunk – Johnny Walker could not reach that far and there were plenty of places to hide along the broken coast. The temperature gradients in the St Lawrence are sharp and salt water and fresh flow close together and the Allied sonar signals were reflected before they reached their quarry.

In the museum at Liverpool we had seen a torpedo – I wondered why stricken ships went down so quickly, until I saw a twenty-foot torpedo.

The Battle of the St Lawrence – fought in the currents and the temperature layers against twenty-foot torpedoes and deck cannon. A battle of invisible predator and defenceless prey – terrible, vicious, forgotten.

But the St Lawrence was smooth, and the U-boats were gone, and Hitler is dead, and Doenitz is dead, and you are a young man with his lovely family, it is evening, and look, *par ici, Monsieur Terry, un oiseau-mouche* – a hummingbird – right there by the rail.

★ ★ ★

Jim, the original narrow dog, is my whippet and Jess is Monica's whippet but on the *PM2* it's every man for himself, or every woman, or every whippet.

Two narrow dogs take up the whole of a narrowboat. They have their little beds how sweet but they spill out of them all over the floor. They lie in the narrowest part of the corridor. They know where you are going to sit for meals and are there when you arrive. They jump you when you are in bed.

When they cannot sit on you the narrow dogs lie and look at you reproachfully – I am sure if you put your mind to it, master, you could find something nice for the poor narrow dogs – a walk, a treat, some love?

Jim is pedigree, patrician, elderly (what happened to Daddy's Little Moon-mouse?), stubborn, bossy but very affectionate, and a grand dog to take for a walk. He holds close and will wait while you chat on the towpath. Jim is a gent.

If Jess were a person you would find her sitting on the pavement outside the pub on a Friday night with her skirt pulled up. She has no control over her emotions. She loves me and cannot let me be – wherever I go I can feel her wet nose against the back of my knees. In fact I can still feel it when she has gone. I can feel it now. She climbs up me and throws her arms round my neck when I am sitting down or puts her chest on my knees sideways.

She is dreadful to take for a walk. Yesterday she yanked out of my hand barking and threw herself on a German shepherd that could have swallowed her whole. Whenever she can she runs away, seeking to rid the world of rabbits.

I took them for their morning walk at Tarleton on the lead and there were rabbits in the lane – hopping about, no harm to anyone. I turned and went back to the boat, but Jess had seen the rabbits.

That afternoon as I came into the boat Jess came out between my legs and was off up the lane. Monica went after her and came back with Jess limping and bleeding. The vet said she had run into a fence and had a bad cut right by her eye and needed stitches there and elsewhere and took her in and gave her back to us sewn up full of dope with a lampshade round her neck.

None was more sad than Jim, who set about licking her carefully and was moved to show his affection in the most obvious way and chased her up and down the boat for days.

★　★　★

It is a truth not universally acknowledged that the climate in eastern North America is a bastard. I have choked in New York in August and near been struck dead by cold in January. I have sweated in Virginia and shivered in Florida, been drenched in Georgia and blown about in the Carolinas. Most European settlers in North America died soon after arriving, and it is a triumph of the human spirit that any raised the strength to reproduce themselves. So to you reading these words down the ages and planning to settle in North America I would offer some advice. You may have heard this before, but – Go West, young man.

Further west than Toronto, for sure. We lay on our bed helpless, the fan whizzing and the sweat lying on us in pools.

Just a few months later we would pass people in the white streets and they would flash the Toronto Salute – a tap on their ear to warn us that our lobes had gone white and the next stage is frostbite and then your ears fall off.

Lever Brothers was air-conditioned and carpeted. I learned to offer my fist to the door, as to a large un-familiar dog, so the bolt of electricity could fly from me with a crack and not harm me or those around me.

The chairman interviewed me on arrival. He was a Brit of traditional cut. In England, Darlington, he explained, we have small houses and small cars, whereas in Canada we have big houses – big houses, Darlington, and big cars.

The danger with these overseas attachments is that they were seen as a tax-free reward for success rather than a serious matter and you finish up poncing around like visiting royalty, bored stiff. So I asked for a proper job and joined the marketing team.

My workmates were most friendly, but I could not understand why after four weeks no one had asked me to the pub after work. I suggested an outing one evening. Very pleasant it was, though there were no women in the bar and apparently it was against the law to drink while standing up. The next evening some of the lads went out again. In the morning they stumbled in with plaster casts, bandages. There had been blows, someone said there had been a knife. We did not go for a drink after work again.

I wonder was it against the law to knife someone while standing up?

I was seen as a harmless if exotic figure, a sort of a Laughing Harry. People would come into my office to chat. To encourage them I liberated from the storeroom a six-foot picture of Lord Leverhulme, the founder of the Unilever empire, in full viscount drag, and put out a call for captions. This was thought rather daring. The winner was Kelly from accounts – *Hello there, I'm your Avon representative.*

★

Monica and our little fat darling and I spread our holidays round our weekends and hired a VW Beetle, which was very good on snow.

*New custom-blended Blue Sunoco is gasoline power at its purest*, gibbered the radio, and the tune runs in my head to this day. Powered with custom blend we drove in every direction – Muskoka, Haliburton, Niagara, Windsor, the Algonquin national park. Near Lake Muskoka we sat by the Moon River and sang the song. The real Moon River was a thousand miles and forty years away – but we'll be crossing you in style, one day. We hired a canoe and at sunset paddled out on to Lake Muskoka, between the dark woods, the water incarnadine.

We saw bears, we met Indians, we saw beaver dams. Mostly we saw maples. Pillarbox red and gold and peach for hundreds of miles, the branches a fascination of patterns and light.

> *When the Good Lord made the Canadian woods*
> *He was in one of his flamboyant moods*
> *Then when he made the Canadian fall*
> *He showed practically no restraint at all*

There are lots of squirrels in Toronto. They are black to soak up the last photon from the sun. They ran along our clothes-lines, and scattered snow on to our heads from the sidewalk trees.

Winter in the city when the lights of Yonge Street, bold as blood, insult the night. Hovering over the morning traffic, with Eddie Luther, the CFRB commentator, as he told the people sitting in jams they were sitting in jams, and the people that weren't that they weren't. We went to an ice hockey match. Our taxi driver explained how he coached his lads to injure the opposition. Our neighbours took us in for Christmas and to a crowded service where people stood up and told how they hadn't needed doctors.

On the day we left, Lever Brothers gave us a patch-work quilt – We thought you would like this, Terry – we didn't know what to get you because you have a funny attitude to big houses and big cars and stuff and seem to be a bit left-wing but we found this made by a special community that lives outside society.

The quilt burned on the *Phyllis May*. Of everything we lost we valued it the most.

Goodbye swinging Toronto. It wasn't swinging really, just people on the radio playing a lot of Beatles records and saying it was Swinging Metro My God look at us swing did you see how we swung?

We picked up our fat little one and headed for Toronto International Airport and from the air the prairies were white and sometimes thin lines crossed them and sometimes ridges but not often and they went on for thousands of miles.

Go West, young man.

★   ★   ★

In Westfields, our house near Trowbridge, my dad would help me with my little tin watercolour box and one of the colours was called Grass Green but I never saw that green again until today.

An overcast day with colours unbleached and the lake of grass a yellow Westfields green, a lake of grass as big as the Serpentine, which is pretty big. The *PM2* looks out from the canal over the lake of grass to a line of pink balsam a quarter of a mile long and then trees a hundred feet high on the other side of the Douglas River – the very river that had borne us on its shoulders past the Asland Light.

A heron a long way up. I had not seen a heron a long way up before. There was a wind and he was flying, not floating like herons do. Perhaps from up there he could check out all the fish in the canal and the Douglas River together, as they flowed each side of the green lake of grass. Or perhaps he wanted to go a long way up, for the hell of it.

We will stay here, we said, for a while. This mooring is beautiful. And it's the only place we have found where the dogs can run free for as long and as far as they like.

Jim and Jess ran on the yellow-green grass in huge circles until they were winded and then they jumped back into the boat and lay panting and grinning, their eyes bright.

We thought we had already seen the best canals, hitched at the most beautiful moorings, sailed the purest waters, but here in the north-west, between the Pennines and the sea, we are having to reconsider our position.

While we are reconsidering our position in the Douglas Valley one day from Wigan, I can tell you of a day on the *PM2*.

★

It begins with the creeping.

At twenty-five to six Jim comes into the cabin, crawling on his belly like a snake. Very slowly he stands up then springs into the air, landing on me with his legs stiff. I shout and wake up. Monica says something disrespectful in her sleep. Jim finds a space near the bottom of the bed and goes to sleep.

At twenty to seven Jess puts her nose under the duvet and then the rest of her and pushes and pushes until her nose is level with my feet, which she begins to lick.

At seven o'clock I get up and put on the kettle just too late for the news headlines on the radio.

After breakfast I get on to the stern and drive the nose into the bank, then swing out and away and Monica and the dogs walk alongside.

The *PM2* is noisier than the *Phyllis May*, with a canally clatter, but never mind, look at the dogs. Monica is a graceful walker, but a whippet, which is no good for anything else, moves like a catspaw of wind on a canal surface, like a swallow touching the water, like a branch swaying. It is not possible to prove the feet touch the ground because they flick so delicately along, and the balance of the narrow body is so subtle, so sure, that part of your mind balances with it. No artwork can compare with the beauty of these animals moving because, no good for anything else, they move exceeding well.

It is important to keep the boat in just the right position alongside the dogs. If it gets ahead they pull and you can't keep your balance and you go slower and slower and the boat gets further ahead and the dogs pull harder and harder and you all finish up in a pile of legs on the towpath.

But if the boat falls behind Jim starts to scream – You fool, you've forgotten Mon. I keep telling you we must stick together. Leave her behind and she'll get eaten or join someone else's pack. Fall back! Fall back! We are a pack! When will you get the idea? We are a pack!

As a treat Monica lets the dogs off the lead and they rush off and Jess works the hedge and as soon as there is a gap she is through it. We don't like her running away but at least these days she comes back.

At the locks the whippets are fastened to a piece of gear and watch the slow-motion fun with all the heaving and the pouring water and lockside chat. If it is sunny they lie down and look blissful and the other boaters stroke them. If it is raining we put their coats on and they look bloody miserable.

We moor up and after lunch we all have a nap and at four o'clock on the button Jim tells us It is four o'clock it is four o'clock four o'clock hurry hurry *Raus! Raus!* and time for my afternoon walk and then my dinner.

The bloody animal can tell the time, Mon. It's Rolex the Wonder Dog, the Canine Chronometer.

A bit of writing and a check through the emails – fan letters and family and the *Lancaster Evening News* wants a special picture down the wire and there is a funny dripping in the engine room, Terry, and why didn't you look at it before when I said and a talking book and a lamb chop and a bottle of Fitou – Remember the vine-yards near Carcassonne?

Boater's midnight – nine o'clock – we just can't stay awake we just can't.

This lovely bed is three inches wider than the one on the *Phyllis May* and how sweet to stretch out and is that the rain on the roof again and the trees are thrashing and the *PM2* is moving like a cradle.

Goodnight sweetheart. Wigan Pier tomorrow.

★   ★   ★

*It was a face which darkness could kill*
*in an instant*
*a face as easily hurt*
*by laughter or light*


*'We think differently at night'*
*she told me once*
*lying back languidly*


*And she would quote Cocteau*


*'I feel there is an angel in me,' she'd say*
*'whom I am constantly shocking'*


*Then she would smile and look away*
*light a cigarette for me*
*sigh and rise*


*and stretch*
*her sweet anatomy*


*Let fall a stocking*

Lawrence Ferlinghetti was a hell of a poet. You could understand what he was on about, which was often girls who seemed real girls like that one and San Francisco which seemed unreal but great. He ran the City Lights Bookshop, where the beat poets and novelists came – Jack Kerouac, William Burroughs, Ken Kesey, Allen Ginsberg. We looked at the noticeboard where the mail was pinned waiting for them to call in.

To me, and many others, the City Lights Bookshop was the centre of our hope for new ideas, for change. It was the most important place on earth.

Lawrence Ferlinghetti came from behind the arras. Where are you folks from?

He was balding, average build, jeans, fifties, could have been a teacher or run a gift shop. But he didn't look like everyone else – he looked more intelligent, more kind. He didn't look more brave, though he had commanded a submarine chaser at Normandy.

Lucy waved at him from her stroller – Tookie, tookie, she said.

Her first word was an attempt to say cookie. Her second was Woof. Lawrence Ferlinghetti stroked her hair.

We live in London, we said. Your city is lovely. We have driven down Route 101 from Seattle, down the Redwood Highway and El Camino Real, and we have seen some grand stuff, but when we came over the Golden Gate that was the best moment. We have ridden on the cable cars, been to Chinatown, cruised on the trip boats in the bay, eaten at Fisherman's Wharf. San Francisco must be the best city in the world. There is nothing missing here, nothing wrong.

It could be nearer to London, said Lawrence Ferlinghetti.

In the sixties London was a long way away.

Lawrence Ferlinghetti talked with me about my writing as if I were a real writer not a piddling amateur and thanked us for coming into his shop and suggested a bookshop in London where we might keep up with the news and gave us a book of his poems and signed it with a message. If I had had a book of poems I would have given it to him but I didn't have a book of anything, but Lawrence Ferlinghetti didn't expect anything. He knew I was a piddling amateur but he still accepted us and wished us well, though we made him sad for London.

A young man with long hair came out from behind a stack of books. I think he had been listening. If you are looking for up-to-date writing I can heartily recommend this book, he said, holding out a sheaf of stapled papers printed and illustrated with stencils. Only fifty cents.

Fine, I said, and added it to my selection from the shelves. It was in the style of *OZ* magazine in England – crazy, ill produced. I have it still.

I am Craig, said the young man.

Woof, said Lucy.

Craig explained that he was a starving writer who often came to the City Lights and he lived in a special house down by the Bay and we should all stay there and save money on hotels and meet his other starving friends.

We thanked him but explained we were leaving the city the next day. But by the way our fridge had become overstocked and perhaps he would like to join us for dinner that evening and help us out.

When Craig knocked on our door at the Mermaid Motel he had brought with him a friend who was mainly beard. David was joint editor of the magazine. I guess they both lived by selling it on the streets. David was a quiet soul, skeletal, with a religious air.

I broke out a case of Japanese Kirin beer and we sat down and did a grand job of emptying the fridge. After the meal we read poetry to one another. We didn't understand their poetry, and though they were very polite, it seemed they didn't respond to my favourites.

Then I picked up the Gideon Bible and read the verses from 1 Corinthians 13, substituting love for charity.

> *Love suffers long, and is kind; love envies not, love brags not itself, is not puffed up. Does not behave itself unseemly, seeks not her own, is not easily provoked, thinks no evil. Rejoices not in iniquity, but rejoices in the truth.*

David put his fingertips together and leaned forward and nodded and closed his eyes and Craig said Man, man.

Encouraged, I read one of my own poems. It was not as good as 1 Corinthians 13 but seemed in the right key —

*I am a butterfly*
*And I live in the summer sky*
*Winter's first breath*
*Will chill me to death*
*I used to feel sad*
*Till I heard someone say*
*The best works of God*
*Only live for a day*

The world was going to change and the change had just begun and we were where it was beginning. An alternative to the military blockheadedness of the fifties, a view that looked forward not back. A view with its own stupidities, and its sweetness would decay soon enough and start to stink, but not yet and at least we had movement again.

The Summer of Love had not yet arrived, and the first time I heard the word psychedelic was from David, and Scott McKenzie had not sung his song, but we had come to San Francisco and met some gentle people there.

Have these cigarettes, said David – smoke them down the coast. You won't find better. Monterey tomorrow? Very nice.

Peace, man said Craig to me, and Peace, man to Monica and Peace, man to Lucy in her carry basket.

Hush little baby sleep there soon, said David.

Tookie tookie, said Lucy.

★   ★   ★

It's a sort of a turning point, I said. It's where we leave all these little towns and the lovely country and start to move on Manchester. And it's very famous – *The Road to Wigan Pier* by George Orwell and all that. It's sort of symbolic of the real north. Anyone writing about the north has got to do Wigan.

A thirty-foot plastic cruiser had paired up with us to share the double locks, and Monica and I were fully exercised trying not to crush it like an egg. The two chaps on board were in their fifties, small, fat, and one wore a hat that looked like a cross between a fishing hat with flies and the headgear worn by Jeff Chandler as Cochise for the more formal moments of *Broken Arrow*. (I always admired Jeff Chandler – such a manly figure, and was disappointed to read in his girlfriend Esther Williams's autobiography that he was never happier than when he slipped into a polka-dot dress.)

Anyway the hat was as I say a fishing hat, but bristling with tall feathers, hung with charms and loaded with badges. Our new companion appeared without it – Has your hat been arrested? I asked.

He put it on again – It is very popular in public houses, he explained. It is even better now I have had the lights fitted. I have had a number of proposals of marriage.

He turned on the lights. His hat now looked like a pheasant that had flown into a Christmas tree, and after a terrible struggle had strangled itself in the light flexes.

It is very popular in public houses, said his friend. He has received a number of proposals of marriage.

★

Here comes Wigan – a house, a garage yard, a tip, a ruined factory, sliding towards us among the dark greens of high summer. Wet high summer. Here we are – this must be it. Broken windows, walls defaced, and the George Orwell pub. We had been told not to approach the lock round the corner or we would be vandalized, so we pulled in to the right, or starboard side, as we sailors like to put it.

This is the back door to a nightclub, said Monica. They come out on to the towpath to smoke. They will throw butts at us and break our windows.

OK, I'll pull back to Wigan Pier.

Of all the works of man Wigan Pier is among the most hopeless. It is a slight increase in the width and height of the towpath, maybe for twenty feet, and a couple of wooden beams and steel girders hanging into the canal. The beams and girders were installed by students in the eighties. No one knows whether they are in the right place.

Opposite is the large and inviting George Orwell pub. Inside were many mansions, and a big kitchen off the main bar. In all the saloons and snugs and lounges there was not a soul. A cheerful Chinese gentleman appeared. Why are you so empty? I asked.

A bit early perhaps.

It was twelve thirty on a Saturday.

The only bitter they did was John Smith's. We ordered two Lancashire hotpots and while we waited we could hear the chef singing in the kitchen. Does he do 'Love Letters In The Sand'? I asked.

He normally favours a more modern repertoire, said the Chinaman, but I'll ask him.

The hotpots were salty and the potatoes were hard. We were drawing to a close when the chef appeared – a tall ginger lad. You have not finished your vegetables, he said. But because you have come to our pub, as a mark of appreciation I am giving you a free sweet – a cinnamon and apple pudding.

He put it in front of us and watched us eat it. It was OK but each mouthful was a hundred calories.

We had nearly got back to the boat when a large man shouted from the other side – You mustn't moor there – they will throw butts at you and break your windows. You must go round the corner.

Round the corner was the lock, where we would be vandalized. We moored up equidistant from the night-club and the lock, hoping that by careful positioning we had found a spot where we could last the night. We screwed up the special lock on the saloon door and left a light on so the criminals would know we were in. That'll terrify them.

I wish I could leave a warm glow in the heart of any Wiganer who reads these words, but the waterside around Wigan pier is a disgrace. When you see the broad canal, all the space, and the patches of civilization – a cottage with roses, an apartment block – and you see these amenities surrounded with junk and desolation you are tempted to set to and clean the place up your-self. And look at what is not there – no waste bin, no water tap, nothing for boats. But miles of rings along the towpath – pathetic rings because no one will want to moor.

The very heart, the very centre of our voyage, and we were crouched between threats on a deserted waterfront, among dirt and disappointment. And what should have been the wharf, the heart and centre of Wigan, was a failure and a reproach.

But the chef and the Chinaman were a lot of fun, and as we sailed away unharmed we concluded that in Wigan you get friendly attention in a public house and will not necessarily be attacked. Perhaps the tourist office can do something with that.

Or perhaps this from Monica's write-up in her parish magazine –

*On the Boater's Christian fellowship list I found All Saints Church up in the town with Holy Communion at 9.30. What a contrast! A beautiful church in wide grounds with flowerbeds. Cream paint and angels everywhere with gilded tips to their wings. A stained glass window by William Morris – four angels surrounding St Christopher as he carried the Christchild. The New English Hymnal full of the dear old hymns I know so well. And the warmest welcome I've had all boating year. I went back to the squalor of the canal singing praises. The real Wigan was there in that church among those friendly faces.*

★   ★   ★

It would be a withered soul who would not enjoy a night in a motel with a beautiful spouse, a bottle of local wine, a cut of smoked swordfish, and a joint. We were Picasso's giants, running in slow motion along a sounding beach which was Monterey beach because it happened in Monterey, a long time ago. Lucy was in her basket in the bedroom and sometimes I was here and sometimes I was not here, and I thought What happens if there is a fire?

Even a few seconds in the fourth dimension do not make good sense when you have to protect your chromosomes for future generations.

I never took dope since, apart from a quiet drag with Howard Marks, the famous criminal and international cannabis smuggler, but that was nearly fifty years later and it doesn't count because Howard Marks makes his own rules and yours too.

When we were old we would attempt the East Coast in a narrowboat but now in our youth our great green Ford hummed down the West Coast staying firmly on land. We had joined the Royal Road in Oregon a thousand miles before and we were closing on Los Angeles, to change our lives. We were going to a slum to see a miracle.

> *Simon Rodia*
> *Funny little guy*
> *Built him a tower*
> *Six storeys high*
>
> *Launched him a ship*
> *To hunt down the Lord*
> *In a desert of slums*
> *Flowered his word*

*Built him a church*
*With masts so high*
*That they draw down tears*
*From a pitiless sky*

*Didn't know what he was doing*
*Too mad to care*
*He climbed like Jacob*
*Through the holy air*

*Here the birds sing sweeter*
*The air tastes good*
*While the gutters of Watts*
*Choke with blood*

*From piles of junk*
*This simple fool*
*Made him an image*
*Of the human soul*

Watts County, Los Angeles, is wide roads, low tatty houses, gas stations and hamburger joints. The sun blazes on the dust, and the roads reflect it back. Thirty-four people had been killed in riots last summer, and a thousand injured and Watts set ablaze.

We drove along a littered street and the towers stood like grey pylons ahead – mystic, wonderful. We stopped the car and an African-American gentleman let us in. We were in someone's back yard.

Are you an artist? I asked.

We are all artists.

As you enter the Watts Towers the air seems to cool. The yard has become a ship, bearing us forward and up. Every part of the walls and the structures is encrusted with glass, shells and ceramics, gleaned from the rubbish of the city. A drinking fountain, offering no water for the body, is concrete set with hundreds of green bottle-ends. Just overhead trellises of iron cased with cement are jewelled with tiled fragments, shells and broken glass. The two central towers rise over a hundred feet, linked with interlaced iron bars, all decorated. The towers are circular like the spires of a church.

*I never had a single helper. A million times I don't know what to do myself. Some of the people say what was he doing? I had it in my mind to do something big, and I did. A million times I was wake up all night.*

I sat down and wept.

It was so simple – If Simon Rodia, the immigrant who had nothing, could do this – I could do something. I could at least have a go. Do something, do something, Terence my son, and if you can't find anywhere else where you are happy – do something, like Simon, in your own bloody back yard.

# CHAPTER SEVEN

# ASTON

## *Stone-next-the-Sea*

*The spiders were gathering round*

*He fastened his teeth in my neck – Dad didn't say much – The fastest narrowboat they had ever known – Old Joe Guyer pissed in the fire – Gold and silver poured from the heavens – A life-saver's embrace – An ironic ice machine – The lights going up street by street – No one would publish my poetry – The first jogging club in Europe – The Stone Steeplechase and the Dog Derby*

They had not met for seventy years and the boater had no thought of anything but the cool morning and the greenery and the dogs ahead and the boat that hummed alongside, heading for Manchester. How blessed I am, he thought, all going so well, and a shadow slipped out of the bushes on the towpath behind him and folded its arms around him and whispered Hello again and fastened its teeth in his neck.

The next day the side of my face was covered in small sores. It had swelled up and I looked like the Fungus Man from Outer Space. No amount of wine would drown the pain.

You have shingles, said the specialist at the Manchester Eye Hospital – alongside your good eye.

You poor chap. You have had chickenpox as a child and the virus hibernates in your nerves and then when you are old it comes back as shingles and infects a branch of your nervous system. In your case the branch affected is the one that runs up your arm and your neck and up the side of your face by your good eye and finishes exactly halfway across your scalp – here, feel where it stops. You are going to have a bad time.

What is the prognosis?

Good.

How long does it last?

Could be weeks, could be years.

Doctor, the pain is awful – harsh and raw – and painkillers don't work. It feels as if some creature from a distant and hostile galaxy, some alien the size of half a pineapple, has fastened itself on the side of my head and is eating out my brains. You have got to give me something or I will lose my reason.

We don't know much about specialized pain control – we are an eye hospital. See your doctor back in Stone. There are new drugs.

I was driven back to Stone clutching my sick bowl. At home my old friend would tighten his grip and I would drop into a chair or sit on the side of the bed trying not to sob.

The doctor explained that the pain of shingles hits the nervous system direct – normal painkillers can't touch it, but the pharmaceutical industry had produced special drugs that act like tranquillizers or hypnotics. I looked up one of the new drugs and found that it was used in northern Canada for recreational purposes.

For the next month I could not eat, or sleep, and my eyes hurt all the time. I lost a stone. Time slowed to nothing as I fought with pain and nightmares.

In the morning I would stumble over to the window and look out on Stone promenade, with its row of pretty lamps. The sea was always calm and shining and the sand was clean on the little beach. Ripples lapped on it slowly. There was never anyone around, because it was winter – no shops, just lawns and beds planted ready for the first warm days. There were no birds. I looked out, following the inlet towards the ocean, letting my eye run along the hills and headlands, and forgot the pain for a moment.

In the bathroom the spiders were gathering. Not quite spiders, a bit more like centipedes, the size and shape of large paperclips. They ran around the bowl and up the walls and across the carpet, and when I went back to bed they came up from around my feet towards me. But when I stared at them they backed away.

My mother came to see me, and my dad. Mum was very chatty, though worried about the shingles. My dad looked a bit waxen, and didn't say much, but as he had been dead for twenty years I shouldn't complain.

Do you realize you are going mad? asked Monica. You have not made any sense for ten days. Spiders, and the duvet coming up at you with lizard heads. Stone-next-the-Sea. Talking to your parents. You are raving. When I came back from handing over the boat to Roger and Dave you were lying on the floor shouting. I was terrified.

I must have gone to sleep, I said, and then the pain woke me and it had gone dark and I couldn't remember where I was and the pain was awful.

*Why, this is hell, nor am I out of it.*

Our friend Dave came to visit – my mate had those pills, he said, new ones, same as you. Sent him bonkers.

We read the leaflets from inside the pill boxes. Side effects – *seeing, hearing, or feeling things that are not there, confusion, depression, swelling of the extremities, incontinence, impotence, farting.* We flushed the pills down the lavatory except those that they used in northern Canada. (Canadians are generally moderate people.) Stone soon returned to its place as one of the towns in the UK furthest from the sea and the spiders disappeared (I rather missed them) and the lizard heads too and my mum and dad returned to their reward in heaven.

The pain? It was worse for a time and then it eased a little. Six months later it still hurts and I can write for only an hour a day. The specialist said my eyesight had returned to twenty twenty. I thought you had to have two eyes to be twenty twenty, but twenty twenty sounds pretty good to me and I am not complaining.

And the boat – Roger and Dave got her back safely. I think they may have visited a public house or two on their way and enjoyed the trip. They said the *PM2* was the fastest narrowboat they had ever known, like running on Teflon, and she leaves little wake. Roger said he had made a list of design faults and would send it on to us. It hasn't arrived and that would have been an example of British irony. He meant to say there was nothing much wrong with the *PM2*, and we think he may be right.

So she lies in the lovely new Aston Marina in Stone, on our favourite stretch of canal, waiting for the winter to pass and the voyage to York to begin.

★   ★   ★

Dr Lewis's chair was an important chair, black leather with chrome, and his office was important too; wide and shadowy. Dr Lewis himself was pretty important as well – the principal of the Stoke-on-Trent College of Technology. He was small and pink with white hair, like a prawn. *Old Joe Guyer pissed in the fire,* he said.

*The fire was too hot so he pissed in the pot,* I replied.

We both chanted –

> *The pot was too round so he pissed on the ground*
> *The ground was too flat so he pissed on the cat*
> *And the cat ran away with the piss on his back!*

Was Joe Guyer around when you were there? asked Dr Lewis, when he had stopped laughing.

Yes, for a while, and then he died. We used to look in through his windows at the corner of Milton Terrace. Awful mess.

No harm in Joe Guyer.

I wonder did someone look after his cat?

You must have come to Pembroke Dock Grammar School in the forties, said the doctor. Long time after me. Basil Davies was your uncle, wasn't he? Bit of a boyo. He did the funeral arrangements for the firemen who died at the tanks. I remember how upset he was, although he was an undertaker. But everyone was upset — they were only young chaps. Look, Mr Darlington — we can't pay anything like you are earning with Lever Brothers. But a senior lecturer works only twelve hours a week. There are three months of holidays. And we quite understand you want to do three years and then be a writer. There will be an interview with the councillors and the head of the Business Department. Marketing people are not easy to find. How serious are you about a post here?

I'm looking for a house. Where is the best area to live?

I live in Stone — very pretty, seven miles down the road. Last twitch of the Pennines before the plains of the Midlands and Cheshire. Twenty-minute drive. No traffic problems in Stoke-on-Trent, of course — it's a linear city.

And a dirty city, I thought, and a dying city.

As I left the dark office Dr Lewis called — *The ground was too flat so he pissed on the cat.*

*And the cat ran away with the piss on his back*, I called back.

Dr Lewis fell off his chair.

We couldn't afford a house in Stone so we bought one in Walton, which is the area alongside for people who can't afford a house in Stone. The roads were not yet made up and the houses were made of cardboard but they were roomy and our bedroom on the hill looked down the Trent Valley towards Stafford. Lucy learned to walk in the garden and we awaited our second child.

The countryside was so green that the light itself was green. The air was wet and soft. The hills were real hills but not big enough to loom or threaten. Each tree was a work of art and often set in generous space. The sun sank more slowly than in London, with displays of duck-egg blue and rose unmatched in any oil painting. When the evening sun gilded the rain, gold and silver poured from the heavens.

We wandered enchanted – we wanted to consume the scenery, to possess it utterly, to know every path, every view.

At the North Staffordshire College of Technology I taught at several levels, beginning with the dispossessed – HND students who had failed to get to university. I tried to cheer them up with humour – their sad faces broke my heart. In the lunch hours I would go to Cauldon Flower Park.

> *A seed floats through*
> *With the sun in its hair*
> *Between the trees*
> *In Hanley Park*
>
> *God, his touch as sure as ever*
> *Washes the sky with superb attenuated blues*
> *And with his other hand*
> *Fires the bare bushes with sheets of yellow flowers*

I developed my own course for managers. I had no

business degree and my consumer marketing experience did not transfer well to manufacturing industry, but I blundered on, relying on workshops and conferences and export missions. Marketing was in fashion and I won a lot of consultancy work. Not from Stoke – a swamp for the dying trees of the pottery industry – but from Birmingham, Manchester, Crewe. I was approached by the Department of Education, who wanted me to go to Harvard.

My head of department was a real gent and sometimes I would see Dr Lewis around the college. *The fire was too hot*, he would shout.

I put together a group of lecturers from my college and Keele University. We called ourselves Research Associates, and carried out market research jobs, mainly for my consultancy clients. On this frail craft when my three years was up I launched out to enrich the canon of English poetry.

★　★　★

The wind came across Stone's new marina like a knife. Winter was here – an inverted Tupperware bowl for sky and the frozen spire of Aston church could not pierce it. We were not far from the field and the sheep and the dread pool where my hooligan dogs had disgraced me a year ago. As for the farmer, may flights of angels bear him home from the pub and roost on his roof.

Aston Marina is new. It has everything you would dream of in a marina and one or two ideas of its own.

There are two basins, each with a hundred pontoon berths. It has a humpback bridge. It has a farm shop that sells olives and smoked cheese and a bistro with Peroni, which is the next best thing to beer. There is a round platform where you can sit and do nothing and watch the boats doing nothing, and little Cedar Houses where you can go and mess about with your girlfriend. The marina staff will lay down their lives for you.

One afternoon I was manoeuvring the boat and Monica and the young Dockmaster were holding ropes. They were pulling the boat in when the rope came off the cleat and both were thrown into the water, which is deep. Monica brought into play the technique of treading water that she had learned before we crossed the Channel, and was just about staying afloat. The Dockmaster made no attempt to regain the pontoon but turned towards her and took her in a life-saver's embrace and paddled with her to safety.

We had not been to the *PM2* for two months. The shingles in its fury had kept us at home. Now on this freezing day we reached the boat and heaved the dogs inside. They hate the boat and today it was sepulchral – cold and wringing damp. There are few colder places than a cold boat – it takes three days to warm one up. It feels damp, said Monica.

And indeed twenty degrees of frost in December had smashed all the plumbing fixtures and the water tank was empty and the bilges were full and the cabin floor by the bed was squish squash.

We set about reclaiming our second home – pumps, dehumidifiers, stove, fan heaters, a giant American fan, the central heating, and after a month it was habitable again.

Time to install the ice machine.

We had obtained at Christmas a book about cocktails. Cocktails were once considered a sophisticated way to drink and reading the cocktail book you get a feeling for our Art Deco past. Many cocktails have stories attached – like Pink Gin, which relies on bitters found in a cupboard in a ship's surgery. In the thirties new cocktails were discovered and noised abroad and talked about as if they were more than a way of getting drunk before dinner.

Most cocktails taste sweet today, and I cannot understand the habit of shaking them with ice – you leave half the drink in the ice. In our household you have them in a glass with ice added. Not that many of our friends will drink them anyway.

We built up a store of rather exotic spirits to support our cocktail hobby and look forward to six thirty when we can choose from our cache of vermouths and bitters and spirits and conjure up tonight's ice-cool treat. But on the boat, on the super-efficient *PM2*, we have no freezer compartment in the fridge.

Monica can work the auctions on the internet and soon an ice machine arrived in a cardboard box. It was expensive and the size of a small fridge. We filled it with water and pressed its buttons and it whizzed and clanked and hummed and rattled and after a long time brought forth a handful of caterpillar-shaped pieces of ice. The mountain has laboured, I said, and brought forth a mouse.

We found room for the ice machine in the bedroom on the *PM2*. It's a ridiculous machine, said Monica. Our friends will mock us.

We can tell them it's an ironic ice machine, I said, to provide laughter and a talking point, no serious purpose, no good for anything. The *PM2* – the boat with an ironic ice machine and two ironic whippets.

Jim and Jess and I were in a corner of the Star, waiting for the winter to end and treating my disease with a couple of pints and two bags of scratchings between three and this old chap came in. By God, he said to his friend, we had some parties. Most weekends it seemed. In each other's houses. We lived in Marlborough Road. The music, the music – sixties, when the music was best. Home brew of course. Much cheaper than pubs and off-licences. And strong! And the pretty wives, always up for a dance and cuddle. Yo ho, that was the stuff! Wonder if they do it still.

I thought – That was the next street to us. It was certainly going on in our street too. I bet it was going on all over the country. The lights going up, street after street, people liberated from the fifties, able to afford alcohol, hooray hooray, party after party, dancy dancy, hold me sailor, squeeze me tight.

Making your own wine was a way of consuming the countryside, its smell, its colours, its wetness, its heat. The crispness of dandelions, the blood of the elderberry, the grip of the crab, the drowsy elderflower. I would as soon have a glass of Monica's elderberry wine as any beaker full of the warm south. I remember how proud

Monica was when she got a letter into the *Amateur Winemaker*, and I remember the home brew magazine where each picture of the editor showed him fatter and fatter, then he died.

Whether it was the parties or the spirit of the times I don't know but all our partying neighbours became very close. Everyone joined the local drama group. We would go on holidays together.

Associated with our less than orderly evenings there was a certain amount of jiggery-pokery as sex moved with clumsy haste from being illegal to being obligatory. Monica and I would flirt cheerfully with our beautiful neighbours but a Welsh low church background fits you ill for adultery. And those who strayed did not seem happy about it.

> *But I was desolate and sick of an old passion,*
> *Yea, all the time, because the dance was long*

★ ★ ★

One of our neighbours came across with a *Sunday Times* magazine. There are poets, in Liverpool.

Roger McGough was supervising his class when I walked in. He looked at my poetry and asked if I would like to read with him and his mates that evening.

It was a cellar and there were a hundred people. Roger read, and Adrian Henri, and Brian Patten, and there was some jazz. Then me.

I read a few pieces about Stone and then some animal poems.

*I am a fish*
*And I live in the wash*
*Of waters that pour*
*Over the weir*
*Where my body ends*
*My head begins*
*Oh I'm smooth and I'm sharp*
*Like a bullet with fins*
*I'm a real work of art*
*But I have been told*
*Although I'm so sharp*
*I'm a little bit cold*

I was recalled for a second go later in the programme.

*I am a rook*
*And I live in an oak*
*I'm black you know*
*From beak to toe*
*All I can say*
*Is caw caw caw*
*I suppose in a way*
*I'm a bit of a bore*

The Liverpool Poets were charming. Brian Patten gentle and withdrawn, Roger the steadying hand, and Adrian bumming a lift.

We drove around Liverpool most of the night, stopping here and there and finishing in a party. Adrian said they had become famous a few days ago and they were off to London and would I like to come. But I was not writing their sort of poetry and I had three kids.

Back home no one would publish my poetry. Encouraging notes written on rejection slips were fine, but they were written on rejection slips. And after a while I had said all I wanted to say celebrating Stone and its countryside, my main theme.

Driving home along the A34 I would see his face, long and white, in my headlights, and his shining eyes and his flapping shirt and white legs as he laboured up the hill and he was a moth transfixed by the light.

But today this is broad daylight and here he is beside me as I toil up the hill back to my house – my neighbour, Fred. Glad to see you jogging, he says. The way you live you need the exercise. You and your parties.

I did not know what the word jogging meant.

I got fat, I explained, because I had two jobs at once, being a lecturer and running my research. Working too hard – no exercise, too much booze. I lost a couple of stone dieting and now I want to get fit. I used to be fit – rowing – but there isn't much of that round here.

When you get to thirty-five, said Fred, your arteries start to harden and you have to work hard to keep healthy and alive. When did you last see a fat old man? We'll start a jogging club like they have in America and get you and some of your fat drunken friends fit so they might live a bit longer.

All manner of men, twenty or thirty of them – tradesmen, shopkeepers, lecturers, workmen, a vicar, a judge. All my friends and all my friend Stanley's posh friends. Twice a week we would meet in the changing rooms of the local school and head out into the incomparable Stone countryside – we were the first jogging club in Europe.

*How I surfed the fields lady*
*Green fields lady*
*Breaking at the top*
*In showers of trees*
*The lane bucked under me*
*Nailed with primroses*
*How I surfed the fields lady*
*Green fields lady*
*How I surfed the fields lady*
*Move move move*

We would run three to six miles and then go up to the Brushmaker's Arms in Oulton and get pissed. Our resting pulse rates dropped into the sixties. The optimal amount of exercise – forty minutes twice a week – and the jocund company made us healthier than any exhausted athlete.

As the symbol for our shirts I chose the great bustard, which is the world's heaviest flying bird. It is not very good at flying so most of the time it rushes about the moors on foot. It has large bald thighs. In the mating season it will nearly turn itself inside out to show its brightest plumage and attract the female. Rather like our members really.

We were a happy club with a high standard of locker-room banter and abuse.

*Look at those shorts! What poncey little shorts! Are they your wife's knickers?*

*No, they are* your *wife's knickers!*

Innocent days – what we were doing was new and fun and good for us. Old men forget, but when old joggers meet we smile and remember with advantages what feats we did that day.

These were the times when runners were mocked in the street. I would not myself lean over a fence and mock a man mowing his lawn or shout at someone walking his dog, and I was damned if I would put up with disrespect because I was jogging. I developed my own response. I would walk slowly up to the offender and stop six feet from him and pause and look at him. Usually the colour would drain from his face – I am a big chap, and ugly. Then I would suddenly flap my arms at my sides like a monkey and shout WAH WAH WAH! I would pause a moment then run on. It never failed and one day in Galashiels I got a round of applause from bystanders in the town square. Had some oaf come after me he would probably not have caught me because I was fit, and that was nice to know, but it never happened.

Fred Wrigley was a recognized athlete of talent and he had thought of the club so he was the club captain. His job was to shout at the joggers on the runs to add a bit of drama and in the locker room he offered manly athletic advice. I was the secretary, who did the organizing. Our runs got longer and longer and included field and lane and road – there were not many cars in the early seventies. We developed our own names for our runs, and grew our own culture and hierachy, with our own heroes and jesters, the swift and the halt.

I set up a run in relay to Llangollen and back. We were received in the council chamber and to the delight of the lads an address of welcome was read. Next year we ran from the top of Snowdon, and the next year from the Eiffel Tower. After that one I went to bed for a week.

We became involved with the Stone Festival. I found an old race in a history book and plotted a course through the water meadows and across the Trent – the Stone Steeplechase, which runs to this day, and then Monica and I established the Dog Derby on the same course.

The club grew to forty, fifty.

But where do we go from here? How do you follow the Eiffel Tower? Could we try our luck in athletics? But the jogging club was a jogging club and the joggers were not interested in racing.

I resigned as secretary and began to drift away. Unfortunately there was nowhere to go. I was not a fast runner and stood no chance on the local athletic scene. I took up gardening and clearing waste land but missed the friendship and the banter. You might turn up the odd hedgehog but they don't have much to say.

I missed the company, the popularity of club office.

I flapped in the wind like a pair of wet drawers.

# CHAPTER EIGHT

# WILLINGTON

## Sunlight Crowding through Tall Windows

*Like everything you have ever loved*

*A little academe – A mistake of forty thousand pounds – Loathsome creatures couple in the bilges – A reproach to the colours of spring – Sideways to a strong wind – My solicitor was in jail – How do you know I'm Roger McGough? – Plaisir d'amour – Lights for only three days a week – We will barbecue your dogs on the lawn – A sweet opiate – The cathedral of trees – Everything you have ever loved – My wife wet herself – There are two types of anteater*

Before long my business had expanded from a corner of Monica's dressing table to a little room off the lounge. I glued cork tiles to the wall and bought a copper lampshade to hang over my desk. I bought a stencil machine for four pounds. The Research Associates team was working hard. We all billed our hours at the same rate but as I did more hours after a couple of years I had saved quite a lot of money.

With reports drying all up the stairs and secretaries sitting in the lounge I asked my builder if he could extend the house. But Terry, you have already got one extension – you have pushed this house to its limit – have you thought of moving?

We looked at just one house. Georgian red brick, on a hill looking down the Trent Valley. The long hall, the sunny kitchen, the bay windows, the stables with the hooks where you hung the torches to guide your carriage. It was the most beautiful house in the town, and one of the biggest. It was called The Radfords. I had a photograph of Westfields and you could hardly tell them apart.

A couple from our local gang agreed to buy the house with us. There were nearly thirty rooms and plenty of space.

I had recreated my past – two families in a country house, but this time Hitler and the Air Ministry would not take it away.

We will have a commune. Our house shall be a little academe. We will show the world how to live and share and work together. We will have a compost heap and gas the rats with exhaust fumes. Monica and I will see our love flower in these high rooms with our sweet friends and the children on the wide lawn.

> *These two*
> *Emparadised in one another's arms*
> *The happier Eden, shall enjoy their fill*
> *Of bliss on bliss.*

You have done it now, said my accountant. The deposit on The Radfords has taken all your cash, and you have got no new consultancy coming in. Five weeks and it's all over. I kept telling you but you say you are not interested in money because you are an arteest. Well, now you are a busted arteest.

Something will come along, I said, and didn't sleep all night.

Next morning I called in my secretary to tell her I had decided to change course and perhaps start a grocery business. Just a moment, she said, it's a call.

I would like you to join my board, said Alan Elkes.

Alan Elkes was the millionaire chairman and managing director of Elkes Biscuits, a firm which employed a thousand people. I had done some research for him and chaired a product development committee. He was a small man with a large enveloping personality. I came to love him dearly, then to doubt him and in the end to marvel that he had been allowed to run the firm for so long. (Perhaps it was because he owned it.)

I was dazzled by Alan Elkes – by his wealth, his warmth, the size of his firm. What I did not do is look back at the history of Elkes Biscuits and its performance. I negotiated a high salary and a two-days-a-week job.

After just over a year I walked out saying that we had to face the fact that the board was not competent to run the firm. I am sure I was a terrible marketing director, weak and out of touch, but I was not alone in my incompetence. We were tittering on the edge of cash crises all the time. Alan Elkes was a secretive and un-reliable colleague, making decisions all too often on the basis of vanity. He had little support from his colleagues. One day the financial director made a mistake of forty thousand pounds in his monthly statement because the production director had decided to hire two hundred people and not told him. Forty thousand pounds was a lot of money in the seventies. But Harry, I said – you saw the buggers coming in past your window every morning!

At the same time The Radfords commune broke up. There were differences over housekeeping and hygiene, but the real problem was that the lady of the other family thought she was in charge of the commune and I thought I was. The others knew how much money I had and decided that I should give it all to them before they would leave. What the hell, I thought, I have no choice, I'll make it back, and I forked out.

They have several times tried to get back in touch and make friends again but you took all my money, my dears, and what do you want of me now?

★ ★ ★

If you do not visit a boat every fortnight it starts to die. It's a subtle death – not a clutching of the chest and keeling over like a diving pelican, not a collapsing on the stage like Tommy Cooper. It is an example of entropy – the law of physics that says that any boat left on its own goes to hell. Bacteria divide in the fridge; flies die inside the light fittings; weeds trail from the hull; rust brings your steel out in spots and then begins to eat it. Loathsome creatures couple in the bilges. Your batteries give up. Your panelling starts to separate and your carpets mould over and the stern gland fails and the lungs of your beloved slowly fill with water and she drowns.

Never buy a boat unless you are intending to live on it for at least four months in a year. *Vanity of vanities, saith the Preacher, vanity of vanities; all is vanity.*

*We have a boat you know, and you haven't. We can go on the canals any time we wish free of charge. We don't have to hire. Hiring is so expensive. Named it after my uncle that left me ten grand. You must come down and drink cocktails on it with us and we can be like the beautiful people in Cannes except we are at Great Haywood.*

Ten grand will get you the first ten feet of a narrow-boat. Then it has to be furnished. Add to that three grand for a repaint now and then and three grand a year for mooring and licensing, and a couple of hundred for annual service and a few more hundred for a biennial bottom blacking and a couple of grand for endless incidentals in fittings and clothing. Each time you pump out the waste tank there goes another fifteen quid.

You see them rotting on the side of the cut, folly after folly: neglected, patched with rust, nettles growing out of the rudder fittings, slowing down all the people who actually use their boats, a reproach to the bright colours of spring, collecting the leaves of autumn on their stained roofs.

You can't do that to a boat – in the same way that a whippet is human, a boat is alive. They have a personality – they are female of course because they carry you in their belly.

The *Phyllis May* was Carmen, with her colours and flowers and exotic past, and the *PM2* is Lorraine Bracco, the lovely psychiatrist in *The Sopranos* – the one in the tailored suit who sat upright and talked softly but you knew that if you were patient and played your cards right, one day, when you least expected it, you would get The Lot.

The time is getting closer when we shall head north towards York. My eye still hurts most of the time but will probably feel no worse if we are under way.

We looked around at the jobs to be done before we set out.

First the brasses. The main brasses on a boat are the ventilation mushrooms on the roof. Whichever way you moor the boat, they are always on the side of the roof away from the towpath and you have to hang on to the grab rail by your teeth to polish them. If you have polished them the day before it doesn't take long at all. If you have left them for the winter allow an hour for each mushroom. When you are near tears you will see that your mushroom has come up to a greeny silvery gold excelled only by the glow of a new-landed fish. By the time you have worked along the gunwale and climbed back into the boat it has started to discolour.

Like most boaters I have tried varnishing – and threw the brasses away when the varnish turned brown and would not come off – and I have applied lotions sold with false promises that they would stabilize the shine. Now like most boaters my brasses are tarnished and I live with a small guilt to join the other burdens of a life with so many little shames and failures.

Very near the *PM2* is the pump-out station. Back out of our mooring station and settle alongside the quay and push the hose in the orifice and the money in the slot and five minutes of gurgling and the job is done. Then drop the ropes and back out into the marina and the wind coming from Ireland hits us like a truck.

Sideways to a strong wind in a narrowboat and you might as well leave the tiller and go below and have a cup of tea and wait for her to roll over the weir and end it all.

On the old *Phyllis May* I might have stood a chance but I am slower with these new controls and we were flung into the pontoons across the basin and trapped there until night fell.

★   ★   ★

Monica and I and our Lucy, our Clifford and our Georgia wandered the halls of The Radfords: sunlight crowding through the tall windows. We were bruised by the break-up of the commune. Monica became depressed and more than once tried or pretended to run away, and the children suffered as her illness took hold. The psychiatric resources in Staffordshire were poor and we soldiered along as best we could. It was a long three years.

One day I realized I could not cope and rang the lady who had been the children's nanny when they were very young. Margaret left her current job that day and pitched in. The dear soul was typical of the people of

Stone who worked with us in the house, the family, the business.

The professional classes in the area were a different matter. There were a few first-class people but not many. While trimming my moustache my barber mentioned that my solicitor, the executor of my will, was in jail. Monica's GP was giving her bad advice, making her depression worse, and I went to see him to complain. A week later his wife killed herself. A dental surgeon from North Staffordshire University Hospital charged me five grand for work that fell out. I delivered Georgia myself when our midwife went into hiding. My accountant began to play the stock market with my money. I will not even glance towards Stafford Hospital, with its twelve hundred unnecessary deaths, and patients lying in pain and filth and crying for water.

I was trying myself to set up a professional practice and learn about planning and finish and I set high standards for myself and others and took all this hard. Oh cheer up, Darlington!

As the saintly Margaret held the pass for the family I looked around – no money, a thirty-room house, three kids. But Research Associates had been chugging along. In fact I would have done better financially if I had never seen a biscuit factory. More work came in and I hired a couple of full-time staff. There was plenty of room in The Radfords.

Sometimes it was sinister, like an old French film –

*Dans la vieille gare solitaire et glacée*
*Deux formes ont tout à l'heure passé*

A man steps off the train and another man appears and they shake hands and speak softly and hurry off into the night towards the great house on the hill.

Often it was cheerful, as when Clifford aged six opened the door of The Radfords one Friday evening, first of the month. You've come to read in our hayloft for Plan B, and you're Roger McGough!

How do you know I'm Roger McGough?

Because you are wearing the sweater you wore on *Top of the Pops* last night!

Sometimes it was embarrassing, like sitting down to dinner with the poet George MacBeth. Sittting down to dinner with George MacBeth was not in itself necessarily embarrassing but this evening Monica presented him with a bowl of ratatouille. George had just written a poem against ratatouille so he was obliged to refuse the dish for artistic reasons. He was proud of his poem and read it that evening. When I had last met George in London he was dressed like a clerk – now he wore a huge moustache and lapels, like a dandy lecturer on the Open University.

Usually it was convivial. The Scottish poets were particularly keen on Monica's dandelion wine, which shone like mother-of-pearl and was crisp and clean, like a single blow to the chin.

Hugh MacDiarmid explained to the audience that critical opinion had decided that there were three great twentieth-century poets in the English language – a Welshman, an Irishman and a Scotsman.

Adrian Mitchell proved evenly matched to a bottle of rose hip wine which had somehow exceeded the physical limits of alcoholic strength imposed by nature.

Dear Brian Patten – summer and I was late but I knew where you would be – asleep in the sun on the pavement outside Stafford station.

Are you Jon Silkin the poet? Will you come and read in the hayloft at The Radfords? It must be wonderful to be rung up and asked if you are somebody the poet. Jon read the poem about his little son dying and the audience of thirty people wept for him and he wept anew.

Dear Roy Fisher. Dear Adrian Henri and his latest teenager Carol Ann Duffy.

Screaming down the hill to Oulton with George Barker in my Morgan as he shouted his poems into the night. As a schoolboy I had loved his poem 'Seal Boy' above all the others in *Palgrave's Golden Treasury* and now here he was, being a poet with me at sixty miles an hour.

I had converted our ruined stables to a reading room, reclaiming the raftered roof space, once the hayloft, with new floors and windows. I built an outside staircase up to the little door where they had swung out the hay into Nannygoat Lane. Lit with oil lamps and with beer crates for seating this was a grand setting for poetry. We got over seventy in once but the average was thirty-five. Downstairs in the interval we would sell Plan B publications and if anyone cared to make a donation to Plan B we would offer them a glass of home brew.

Local poets would come out of the audience and read first and then the famous guest in the second half. Sometimes I would read with the local poets. Monica would sing on her own or with Steve Lewin – I remember 'The Bells Of Rhymney' during the coal strike, and one night 'Plaisir d'Amour', the song she sang thirty years later when we were approaching Calais in the *Phyllis May*.

I loved to hear the poets from the audience because they spoke from their hearts. I understood if they did not come again. They had read their poems; they had had their say; they had told us; they had let us know.

The first Plan B publication was Dave Rowley's *Winter Poems*, which included part of his 'Music of the Mind's Tibet'.

Plan B was hard work, mostly for Monica, who administered it. After five years we would have been asking the same poets for the third time, so we closed it down.

> *We pegged above ravenous ravines*
> *Our makeshift tents of Art*
>
> *We gained nothing but height*

Yes Dave, nothing but height – and wasn't the view great!

On holiday we planted our tent next to a young French

couple who would lean out of their caravan at eleven in the morning and make drinking gestures. This convivial pair had two dogs – an Alsatian and a dachshund. The Alsatian was a peaceful creature, but the dachshund would fire a volley of barks at every opportunity. Prévert is a small dog, explained Louis, who thinks he is a big dog.

Edward Heath was a small dog who thought he was a big dog – a bullying effeminate who promised and threatened and then backed off. The fool who index-linked public sector pay when inflation was heading for 20 per cent. The dolt who antagonized the miners when the country could not afford to buy oil. The oaf who decreed that Research Associates could put its lights on for only three days a week.

RA sought out contracts from industry and government to answer these questions –

*What is the size of our market, how is it divided between us and our competitors, and what is the sales potential of our products?*

*What do our customers want and how good are we at providing it compared to our competitors?*

Within these questions is all the law and the prophets. RA would take them on anywhere in the world, but no one was asking.

We sat around by the light of the Plan B oil lamps, working through the scraps and shreds of business we had pulled in before the oil shock closed down the phones; staying alive, doing the best we could, waiting for the wind to change, looking for a sign.

*Dear lemming crouched in your burrow in Stone*

*My beloved colleagues in the Revenue and the social services have been sending you questionnaires for some time about your house and your activities and have been passing the results to me. So we know all about you and your obscene practices. You are a wretched businessman and you have been conducting your business in your house. Do you not realize, you little swine, that a house is for living in and you have no permission to do anything else in it. You can eat and you can reproduce yourself and make model aeroplanes and that's about it. What did we fight the war for if it is not to keep the power in the hands of the council so we can stop everything else. And furthermore I understand you have a bigger house than me which is not fair as I am more intelligent and well-intentioned than you and work myself half to death. I think you are probably rich and a Tory and in the thirties my parents had to endure the Means Test applied by people like you.*

*You must stop this business nonsense at once – put all your equipment out on the lawn and send home the staff whom you abuse so cruelly. If you do not I will have no alternative but to send in the planning police, who will rape your wife and kill your children and barbecue your dogs on the lawn.*

*Yours hatefully*

*A prat from the council planning department*

*Dear A prat from the council planning department*

*How enchanting to hear from you, and how refreshing to feel that the council is protecting us from overstepping the mark when our enthusiasm bears us away. In the coolness of your office you must see things so clearly. Your power is so great and we are indeed blessed that your Christ-like compassion colours all the desperate decisions you have to make.*

*My wretched business is only some modest office equipment and a few staff, some of them part-time and some absent in the field, and sometimes my little daughter sticks down envelopes if she gets home early from school. We have twenty rooms unused and we can use this space to the benefit of all. Should the flow of business ever interfere with the environment in any way I will at once decamp and set up offices in town. I am deeply sensitive to the need to follow planning laws, which I realize have been designed to make sure that the individual does not do things that would make them richer than you.*

*I would only mention that my little firm carries out research to assist British firms in exporting. One cannot help asking is your time well spent hampering and frustrating a firm that is at the cutting edge of developments abroad for British business. We are entering a recession and unemployment is at a high level already. The press would make a fine meal of an export firm destroyed by bastards in the council planning office.*

*As I say, the moment my firm begins to be a burden on the environment I will move it, and until then*

*Fuck you*
*Terry Darlington*


Research Associates ran in The Radfords for thirty years, and carried out a thousand studies in forty countries.

Ten years after the exchange above, Downing Street

asked Research Associates to carry out a study identi-
fying barriers to business.

*Burdens on Business* was published by the Department
of Trade and Industry in March 1985, foreword by
Norman Tebbit. It recommended action to '*cut planning
burdens . . . and assist people in starting businesses in their
own homes*'.

★ ★ ★

We left Stone on one foot – tired from farewell dinners,
our mushrooms unpolished, our front fender askew, my
eyes hurting but Oh hell let's just go – we won't learn
about the north by sitting in Stone. We have delayed
once because of a second attack of shingles and we have
missed April on the cut. Perhaps things will straighten as
we go south.

South? Ah you picked that up – yes, south down the
Trent and Mersey Canal and down and down and round
and round in a great curve and off the canal and on to
the Trent, which is not for long the little river that runs
through Stoke and Stone. It turns into a beast more
powerful than the Thames and if we are very lucky and
it does not devour us it will swing round and deliver us
squarely into Yorkshire from the rear. There we may feast
on pudding and gravy and fish from Grimsby with
golden batter that is so crisp and sweet that none gets
left for Jim and Jess.

Let us bless the fact that we do not have to go north
again and slog up the deep locks of Stone and through
derelict Stoke, where lovely people hang on in their

dying rose-coloured terraces. We do not have to break our hearts on the locks of Heartbreak Hill. No, we go down my Happy Valley, the Trent Valley, with a lock and a pub every five miles and the skies that enslaved me as a young man when I came from London.

We missed the first impatience of spring but as the air warmed the white May flowers looked to my tired eye like cumulus drawn down on to the cut, and the perfume filled my body with a sweet opiate, taking away pain.

And the trees, the leaves just unwrapped, embraced the waterway with their green generosity.

Jess has decided she doesn't like the engine and when Monica is driving she sticks close to me, panting. Before she came to us her name was Cling. Her mum was Araldite (rhymes with Aphrodite) and her dad the faithful Velcro. Cling sticks close to my right leg, or fastens her nose to the back of my knee. If I sit down she takes up her default position, which is standing between my legs with her arms around my neck.

In Rugeley we walked through the squares and flowers and ate a full English breakfast in the market, as we always do. Then we sailed the long pound through flat country lovely with trees and new crops, to Wood End Lock. There we have a secret place with metal piles where we can fix our mooring chains, a place unknown to all except the other people who moor there.

In the autumn two miles of leaves fall above Wood End Lock. They drift south until the lock stops them and the canal becomes a soup of leaves. This disables the propellers of narrowboats and you are sailing on treacle. Entering Wood End Lock in the autumn requires great patience and a packed lunch.

Jim and Jess love the towpath down to Fradley. From time to time Jess cuts off left into the field to hunt for rabbits but so far she has come back and we process down the cathedral of trees to the Swan.

When Jim was a puppy we took him to the Swan. Two years later we took him to Fradley Junction again. He pulled us to the Swan, and straight through the door to the bar with the scratchings.

In Alrewas there is a house covered in wisteria, like my room in college. When you brush by on the pavement it smells like everything you have ever loved.

We stayed a few days while I tried to get my balance. I had become fat – but the booze gave me an evening without pain and it is hard to exercise when you are junked up and don't see very well.

The steps up on to the stern from the interior of the boat were strait and steep. Even Jim baulked at them. I pulled and heaved and got around, but barely.

My painkillers made me feel dopey, but I could drive the *PM2* as long as nothing unusual came along.

Like the boat at Alrewas. A narrowboat head on has a small profile – and a black one coming out of the shade is nearly invisible. I crashed into reverse and stopped a foot from it and sidled by in a maelstrom of foam muttering apologies and waving.

Next the bridge. There were things sticking out of the water on the starboard side. They were black and sort of like ducks. I focused on them and we got closer. Ducks, funny ducks. What funny ducks, goodness me. Funny black ducks, funny shapes.

Monica was on the towpath – TERRY, WRONG ARCH!

Then I saw the big notice telling me to keep to port. Strange, it was such a big notice – should have seen it really.

I gave up the tiller and tried to get down from the back counter into the bedroom cabin. But the step is steep and I didn't seem to be able to carry my own weight. I got a grip with my arms and elbows but my knees gave way and I collapsed on the floor in a heap of wrangling legs.

In Willington I told Monica that I would not patronize the ice machine this evening – would she like to join me in seeking out a good pub?

No, you go, leave me with the dogs.

There were three pubs in the village. The first was big and black and chrome and clean and nearly empty, because it was early, and the staff were moving about restlessly as if a great threat was closing in. My pint wasn't bad, but this did not feel like a pub to me, and who knows what terrible people would come in – men with Range Rovers and loud voices, or fat women with leggings and visible panty lines.

The next pub was small and brown and stained and there were two men at the bar. Just one brand of bitter on sale. I sat down and one of the men walked out. Something we said? I offered to the other guy. He thought that was quite funny and tipped his hat to me as he walked out. The barmaid had gone, and soon I had gone too.

I don't often visit three pubs in an evening but I knew the third pub would be OK because the others between them did not provide what a village needs. Have you noticed the way it works? Good pub, bad pub, good town, bad town, and so the world balances itself.

The third pub looked like a pub – there may have been timbers. I walked in.

Terry, shouted a man at the bar. Terry, shouted another. My God, it's you.

They came towards me holding out their hands. It's you, isn't it?

I could think of no way to deny it.

Read both your books, said the first man.

Read both your books, said the second. My wife wet herself. Look everyone, it's the chap who. It's him. Where's Jim?

Through our journey so many people seemed to know who we were, and were keen to compliment me on my books and call me Terry and be my friend. The more verminous the boater the more likely he was to call out as he passed. When we moored fans hammered on the boat. Some asked if we found them intrusive.

No, we loved it.

★   ★   ★

I pulled up my Union Jack knickers and adjusted my

bridal dress. I wore Union Jack socks and a tiara of ivy and field flowers. My son Clifford took my arm. He wore large plastic ears.

It was the fancy dress competition on our campsite in Cornwall the day Prince Charles and Lady Diana Spencer got married, and modesty cannot prevent me recording that we won.

Our family drove to Cornwall four times in our VW camper-van towing a trailer tent. I do not remember it raining there.

We made up jokes and rhymes and stories to help pass the miles. Little Georgia was strong with the light verse.

*There are two types of anteater*
*The spiny and the not*
*They walk about the jungle*
*Where it is quite hot*

*All they do is eat ants*
*Every night and day*
*When they get a lot of ants*
*They shout Hip Hip Hooray*

The last time Monica and I went on a camping holiday in France I kept looking round like a cat that had lost her kittens. Are they behind the tent? Have they gone to the lake? Are they safe?

They grew up and left home, explained Monica.

And indeed they did – Lucy is nearly fifty now.

Clifford told me the other day that when his boy Max was sixteen he would take him to London. They would take a suite in a posh hotel and go to a strip club and drink beer and see the Thames at the Prospect of Whitby and the Schneider Trophy monoplane in the Science Museum.

Just like when I was sixteen and you took me, Dad.

Cliff, can I come?

# CHAPTER NINE

# SHARDLOW TO THE TIDAL TRENT

## *Yellow Fish*

*The Japanese turned out to be human beings*

*The moles are closing in – Make the blood green – The most interesting job in the world – I chose life, not art – We bounded over the snow – Walls of white foam – I never got to grips with Bangkok – As if a gunboat lay offshore – He answered even the damnfool questions – The whorehouse Hilton, Taipei – Out with your vippets – In Nagoya little children would burst into tears – I am an old man and I will be dead soon – You are burning the furniture*

You have got to stop at the Ragley Boat Stop, south of Derby. It has a wooden wharf with rings. There is a field. There is a pub. Ten years ago we had a bottle of wine and two steak dinners for a tenner. When I am very old I will go and live there.

We did not stay to live out our days at Ragley but puttered on to Shardlow, where the canal drops into the stripling Trent. A main road goes through Shardlow, and the canal slips under it with such discretion that motorists wonder why there is a Navigation Inn so far from the sea.

A few years ago on our way to the Inland Waterway Association Festival we found a kilo of windfall plums on the towpath by our boat at Shardlow, so Monica put some of that summer into jars.

People do not gather wild fruit as once they did – blackberries, damsons, little yellow plums, pears in dying orchards. At Sandon Lock near Stone there is a garden with an apple tree blessed with a bumper crop year after year, and every year the apples fall and rot.

We go to the Inland Waterways Festivals from time to time to sell books. We have a tiny stall in the corner of a tent, and Jim and Jess sleep under the stall, coming out for photo calls, or rushing out screaming if a dog passes by that they don't like. We love meeting the fans – *I like that bit where you say If you don't shut up Jim it's into a sack and over the side* – and the other writers and the magazine editors and the canal painters and the chaps with waistcoats who make belts with a loop for your windlass.

Today we lock down on to the Trent and away to Trent Junction, where the Trent joins the River Soar and flows east, and the Erewash Canal heads north. The river currents heave the boat and I feel the tugging under my feet and the pull of the tiller and I long for the old adventures in the great estuaries of America and check around me for alligators.

Flat country, few trees, wide, light. A mooring by a stony bank. Power stations – they will pursue us all the way to York and back, growing ahead or slipping behind, occupying the sky.

A walk up the Erewash Canal. A lad with four grey brindled creatures on leads. They look like whippets, but they are very small. They are electric with energy, doing star-jumps in the air on the end of their leads. Jim and Jess looked on them kindly – sight-hounds usually get on well with each other. They are whippets, said the lad – small ones. We race them – they are faster than the ordinary ones like yours.

Further on a fisherman. Excuse me, I said. When I came up there were five molehills round you, and now there are twelve. The moles are closing in.

★　★　★

There never was a more uncomfortable and un-controllable vehicle than my Morgan, but love knows no sense and I kept the ridiculous vehicle for six years. It was beautiful with the slits in its bonnet and the strap to hold the bonnet closed and the wire wheels and the flaring wheel arches. There were few flarers more flaring than the Morgan wheel arches.

There was not enough room for both my feet in the pedal well and the canvas top leaked and it steered like a drunken pig. But anyway here I am steering into the drive of Ragdale Hall for a week's break.

When I got into reception I was met by a lady who believed that a loud and rude manner was a sign of high class and distinction. Not a bad soul in fact but no asset to a business.

There were women everywhere but no men! Oh Lord this is a retreat for women who will talk about make-up and exfoliation all day and I will stand out like an idiot and the week will be a disaster – I had better go home.

Then I spotted a man – there were four of us.

There was a programme of talks and exercises and the countryside around was beautiful and I would go jogging along the sides of the fields with the manager. There was very little food – six hundred calories a day, and the hunger grew and grew.

One of the guests looked just like a fat version of Trevor Nunn, the famous theatrical director, and turned out to be Trevor Nunn, the famous theatrical director. He was a pleasant chap, very interested in Plan B. He knew most of the poets who had read for us. I had lately been swept away by his TV production of *Antony and Cleopatra*, with Janet Suzman, his wife at that time. I told him so and he was pleased. I was surprised he was so pleased, but however famous you are and on whatever scale your work is known you can only please people one at a time and it is nice to be told about it. I understand that now in my little way.

Trevor Nunn had seen quite a lot of Yevtushenko, the Russian poet, and told me stories of him. The best was about when Yevtushenko saw Trevor Nunn's production of *Macbeth*. What did you think of it? asked Trevor. Yevtushenko took his arm. Trevor, he said, make the blood *green*!

If you try living on six hundred calories a day you will know what the thirty inmates of Ragdale Hall suffered during that week. There were no classes in the afternoon and a dozen of us would sit in a semi-circle in the bay window smoking and talking and longing for food and home and for anything to happen.

If something does not happen soon, I said, I am going to go mad.

The roof above reception fell in, just missing the rude receptionist. Masonry crashed through her desk and glass and plaster covered the floor.

At the Department of Industry in Whitehall there were civil servants on the other side of the table like a row of stoats. Research Associates had been invited to bid for a worldwide study into a new type of ceramic manufacturing machinery.

I opened my briefcase and my papers exploded across the table. Now I have your attention, I said, we will begin.

We had a few things to offer – as the oil shock eased I had recruited some multilingual staff who were pretty good – alone in the market research industry we recruited via national advertising. Oxbridge recruits we found risky – too often they cracked under pressure. I suppose the best Oxbridge people were not going to work for a little firm in the sticks. A star from a provincial university might better realize the level and romance of the work. After all, market research of the type we carried out is the most interesting job in the world and the only profession I know where you are paid to tell the truth.

Three members of my staff sat with me, looking keen. I gathered my papers and the examining board tried to look serious. We have a few worries about your proposal, Mr Darlington. You do not have any engineering experience in your firm?

But this is a marketing job – you want to know how many of these dust-pressing machines exist, and the speed of future uptake, and the opportunities for our chaps to make them and sell them. That's nothing much to do with engineering.

How do you propose to get this information?

From the big ceramic manufacturers and also the dust-press suppliers themselves. Research Associates interviews competitors as a matter of course.

But no one does that!

We think of ourselves as investigative journalists. We will wait for days to get our man. There are people who can get competitor interviews and people who can't – we can.

Your proposal is well written, Mr Darlington, and your price is right.

We filed out alongside the civil servants. One of them spoke to me – Last month a chap came in to give a presentation. He was very nervous and at the end of the presentation he got up and walked into a cupboard and stayed there until we had all gone.

The contract came in the next week. There was work in a dozen countries around the world including Taiwan and Japan. My brilliant new Oxbridge-economist research head resigned instantly at the thought of going to the Far East and getting the big interviews. It looked like that was the bit I was going to do.

In the seventies few people had been to the Far East from England. I was forty-two and scared. I sat in my Heathrow hotel and watched the television. There was a play by a modern author about a chap who worked in advertising and never really grew up. I could have written that, I should have written that, instead of poncing off round the world. I should be a writer – that is what I was meant to be. That is where my skills are strongest, that is where I feel most happy.

But one night not long ago Basil Bunting had read his poem 'Kyoto' in the Hayloft. That was marvellous, Basil, what was Kyoto like?

Never been there.

But I'm going there tomorrow!

This was the turning point. From now on, I decided, I would abandon all hope of artistic success and put my money on this marvellous job I had created, with the travel, the excitement, the experiences beyond price. I chose life, not art.

But as I watched the television play I was sick of an old love.

I had not seen a jumbo jet before. It was like a flying cinema, rather bigger than the Grand in Pembroke Dock, and a lot grander. Pastel colours, soft even lighting.

My seat was near a window. The sunset was unlike the quiet green and yellows in Stone. Under a fierce orange sky like this anything can happen.

I was folded into a space too small for me close to a pretty Australian and her husband. These young people were proud of their Australian culture, which seemed built around tinnies and bottles of sweet sherry for the Sheilas and Vegemite. They rejoiced in the vulgarity of their country, and their jokes made me laugh all the way to the Middle East, where we fell asleep. I lay much closer to the Australian girl than I would to Monnie at home.

When I woke up I considered my position – I was on my way to alien countries to win interviews with people who did not want to see me, on a topic which I barely understood. I wasn't even an engineer, and I spoke neither Chinese nor Japanese. What would these places be like? The Japanese were war criminals, and I knew nothing about the Taiwanese, except that they were Chinese and famed for their corruption.

There comes a point where fear congeals into a sullen acceptance.

But first Thailand, with the eternal snows and the yaks and the holy men with all the wisdom of Shangri-La. A grand place to break my journey for a few days and cool off and unwind. I might even have a ride on a yak – I bet you can! I twisted my fingers into the rough hair and we bounded over the snow.

★　★　★

We tied up the *PM2* opposite pubs and bars, chairs down to the water, all empty, and walked into Nottingham. Soon we faced a thirty-foot wall – mixed facings of brick, daunting and untidy. We couldn't get through this without crossing a lot of roads, and dodging a lot of cars.

Uphill and there was a small market in a large square. Everything was uphill in Nottingham. There were rings on the waterfront but no boats and I wondered why. It was a windy day and windy days make me uneasy. Nottingham made me uneasy. It's like Cardiff, I said, without Cardiff Bay. It's a bit like Cardiff in the fifties.

How can you sum up a city in an hour? asked Monica. But I hope our mooring is safe.

We had a quiet night and moved on early and soon the canal dropped into the Trent again.

At Stoke Bardolf Lock the lock-keeper helped us through and pointed out the moorings below the lock. A wide lagoon, trees trees, low thunder from the weir. Climb out of the lock and here is a broad track through fields towards Newark and Jim and Jess ran free.

England is such a lovely country, secret corners without number scattered like jewels. Old John of Gaunt was right – *this precious stone set in the silver sea.*

That evening we stood on the lockside and held hands and Jim and Jess pushed their faces up towards us. They know, I said, they know how lucky they are to live in England. No alligators or panthers, no blasting heat. How green, and the wind soft in the trees, and the light fading, and the whispering of the weir.

A sudden stench from the sewage farm down the river, and the weir was manufacturing walls of white foam that crowded down the river at us. Jim and Jess began to choke and we all tumbled into the boat, while the foam mounted the windows.

★   ★   ★

Bangkok. A wall of hot air on the steps from the jumbo. Sunlight like an electric fire in your face. At the bottom a chap holding papers – Passport, oh yes, entry visa, thank you.

He took some of my money and gave me leaflets promoting a show, a restaurant and a massage parlour. I did not realize that he had no official status at all.

The airport bus took me through the seething city, hell-hot and flat.

That evening the bar – a five-star hotel bar containing twenty-five whores and the Australian Rugby League team. I soon got into conversation with the rugby players, but did not realize that the beautiful women were for sale. I was wearing my best suit and drinking beer and sitting upright as an English gentleman should. As we would have put it in the Coronation School Pembroke Dock, I must have looked like a tit in a trance. Relax, for Christ's sake, said the Australian scrum half, taking off his shirt and climbing on the table.

The musical group entertaining us, The Regulars, could manage a handful of tunes and then went off into a mish-mash of Western and Oriental music that sounded like sweet and sour Yorkshire pudding. They seemed frightened of the audience, and frightened of being fired. We are The Regulars, they kept explaining, we are the regulars.

A girl under the mirror turned her face away and looked up so I could see her skin and the curve of her cheek.

I went to bed fending off messages from the massage parlour – jet-lagged, confused, a tit in a trance.

I never got to grips with Bangkok. Perhaps the fact that it turned out to be in Thailand, not Tibet, got me off balance. I had been looking forward to the yaks.

The heat bothered me, the dirt, the size of the place,

the corruption in every corner. I saw some gold Buddhas, bought a ring and some silk, and lay on my bed in the hotel trying not to worry about Taiwan. In the evenings I would chat with my friend the scrum half, who explained that his team had won a cup, *the* cup even, and had been sent to Bangkok as a reward. For Christ's sake, relax! You English are as stiff as boards!

He and his friends kept going for short breaks upstairs. I looked for the girl under the mirror, but the girls were changed every hour.

We are the regulars, sang The Regulars.

It was a relief to be on the way to Taiwan. The island lies off the coast of China south of Japan. It was big in the ceramic industry and the UK government was encouraging trade. This was where my research would begin.

My interpreter, supplied by the British export office, was a man of a certain age, a real gent, who arranged interviews and set up an atmosphere of goodwill. He came with a car and a driver, and another guy as a reserve. There were always a lot of guys available in Taiwan.

People in the ceramic industry were happy to see me, thinking that I was a direct representative of Britannic wealth and power, and could be a customer. A formal lunch was set up for me by the Taiwan Ceramic Federation.

I was being treated as if a gunboat lay offshore so I tried to be as official as I could, moving slowly, making considered gestures and talking in proverbs. This went down well enough. There were a dozen of us at a round table – mainly people from the Federation and some manufacturers. Rice wine was poured. Tell them I do not doubt our countries will flourish together in the new dawn after the oil shock, I said.

They all raised their glasses. We look forward to your orders pouring in, they replied.

There must have been a hundred dishes on the table and we were to help ourselves. The food was mainly those white plastic erasers that compete with the rubber type and rub out more cleanly – the ones with square edges. They had been drizzled with black stuff that smelt like oil from the sump of my Morgan. They were served in bowls and alongside were boiled nettles and white noodles and rice. There were raw pink creatures that I was not familiar with, though I may have seen one under a stone in Swansea Bay.

What is the output of the type three dust press? asked a manufacturer.

More than sufficient, I replied, and capable of cost-effective upgrade.

We toasted each other and my glass was refilled. Then there was a crash of gongs and a man came in carrying a flower, and behind him a man with a silver platter with a dome and behind him a man with a sauceboat. The platter was set on the table and everyone put their fingers together and moaned. It was lifted to another clash of the gong and there was a yellow fish, several pounds in weight, on a bed of rice. It was not shaped much like a fish – it had too many corners. I could not see it doing well in the deep. Reverently it was broken up and served.

It is an important dish, whispered my interpreter.
What is it called? I asked.
I will enquire.

My interpreter had a long discussion with his neigh-
bour and then checked a point across the table.
Someone went into the kitchen and there was banging.
A man in white came out waving a knife and shouting.
At our table there was a lot of conferring and nodding.

My interpreter leaned towards me.
It is called Yellow Fish.

The car was prompt the next morning and we chatted
as we drove south. Taiwan used to be called Formosa, the
beautiful, but all I saw was jungle.

My interpreter explained that people in some
different eastern countries would use the same
ideograms when writing, though they could not understand each other talking. He drew me the ideogram for
*happy*, which looked like a smiling face, and the one for
*exit*, which was an empty square.

On a hill a factory. A small meeting room with three
men waiting. Three more men arrived and one climbed
out of the filing cabinet. Four more came and sat up on
the window-ledge. We were leaning on one another.

All these people were extras and the man to whom I
should be talking would arrive late, to show his im-
portance. The extras smiled and looked with disbelief at
my great black beard, my round eyes, my long legs. They
looked at my Italian suit, my Rolex, my Pendragon
briefcase, my Church's brogues, pricing them carefully.

I explained the principle of the dust press and asked if

they would buy some if we could supply from England. Yes, one of them said, if it gives us cost-effective production and does not break down.

They could not have said anything different, and I began to realize how stupid many of my questions were. I should be concentrating on locating all the dust presses currently in the field, finding out who made them, when, what they cost, were they working – and then size the potential market myself.

Three more people arrived and sat on the ones who were there already.

Then there came a hush and the important respondent arrived smiling. A space was cleared for him and he answered my questions, even my damnfool ones, with courtesy, as best he could.

My afternoon respondent was several hours further south. We got out of the car and struggled through creepers to reception. Here was a jewel of a factory, clean and quiet, with happy staff and shining equipment. Tarzan had come upon the hidden city. A single charming manager gave me some useful answers, and a mug that was made by a special process. I knew he liked me and it was a real gift and I kept the mug for thirty years then Monica dropped it last week.

We were very late back at the hotel, just in time to see the butterflies.

When we were in Monterey Monica and I had seen the monarch butterflies on their way up the coast, flooding the sky and hanging in bunches from the trees. But the migration of the monarch butterflies did not rival the midnight hour at the Taipei Hilton, when the whores were sent home. They glided down the steps and tripped along the pavement, their silks floating, colours of sunset and sea, their teeth white and sharp, Red Indian skin, coffee skin, blanched white skin, tittering and laughing as the Hilton shift came to an end and now the next act of the night could begin.

You wanna woman?

I knew my room boy went through all my possessions each day seeking something to steal, some leverage to gain. He had produced a drama with a couple of other boys crying and shouting. I didn't really know what it was all about but they made it clear that a modest amount of money would save one of them from slavery and disgrace and probably buggery. It was so unfair and only I could retrieve the situation. I gave them a fiver and told them to clear off. I wished I hadn't given them anything but they had access to all my stuff and might piss into my camera or something.

You wanna woman?

Yes, I said, but I will wait until I get home.

Woman only forty pounds. Until midnight. All on room service, no trouble. Very pretty, very clean. Put on bill as dinner, or translators. Speak English.

Oh clear off.

I went down to dinner. A drink in the bar first. The barmaid was gorgeous. There was a mix of races in Taiwan – the Chinese with their flat yellow faces and the original Taiwanese, who were the colour of oiled teak – smooth brow, with very high cheekbones and narrow eyes. They did not look like human beings, but were pretty, neat — wooden toys. There were some Japanese faces, oval, delicate.

Anyway this girl behind the bar was Japanese and European and perhaps a bit Chinese too and drop dead gorgeous and she made it clear that for a modest contribution I could have her as well as my beer. I fled to the dining room.

I sat at my little table in the middle of the room. Everyone was looking at everyone else, and there was a silence, as if a great storm would soon break, or a tsunami come tearing into reception and up the stairs. A young man walked through slowly holding a packet of cigarettes behind his bum. It was clear what he was saying.

Back in the bar the barmaid whore had gone and on the stools there were a couple of Brits holding beers. One of them was old and distinguished-looking. He looked a bit like Dr Lewis.

My God, I said, I am just realizing what this place is like. It might be called the Hilton but it is a whore-house. The whorehouse Hilton, Taipei. I didn't know there was anything like this in the world — it's shocking. Everyone is for sale — the receptionist, the barmaids, the waiters, the room boys. They have whores on room service — I have seen them leaving at midnight. I have seen them with my own eyes — hundreds of them. Corruption stewed in corruption — it's Babylon.

It's a disgrace, said my new friend, and put his hand on my knee.

★   ★   ★

A pleasant mooring on a pontoon at Newark – thank you Newark – and I am sitting under the black canvas of the cratch in the bow and a big man is coming towards us in a blue duffel coat. He was walking in a shuffle and I could see a shadow behind him. Are you the chap who? he asked.

Yes, I said.

Is this the *Phyllis May* that?

No, I said, she burned.

My wife has read your books and has always wanted to meet you, but she's shy.

He moved a little to one side and I could see his wife hiding behind him, smiling at me with her eyes open as if I was Jesus Christ. She hid behind him again.

She likes the bits about Jim, said the chap. She reads them to me. I like them too. She liked it when he danced with Monica in the square. Is Jim on board?

Jim came out of the boat. This is the dog which, I said.

Jim greeted the fan and his wife. She's very nervous, said the chap. Never met a writer before.

He turned to go and his wife went with him, moving round him as he went, like a squirrel keeping on the other side of a branch.

We went below.

Vippets, came a cry, vippets! Do you have vippets in here? Out with your vippets! I will see the famous Jim! Is that him? Is that the dog who?

Heidi was a pretty lady entering middle age – she had a little accent and a smile and a personality that would defrost the roof of a Dutch barge in a February dawn.

Thirty years ago she had fallen in love with a man in blue in Mönchengladbach and he had left the RAF now and they lived in England on their sixty-eight-footer.

We decided to go to Cromwell Lock with Heidi and Tony, where we would brave the Trent, which went tidal there and of which many tales were told.

★   ★   ★

The South China Sea. *The South China Sea!* I was flying over the South China Sea! Only people in the forces went to the South China Sea, a long time ago, and not all of them came back. There were the films of course, usually with Stewart Granger and Ava Gardner and Grace Kelly or was that Africa anyway this is incredible. I can see the ships making their white trails on their way to Rangoon and Sumatra and places and here is old Terry from Stone Staffordshire, with its canal and its pubs – here he is deep in the mystic orient. I didn't think much of the Japanese in *The Bridge on the River Kwai* – poor Alec Guinness – My God, we're going down!

This must be Nagoya, the heart of the Japanese pottery industry, a city bigger than Cardiff, on a great bay. It's so white!

White and modern. No real high-rise buildings. Most unlike the scruffy unexpectedness of Cardiff – this was glass and concrete and shops and cafés tucked into the ground floor. I wandered around without a hint of danger, never propositioned. I explored the underground markets selling those erasers that you drizzle with Morgan oil and horrible creatures from the deep.

The passers-by would try not to stare at this huge man with his strange skin colour and clothes and his terrifying beard, but little children would burst into tears.

My hotel was comfortable when I had learned the trick of sleeping with my feet out of the window. The television poured out a stream of idiocy.

I went to the desk manager to get a translator. He did not have much luck and was hours over his time. My dear chap, I said, don't worry about me, go home, we'll try tomorrow.

But it is my job!

I thought of the uncollected rubbish in the streets in the UK, the unburied dead, the strikes, the laziness, the hatred. But the desk manager worked later and later, and produced Itsi – efficient and charming, dark skin, from the north, a true lady.

But it is my job!

So I could begin my fieldwork. With Itsi at my elbow and a friendly Japanese Ceramic Federation I got the interviews I needed and had time to make friends.

The Japanese turned out to be human beings, very like the Welsh – small, sensitive, emotional, chatty. To my surprise the detail of their body language and facial expressions was the same as ours. They loved a joke and could pick one out of the tangle of translation and we would laugh together. I think they were surprised too that we were of the same clay. I could see, said the head of one of the pottery firms, that you are a real English Rental Man.

When I left Itsi gave me a picture she had painted for me, of a flower.

I have a photograph of my return taken on the lawn of The Radfords, with Monica and the children joyful in the evening sunlight under the great trees.

We don't need a presentation, Mr Darlington. Your report is clear and we know what to do. Look, we have a number of other projects coming through – would you be interested?

★   ★   ★

Heidi and Tony went down the Trent yesterday, said Monica. Today it's eleven o'clock, for the tides. We go out at Cromwell Lock then it's sixteen miles due north to Torksey. Then next day thirty miles to Keadby. That's as long a passage as the Albemarle Sound, or Lake Okeechobee, or the Channel. And the Trent runs fast and it bends. It's different up here – bigger locks, bigger rivers, bigger currents, bigger bends. The North Sea tides reach forty miles up the Trent. That tells you the country is flat, and with such a small drop you have meander after meander.

The Trent was pouring out towards the Humber, pulling at the trees and grasses on its banks fifty yards apart, as the tide was swept back out by the river. No more crystal Trent with dragonflies and trout – the wind over the low banks would blow away anything smaller than a cow, and it would be a strange and dreadful fish that could breathe in this torrent of mud.

A narrowboat is difficult to steer, if only because the bow may already have arrived somewhere you do not want to go. Bow thrusters, which are propellers set into the sides of the boat, can help though they take half the fun away. Narrowboating is a contact sport. To enjoy a boat you have to drive her on currents, into the wind. You want to struggle with her, chuck her about, bang and bounce. I love to feel her move under me har har.

I pushed the throttle down – let's see you go, baby! I knew the *PM2* was fast but she could overheat and this was my chance to check her safe top speed. I squinted down at the temperature gauge and ran her for five miles at between 2500 and 3000 revs, backing off when the temperature needle tipped over vertical. With the tide and the river behind her the *PM2* went along the Trent like a rat up a drainpipe, roaring and splashing. I don't know if there is a speed limit on rivers – I suppose there is – and I must have been breaking it. If there are any vigilantes out there I am awfully sorry and I won't do it again, promise. I am an old man and will be dead soon and won't get many more chances to do silly things, and I do so love doing silly things. And by the way, Go to Hell.

On a river there are two things you must never forget. The first is *Wear a Life Jacket*, and the second is *Don't Cut the Corners*. One of the biggest moments in the life of a geography teacher is when he explains how the water on the outside of a river bend moves slowly, and on the inside of a bend moves quickly. This means that the river drops mud on the inside of a bend. So when you come up on a bend in your boat you must never take the obvious short route and cut the corner.

So go painfully round the outside, round the outside – yes, I know it can mean you go to the wrong side of the river, but stop kidding, you are meeting only three boats a day. And you have got to take that route every time, every time, however unnatural it feels. Relax once and forget and you are on the mud and waiting for the next tide, unless you got stuck on the top of the tide, in which case you can be there for weeks.

Monica took over and I opened the engine-room door and there was Jess, with Jim hard behind. Poor Jess was panting and trembling and as I went into the saloon she fastened herself to the side of my leg and walked along with me. Jim lay down beside me and Jess flung herself into my lap. I stroked and comforted her and though animals, particularly my animals, do not normally respond to my wishes she calmed down and put her head on my chest.

★   ★   ★

*I fled Him, down the nights and down the days;*
*I fled Him, down the arches of the years;*
*I fled Him, down the labyrinthine ways*
*Of my own mind, and in the mist of tears.*
*I hid from Him . . .*
*From those strong Feet that followed, followed after.*
*But with unhurrying chase,*
*And unperturbèd pace,*
*Deliberate speed, majestic instancy,*
*They beat – and a Voice beat . . .*

Well done, mate.

But the voice was not for me. The voice was for the

figure in the wheelchair, crouched to his task, his wheels fizzing, overtaking on my left as a thin man nearly seven feet tall swept by me on the right at nine miles an hour. My eyes filled with tears for the heroic wheelchair athlete and the respect shown by the tall man who was whole and clearly a star and the world is full of love really don't you know and I dug in and tried to go after them. But they are faster than me; I am out of my depth. Still twenty miles to go. I should not be pushing – where is Leslie?

Leslie was ahead where she should be. They said she put make-up on her legs but one so favoured by nature needed little help from artifice. Black hair, pale skin, a beauty with a heart that had powered her to so many sub-three-hour marathons. Leslie knew what she was doing – that was why I was following her. Oh, you're pretty, shouted a child.

The Harlow Marathon was a respected event, but it was 1978 and there were fewer than three hundred runners.

I had been told that the qualifying time for the Boston Marathon was three hours. Most marathoners never reach this time, especially veterans – men over forty, women over thirty-five. To run under three hours you have to run a mile at nearly nine miles an hour, and then do it again twenty-five times.

The human body when match fit can react explosively for ten yards, sprint for a hundred yards, and run for sixteen miles and then it starts to eat itself from the inside.

An hour a day, my marathon coach had said, and none

of your smart-arse excuses – an hour a day and two on a Sunday. Did you do two last Sunday? Look, do you want to do Boston or not? What chance have you got of making three hours to qualify? You are a jogger, not a bloody athlete. You are a businessman, all booze and schmooze, and I bet you and your fat mates hang around young girls. Athletes are hard, they are dedicated: they have balls of steel. Come on, dig in, up this hill. Lean forward and pretend you are pulling on a magic rope that will take you to the top. Push, you fat bastard, push. Afraid of a bit of pain, are we?

My children used to laugh at me as I set out into the night mummified against the cold. *The return of the ninja!* Or when I tried to climb the stairs, falling forward with stiffness and fatigue.

But it was not all churning through dark streets at night. There were the runs over Mow Cop with my coach and his mates: throwing snowballs, being a boy again. There were the trails in the woods and along the hills, and the chats over a beer, my blood foaming with more feel-good than any smackhead.

Here I am at the sixteen-mile marker – this is where it will start to hurt. There are few worse experiences than a bad marathon, when your blood sugar has run out and you are burning fat and your body is shouting No, no – you are burning the furniture you fool you will be sorry oh God I am hurting hurting.

And the pain settles into your muscles and flares up at every move and you get slower and slower and you are a loser and there is no sugar in your brain and you think Why am I here? I shall disgrace myself. I shall have to drop out I shall have to drop out everyone is going by me I can't stand it.

But this was a good marathon. It was painful now but my mood was good and I could handle it. A cool over-cast day and a flat course and I did not have to think with Leslie setting the pace. I had spent the summer training slowly after an injury and holiday runs along the Pembrokeshire coast path had given me strength without burning me out.

Twenty miles – they say this is where the race begins. I was fifteen yards behind Leslie, too shy to make myself known. I was sure she was heading for three hours – the timing was just right so far. At twenty-four miles I moved alongside her and passed her and her small cohort of admirers. No one said anything.

On my own now.

Pick up a drink, try to get it down, Oh sod it chuck it over your head.

Just enough runners ahead to avoid getting lost. Feet hurting perhaps a blister but who cares who gives a damn now round this corner and there is the tape but oh it hurts it hurts just push and push and over.

The clock read two hours and fifty-eight minutes.

I hung on to the chicken-wire fence. Under three hours – I had qualified for Boston. And I was an athlete – I had my union card – I could even captain an athletic club.

I realized I was crying.

# CHAPTER TEN

# NORTH TO YORK
## *Bends and Meanders*

*Yellow claws and mad staring eyes*

*Never forget your geography teacher – Fighting outside with guns – An international sportsman – We headed for Thorne sideways – Could you train me for the marathon? – The wind blew me down in the mud – It had carved up one of those whippet dogs – One day soon I will knock on the door – Pirates that run down narrowboats – Outrageous old boats – This cancer must be cut out of our economy – The only way to appoach a city – On the left was Mama Cass – Jim was in love – A sixty-pound anchor coming at my chest – A man shuffled towards her – Under the fence, bloody, helpless – We have her on a morphine drip*

Out on to the stream again for the thirty-mile passage from Torksey. Taking it a bit easier, enjoying the wide skies, the high-builded clouds, the slap of the ripples on the hull, the green banks and now and then willows and the foliage and swans and Is that a hawk?

The noise and movement of the boat is not upsetting Jess today though she is still with me like the poor. Jim should be well used to long passages after France and the USA and he has remembered that and returned to his bed.

How quickly the hour passes when you are off the tiller. Hardly have you stretched out in your chair when the clock bongs out the half, and gives an apologetic coughing click bong on the quarter and then – WAKE UP, you are on!

In my early days of affluence I bought a mechanical marine barometer and a matching chronometer with bongs and hung them in my office. When we bought the *Phyllis May* we hung our brass beauties by the door but they stopped working and so we bought a new set, with modern quartz movements that did not break down all the time. They burned with the *Phyllis May*. Then we found a gentleman who mended clocks so we now have the original set on the *PM2*. I have learned to tell the time by the bongs – eight bongs at midday and then one at half past then two at one o'clock and so on until eight bells at four o'clock and then start over. I hope I am not boring you.

Oh My God I have got a wave behind me, and a big wake on one side – I am running ashore! I flung the tiller round and the boat slowed and sand and mud rattled against the rudder and I revved up hard and the *PM2* swung round and back and was free. I was a hundred yards from the bank but was I on the inside of the bend?

Yes, I was.

Never ever forget your geography teacher. He may wear tweed sports jackets and grease his hair and keep rabbits but one day his teaching will bear fruit – for instance if you are trying to work out which side of the river has the sandbanks or if you are going to Thailand and think you are going to Tibet.

And now what's going on? We are there! We are at Keadby, at the lock into the South Yorkshire Navigation. But where is the lock? I can't see the lock!

Go back, go back! shouted Monica and I turned against the current and inched back along the high broken quays.

There, there!

An entrance concealed among the twists and folds of the quay, an entrance that would have confused an invading force of boat commandos with years of training and a global positioning system. I swung in and bashed the *PM2* against the throat of the lock. I used to be able to do this, I thought.

There was a plastic cruiser waiting for us and we rose slowly. When we had risen we were parked in a little holding basin to await the swinging of a road bridge while the lock-keeper bustled around, interrupting his British Waterways duties from time to time to arrange his daughter's wedding on his mobile phone, or pop up to Thorne for some root canal treatment.

★   ★   ★

The town of Boston Massachusetts has many marvels.

The John Hancock Tower, a blue mirror sixty storeys high, was completed in the late seventies, and at once began to shower the citizens of Boston with glass panels forty-four feet square. Every pane had to be replaced. And it swayed so much that many on the upper storeys were seasick. A huge machine of weights and cables was installed on floor fifty-eight to stabilize it. It is the highest building in Boston and everyone loves it.

On the outskirts of Boston is the Paul Revere Motel. Sometimes it was not easy to get a room in Boston and on one business trip I finished up there with my lady colleague. Truck tyres hollered just past my window – I was partly underground. I complained to the manager – Give the room to the girl, he suggested.

In the night there was fighting outside with guns. For breakfast in the morning there was a coffee machine and a basket of doughnuts. Here, give the girl a doughnut!

As well as the worst hotel in the world (apart from the Airport Hotel, Lagos, of course) Boston in those days boasted the best restaurant. The No Name restaurant had no name, as the name implies, but wherever you went in the world travellers would talk of the fish – oysters, scallops, lobster, bluefish. They would talk of the buzz, the fun of standing on the quay in the rain with your crate of beer or bottle of wine, queuing to go in. Do I mean queuing, in the rain, to get into an unlicensed restaurant? Yes, really.

Not least of the marvels in Boston was Boston Billy. Bill Rodgers was a shy sandy-haired man, once a pot-smoking student. He was the winner of the Boston Marathon four times and the New York four times and the best runner in the world. Long-legged, slim, not too tall, he ran easy – he did not pump or throw – he tended towards the style I call the floater. It is lovely to watch. The feet do not land on the ground – they caress it as they pass. Bill Rodgers could lay one five-minute mile on another and not give a feeling of speed or of trying but he was here and now he has gone.

Nice of you guys to come over, said Bill Rodgers.

I did not find it easy to reply – I was in the presence of one of the greatest athletes in the world and he had spoken to me! But I told him that Tom was thirty-seven and a bank manager and Major Bill was forty-five and had his own research firm and I was forty-three and had my own research firm too and we had started a marathon club just for veteran athletes – the only one in the world – and this was our first club event. Then I told him that the bats printed across our crimson tracksuits were Indonesian flying foxes, which were primates and very clever and made love upside down and the motto on our tracksuits *Sapientia atque Levitas* meant wisdom and lightness of heart or cunning and low body weight, whichever you prefer. And I told him he was marvellous and he signed me a flyer for his running shop and said we were doing good for the sport of road-running and wished us all the best and our new club too.

I don't think I bored him, but he would not have shown it, and not many people spoke to him as he sat in his corner.

> Weave a circle round him thrice,
> And close your eyes with holy dread,
> For he on honeydew hath fed,
> And drunk the milk of Paradise.

I left him drinking a Bud light, resting, waiting his hour. Gentleman Bill, Boston Billy, King of the Road.

★

It had been nice of Bill to ask us to his pre-race party just because we had visited his shoe shop, and now we are in a room packed with international sportsmen and Harvard jocks. Marathoning was not so well known in those days and veteran athletics was not so well established and old men like ourselves were figures of some interest. Track stars, quarterbacks, basketball players, expat stars over on attachment approached us and spoke to us as equals – spoke to me, the second eight oarsman, the jogger, the despair of my PE teacher at school, the bearer of sick notes, the coward, the one-eyed weakling – they spoke to me as an international sportsman leading an official UK team! I think we were indeed in some way official – my coach had told me. But he had also told me the veteran qualifying time was three hours, when it was three thirty. What the hell – we were here!

We were walking back to the hotel when a young woman approached us, pointing at the bats on our tracksuits – Gee the bats – the Sumatran fruit bat of course – you know I work with bats.

She told us about working with bats, taking her time. As her conversation did not seem to be moving towards offering sexual favours to the intrepid sportsmen from a foreign land we let it run out and said farewell.

The next day Major Bill and Tom and I ran from Hopkinton to the Prudential building in company with ten thousand others and finished the marathon in close to three hours.

Major Bill stopped outside Wellesley College at mile thirteen and from the hundreds of yelling babes chose the prettiest and took her in his arms and kissed her with enthusiasm and ran off to storms of applause, his Union Jack shorts helping to brighten the rainy day.

Some way ahead Bill Rodgers was breaking the American record.

★   ★   ★

Up on the South Yorkshire Navigation the wind was like a runaway train. It spun us round and flung us into the bank behind two barges, and Monica had to pole off the front of the boat while I did what I could with the engine from the back.

We have listened to tropical storms machine-gunning the roof; we have seen raindrops that would fill a pint tankard and watched them explode as they hit the cut. We have seen these things in Virginia and in Florida and now we have seen them in Yorkshire. They last much longer in Yorkshire.

We stayed for a couple of days waiting for the wind to drop, lying in the cabin at night as the rain drummed on us and the wind rocked us, little kids with Mummy and Daddy downstairs and you can just hear their talking and their laughter.

I don't think it is quite so windy today, I said on the third morning, knowing that I lied. Anyway we can't stay here among the ruined pubs and the desolation, visiting the working men's club. Not even Billy Gracelands, Elvis's lost brother, singing the fifties on a Saturday night will hold me.

Monica gave a push to the bow, and I gunned the engine and pulled the tiller round so we held the middle of the cut and we headed west for Thorne, sideways.

★ ★ ★

Here I am sitting in The Radfords on a Sunday night, lulled by a good dinner and a few glasses of dandelion wine and the fact I had run twenty miles in training that morning and the telephone rang.

Is that Terry Darlington, captain of Stone Master Marathoners? Chris Brasher said I should ring you. I want to run a marathon and I understand you are the captain of the only marathon club in the UK. I live in London but I can travel to see you – could you train me for the marathon?

I got so many calls – the marathon club had become a national club, with members all over the UK. We did only marathons, in the UK and overseas, with no one under the ages of thirty-five for women and forty for men. This caller sounded as if he was in his twenties and I was bored turning away people who did not qualify and wanted me to bend the rules.

Look, I don't want to waste your time – my club is just for veterans. I am so sorry to disappoint you, but it is the unique thing about the club. There are lots of general athletic clubs in London that might be able to help. How old are you by the way?

Seventy-three.

Oh goodness me, my word. Sorry to be negative – your voice fooled me. Come up next weekend and we'll fix you up with your uniform – you will always have to wear it training or racing with the club. Lovely red uniform – lots of badges and your name on the front. We'll hit you for your joining fee and we'll chat about fixing you up with a coach in London. Are you moderately fit now?

I used to do some dancing and am in quite good shape.

And your name?

Ernest – Ernest Dudley.

The writer who had invented Doctor Morelle and Miss Thrale for *Monday Night at Eight*.

★ ★ ★

On the South Yorkshire Navigation the *PM2* was going to meet a large number of low bridges that block the canal. These are known as swing bridges, or lift bridges, or bastard bridges that hold up the traffic and don't work and this key is broken and I think I am going to burst into tears.

Monica is on the tiller. The wind, coming hard over the Pennines and across the plains north of Sheffield, over Pontefract and Wakefield, over the green fields and the low banks, had pushed the *PM2* into the bank and held her like a lover. I got my fat and stiff body over the side, and waving my lock key strode up to the bridge.

After five minutes, in a bush I found a tablet of stone. In this tablet was set a bronze plaque with writing on it – a Rosetta Stone for boaters.

It had taken centuries to decipher the Rosetta Stone

and I wondered if the chap who finally did it has got a mobile phone and could offer a few tips. Much of the writing had been attacked with hammers or shat on by birds or just rotted off. Hiding among patches of moss was a keyhole – a British Waterways keyhole for my British Waterways key. I looked hard at the writing again and I could see some shreds of meaning in it. I tried to turn the key. At this point any boater will collapse in tears of laughter – he tried to turn a British Waterways key!

But it turned, and over the road there was a click and a thump. I walked to the red and white pole that was sticking up in the air and pulled a lever and a hooter started to scream and the pole came down across the road.

A tractor appeared and stopped.

I began to walk across the bridge to put down the other barrier and the wind blew me down into the mud.

A Range Rover appeared and the driver hooted.

A train came by alongside us with a noise like an earthquake, and hooted.

I caught hold of the rail on the bridge and pulled myself up and tried to pull the bridge open. The man in the tractor shouted something and the wind flung me against the bridge. I pulled again and the bridge did not move. I wondered what would happen if I ran away. The man in the Range Rover got out and the wind blew him down into the mud.

The hooter on the bridge carried on screaming.

By the railway track was a signal box with a long

staircase and a woman came down this staircase and walked to the bridge and crossed it and stood by me and we pulled at the bridge together. I'm not supposed to do this, she said.

The man from the Range Rover joined us and the bridge began to shift.

Not all the dozens of bridges ahead of us were like that. Some were better, and some were worse.

Thorne is a nice place, though most of its industry is dead and the high street shows it. A fine pub at the waterside and over the other side of the canal are fields where you can run whippets.

Monica took Jim and Jess for a walk. They were on the lead, ready to turn into the woodland, when the cat struck.

It was a heavy ginger cat, with a bell and mad staring eyes. It came out of the hedge and stood for a moment and flung itself on Jess and raked its claws across her forehead, tearing her skin. Monica pulled the furious dogs away and the cat very slowly went back into the hedge and no doubt to its home, looking back as it went, holding close to its heart the secret that it had carved up one of those whippet dogs that chase you but they are cowards really and no match for a bold ginger tom with yellow claws and mad staring eyes.

It's awful, said Monica. They keep trying to find ways to get off the boat and hunt down that cat and kill it. I can't let them off the lead at all. And poor Jess, always in trouble. We can't stay here now. It's the New Junction Canal next, then the Aire and Calder

Navigation, where the great ships used to come in from the Humber.

★　★　★

Ernest Dudley came to Stone on many Sundays to train. There was half the traffic that we see now and most of the population were still in bed getting over Saturday night so we had North Staffordshire more or less to ourselves.

Ernest was slim, not tall, with an elfin face and white hair. He got on well with Sandy Risley, his coach in London, and ran some marathons and wrote a book about it all and lectured on the ocean liners – always wearing his Stone Master Marathoners uniform.

Stone athletes ran marathons all over the world, and our ladies won many of them. We organized our own marathon, the Flying Fox, which became the UK veteran championships. In 1986 Monica became the UK champion over fifty with a time of three hours and thirty-six minutes. For three years she was the captain of the club, and led our successful veteran cross-country team, Hell's Grannies.

Nowadays the club is open to all ages and races all distances and has a hundred members. I feel very proud when I see an SMM pack on the road.

Ernest has gone to sit by the fire with Dr Morelle and Miss Thrale. He was ninety-seven. One day soon I will knock on the door and join them, maybe on a Monday night around eight.

★   ★   ★

Style is what you leave out, and the New Junction Canal leaves nearly all of it out. Take me away, shining road, take me north where all is stripped and simple.

I was born in Lincolnshire, a county which is mainly sky. The RAF is based there, because the RAF needs a lot of sky. I was there long enough for a part of me to be colonized by those plains, those dykes, and the green lines of the crops and the wind and the clouds stacked and chasing. Like the country the New Junction Canal crosses.

From the boat you look across the low towpath over the fields to the horizon. Some drains but little else. No banks, no trees, no hedges. Like a road, the canal is level with the land. A bit like the Canal du Rhône à Sète, which crosses the blue lakes of the Midi as if it walks on water, with just a few stones on each side of the canal – everything else left out.

Always the wind, the wind, on the New Junction Canal and one lock and five miles and it's over and turn left on to the Aire and Calder Navigation, which is where the big boys play. Like the New Junction Canal, but broader, more scruffy. Plenty of water, let's punch into the wind, yo ho ho.

The barges carrying coal, sand, petroleum to Leeds and Sheffield have gone to their last moorings, but here is a black commercial boat some way behind us. Leave the lock gates open – plenty of room. We know how to behave with the commercial traffic. I never put a foot wrong with that one. *Politesse*, respect, is the key. We'll wait for them, we'll wait. These guys are working and I am just an old-timer on a pleasure boat. Soon enough the commercial traffic will be gone, but the system was built for them and they have worked it for generations. They are simple folk, but with hearts . . . OH I SAY! The tug is coming into the lock and coming and coming For Christ's sake I gave you plenty of room look your bow is right over us – black and as big as a block of flats – you'll crush us like a fly!

Look Monica at those buggers on that barge – oily and ragged. They are not sailors – they are pirates that run down narrowboats in the big locks and pick over the bones of the wrecks. OK, OK, you go out first – by heaven that was close. I think that gypsy almost waved. I think I'll go down and have a shudder with Jess.

We don't press on to Leeds, but drop into the River Aire – muddy, high banks. A few miles and hard left up on to the Selby Canal – we are heading for York.

To ease my shingles I was wearing a pair of Polaroid glasses. These show the clouds without the glare of the sky. Each crease, each crevasse, each crag is revealed, each separate shade and shadow. You can climb the blunt peaks and walk in the valleys.

The New Junction Canal has a primitive, empty beauty, but the Selby Canal has the lot. Foliage droops over it, flowers smile from the verges, birds charm from the trees. It has slow curves, and long stretches beckoning you ahead. The water is clear. In the Selby Canal the water is as clear as gin.

Polaroid glasses take the reflections off water and let

you see down into it. Under the Selby Canal there are cities of vegetation – pancake leaves give great platforms, level under level, from which spaceships might lift. Green bushes give cover to wait for the Klingons and you dart out and blast them and run for the shadow of the water lilies, because the Klingon radar will not reach you there. Now give her some wellie – let's have lots of time-warps and we will whizz through the caverns of outer space and we will be the masters of all the green cities.

At Selby you look over the lock into the River Ouse, which at six o'clock in the morning is very wide and very deep, and very fast, and a very long way down. Heidi and Tony in the lock with us – The vippets are below?

Echo their German shepherd stood on the back counter, his orange eyes with their lion strangeness seeming to look in as well as out.

Twenty miles to York.

You feel the currents most as you come out of the lock, then soon you are settled on the tide pouring up the muddy stream from the North Sea and the Humber and Tony is leading and with Tony as cruise control we settle down to muse upon life and the universe. The trouble is Tony keeps changing his speed – I am either up his back or being dropped off behind. On a long cruise you should set your speed and forget it – if you change you should first have to get written permission from British Waterways. I pushed the throttle down to catch up again.

There was a grinding and the boat tipped to port, nearly going over. The grinding went all down the hull and out under my feet and the boat swung the other way and did a bit more grinding before I could get her out in the stream again.

Was I on the inside of a bend?

Look, I'll be straight with you. You have got to understand that in this low country there are lots and lots of bends and meanders in the rivers – hundreds in fact and it is really all bends and meanders and it is not natural, not intuitive, to hug the outside line and sometimes you forget – you are bound to forget, especially if you are full of medication and an idiot.

Oh see over by the bank – lots of outrageous old boats hung with tin sheets and tarpaulin and ladders going up the bank and shacks – a riverside city for people who like living in hulks and shacks and perhaps are poor or not favoured in their wits.

As we get nearer to York Marina, south of the city, the boats get cleaner and bigger. They are mainly plastic cruisers, and here are some big beauties that could set out to sea any time, and hold a lot of gin in their great marine refrigerators.

★　★　★

Research Associates had many hundreds of customers, and lovely blokes and ladies most of them were. Some were not, of course, and I suppose they are in some ways the more interesting.

As our firm traded through the seventies and eighties

Monica and I saw the terrible deaths of many of our large and world-famous corporations such as Leyland, British Shipbuilders, Bedford. These organizations were aware that something was wrong with them and were interested to find out just what it was and what they should do about it, until you told them, and then they weren't interested any more.

I remember going with a couple of my senior people to give a presentation to Leyland at their plant about the prospects for the Range Rover in Germany. I would not normally write about studies which we carried out in confidence, but that Leyland company does not exist any more and it was a long time ago.

We arrived at the plant at 10.30 as arranged and were asked to be kind enough to wait in reception. There is a board meeting and then it's you.

By 12.30 nothing had happened and I began to realize what was going on. I took my chaps – one was a girl chap – out to a good hotel for a long lunch and we returned and took up our station in reception. At half past four we were told the board was ready.

The boardroom was full of junk. No one had been interested to have it cleared out. I was used to clearing out and tidying the room for our presentations to failing firms and public bodies. Once in British Telecom I refused to use the lavatory provided. I was offered the lavatory used by the board and that was fine.

Among the junk was the Land Rover board, half a dozen men, looking murderous.

We began our presentation. The company's distribution system in Germany was scruffy and low-grade –

not suitable for a luxury vehicle. We showed photographs of vehicle dealer outlets crouched in dirty corners of industrial estates, and we showed the proud Mercedes outlets. We told the board that the Range Rover was not trusted for its reliability, and that many Germans were scornful of British engineering. There was little advertising support in the German market. We showed a breakdown of vehicle sales by price band and we forecast for the Range Rover the next year a static sales picture, perhaps two thousand vehicles.

The half a dozen men began to throw the furniture at us.

Did we not realize that all their forecasts were based on four thousand units a year? Did we not realize that they had been selling Range Rovers for a long time and knew what they were doing? Did we not realize that they were a new board and they had come in with guns blazing to sort out the firm? What did we know? Who was this young man who spoke German and had done the interviews, and that girl who had done the forecasts? They are not vehicle specialists! We understand that the first draft of the report that you sent us had spelling mistakes in it! Spelling mistakes and we are spending tens of thousands on this research!

You learn early on in research and consultancy to keep cool under fire and my chaps did very well. These are the outlets, these are pictures of the senior respondents we interviewed – very informed people, these are the vehicle segmentations by price. What evidence do you have, sweet sirs, that you will double your sales next year with a weak distribution system and an unreliable product? Could it be reverse accounting, I suggested, setting your sales to the level you need to finance what you want to do rather than looking at the market and then calculating the sales?

Bloody amateurs, said the board. We are being advised by young men and girls and Mr Darlington who is not always polite. You should be ashamed. We will pay your bill but we will not use you again and we cannot recommend your services to others. Two thousand – that is an absurdly low forecast. You have no idea of what this new board can accomplish.

They sold nineteen hundred. There was never any way they were going to do better.

These fantasists were the sort of people running our big industries at that time, the industries that one by one failed. And now German companies are making the Range Rovers, the Minis, the Rolls-Royces.

Industry and trade were unfashionable, low-class activities compared to the law or education or the Civil Service or the BBC and the best people avoided those careers. So second-raters had risen from the ranks to fill the boardrooms. They lost control of the workforce and lost control of their finances. *This cancer must be cut out of our economy*, said one customer of a failing engineering industry.

One day Research Associates was telephoned by Doulton, the pottery company. We are angry and disappointed, Mr Darlington. We are sitting in the boardroom waiting for your team and you are nearly half an hour late. You are supposed to be specialists in business efficiency. It's a disgrace. Why are you not here?

We are not there because you have not asked us.

★　★　★

The only way to approach a city is by water. The water is why it is there in the first place, and its shape, its purposes, are revealed as you approach. The old warehouses, the quayside pubs, the remains of the docks, and over the top the Minster.

No quays for pleasure boats and then just the other side of the city centre some rings and a sort of wharf.

I would like to take some York councillor along the quay where I went for a walk and nearly fell down a hole into the river and see if he can make it along the quay safely. With any luck he won't and I will pull him out and save his life and he will go back to the council chamber and say Complete refurbishment, water, electricity, pontoons, a laundry and a convenience store and a nice sculpture or two and room for a hundred boats because a great city with a great river deserves an inland pleasure port at its centre.

Here we are – the chap on the bank looks friendly – holding out his hand to take a rope. In his other hand a bag of pork scratchings and a bottle of champagne. Where's Jim? Where's the narrow dog?

What a welcome!

John is a fan and he came on board for a chat.

In my Father's house are many mansions, said Jesus Christ.

Some of the mansions are in the roof of York Minster

– up there in the incense and between the woven stone where music dwells lingering – how was that ceiling ever built? It could not have been made by human hands – it is too beautiful, too high.

The choir was visiting from Rugby. On the left was Mama Cass and in the centre Michelle Phillips – from the Mamas and the Papas. They sang like angels and I tried with no success to keep my thoughts pure about Michelle Phillips, the lovely hippie Mama. The voices rose into the roof and bounced around its pillars and valleys and fell down again, even sweeter than before.

The sermon was delivered by a toff who had a toff's voice and thought like a toff and no doubt walked like a toff. He was a long way down at the altar and we were back here by the door with the Japanese but the sound system was good. The toff made it clear he wasn't very interested in being here (toffs never admit they are very interested in anything) but as he found himself address-ing a crowded congregation on Ascension Day he could spare a few thoughts for those ignorant people in the USA who had said The Rapture was going to happen today and the righteous would ascend to heaven but it didn't happen so sucks to them ho ho. I'm going now – I've got a lot of interesting things to say but you will have to come to my next sermon on Sunday and it has been mildly amusing talking to you ignorant fuckers.

I have walked Jim in many counties, and in France and the USA, but I have never seen a lovelier field than here in York. A raised path and you look down on ten acres of level green, where Jess and lion-eyed Echo tore about. No living creature is faster than Jess but Heidi's German shepherd is strong and agile and Jess runs in great circles so he cut the corners and gave her a good game. I do not know what he would have done if he had caught her.

Jim had met a terrier, a puppy. He wrestled with the puppy and chased the puppy and tried to mount the puppy. Someone told me once that a puppy seems to a male dog rather like a girl. We stopped that nonsense but Jim was in love.

He stayed with the puppy after we had set off home and I had to go back for him. The Lady Who Knows about Whippets was right, I said to Jim, who was pulling back and whining. Come on – you have got no idea – you are useless.

York seethed with tourists and the sun shone and we untied our ropes and let the bow come round slowly in the current and there were Heidi and Tony ahead and we followed them down river. We were going home.

Past Naburn Lock the Ouse is tidal and the mudbanks were high and the tide was low. As we pushed down, the tide pushed up, getting fiercer and fiercer. And towards us in the centre of the stream a river of strangeness came at us, thumping and threatening. There is the arm of a drowning man, helplessly waving. Look, that's an alligator – I would know it anywhere. Here comes a chest of drawers. Snakes ten feet long writhing and knocking – knocking, how can snakes knock? The antlers of a stag, half a piano, truckloads of firewood, all streaming down on to us. What if some of this flotsam gets round the prop?

Keep going, try to avoid some of the big stuff – look, the tide is slowing. Soon we were bumping through a stationary Sargasso Sea of junk, and then it all began to run back out towards the sea, and we were travelling with it at the same speed, so we could forget about it.

Nice day – river a bit bendy, but the secret is relax and let the boat find its way. Let the boat do the work – it will find the stream. The number of boaters who fight the currents and the wind. A sensitive boater, an arteest like me, uses the forces and currents of nature as his friends, and reaches down to find that mystical connection with the world that – watch this one – Oh Lord!

The current running hard on the outside of the curve caught me and pulled me under the trees and bushes hanging off the bank. They scratched along the boat.

I was on a tight right-hand bend in a current. If I pushed the stern in, the back of the boat was going deeper into the dark and hostile canopy, and if I pushed it out the bow did the same. The stream thrust me in further – four knots flat against the side of a fifty-eight-foot boat. Work out the foot-pounds in that one. I was being held hard into the canopy and dragged through it and had no control of my boat. To use the phrase favoured by my old rowing partner Dave Morgan of Llandaff, I was buggered, literally.

It was all happening so fast – a thick branch swept down the roof and took off a chimney and came at me and now a sixty-pound anchor was coming at my chest at four knots. Sometimes when dreadful things are happening you become transfixed and just stand looking. I became transfixed and just stood looking, like a tit in a trance.

The anchor hit me on the chest. I fell down on the back counter, my Breton sailor's hat flung wide into the stream. I reached up and pushed the tiller hard to the right and the branch was gone over my head. The anchor had jammed in the hatch just before it had the chance to break half my ribs and sling me into the river.

Mercifully here was a bit of bank with no trees. The bow hit the bank and I carried on pushing the tiller and the stern came out and then I straightened the boat and gave it full revs and it struggled out into the stream. Tony ahead was beginning to turn round to rescue me and I waved him on. I carried on down the river, bare-headed, the boat hanging with branches like a hippy festival.

I made a bad entry to the lock at Selby, banging and thrashing. I used to be able to do this. Lock-keepers would congratulate me, not talk to me as if I had started boating on Tuesday. OK, OK, I'll take her into that side and of course I'll be careful – I'm always careful. What makes you think I'm not careful?

All down the port side of our new boat there were scratches. Oh hell, it's a contact sport. They'll polish out. Could happen to anybody.

Monica was very kind and has said almost nothing so far, but I couldn't help wondering if the loss of my captain's hat was some higher power trying to tell me something.

★

At Knottingley we tied up to a fence just above the lock, and around us was desolation. Empty factory sites, broken walls, barbed wire.

Monica wanted to buy a Calder and Hebble handspike. We didn't know what a Calder and Hebble handspike was but the book said that it was essential. Among the desolation was a big shed declaring itself to be the terrestrial headquarters of a shipbuilders and marine engineers. Monica went into the shed. The shed was empty, waiting for a ship to build.

A man shuffled towards her from the junk and shadows at the end of the shed. He was smiling broadly and his eyes shone. Monica asked him if he could sell her the handspike. Oh no, we don't do that sort of thing here.

Monica did not wait to enquire what sort of thing he did here.

Meanwhile I was away up the towpath with Jim and Jess. A pleasant lawn and here is the towpath, narrow between these low garden walls and the canal. And look, along the towpath – roses, lupins, delphiniums, granny bonnets, foxgloves, valerian, ox-eye daisies, peonies. Coming into Knottingley off the river it looked like a hell-hole but someone has planted two hundred yards of the public towpath as a cottage garden.

When Monica and I lived on a shopping parade in Chessington, Surrey, behind us there was the railway embankment. Late one evening I dressed in black and took ten packets of seeds from Woolworths and climbed through the wire and shook the seeds all along the embankment.

None of them grew.

Monica did not want to moor by the beer garden at Horbury because some nasty people might come into the beer garden and talk and then fight and knife each other and knife us and knife the dogs. I like to hear people talk, I said, and took my rope ashore and through the ring on the bank.

To make peace I offered to take the dogs for a walk back down the towpath. The dogs came out of the boat grinning. I caught them and clipped on their collars.

A few people with dogs coming towards us and then nobody. I realized that on one side I had the canal and over there a hundred yards the river Calder. No roads that I can see. I know how practised these whippets are at getting into trouble but they should be fine unless they are attacked by a duck or something ho ho. They are born to run and I love to see them free. I let them slip and they trotted ahead.

Jess and Jim can disappear at will. Jess will then reappear well in front of you from behind a hedge, regardless of what barriers seemed to lie in her way, and Jim resumes his earthly form just behind you like a pantomime villain. *Look behind you!*

I am always nervous when they are off the lead, because of the terrible trouble that they can generate, but this is safe – canal on one side and down there the river – see here is Jess again, back up from the river, and just behind my right knee Jim has taken shape, quieter than a whisper. It's a gamble every time, but you have to give them some freedom – there they go, down the towpath – we must have come nearly a mile.

A commotion over there towards the river. Oh dear, Jess is chasing those poor ducklings. They have come into the very shallow water on the edge of a pond and she is upon them – they are tiny – she will kill them all – she can't help her instincts – what a disaster.

A dark shape just above Jess, struggling in mid-air. Jess turned and snapped upwards and it was the mother duck, one wing apparently broken, flying two feet above the ground. Jess jumped for her and missed and the duck made for the river, with a lurching broken flight, but too fast for Jess's jaws. Another jump, another miss, cries of despair from the duck. The ducklings meanwhile had got into deeper water.

At full speed Jess and the duck went over the river bank and there was silence.

And silence.

And silence.

I stood behind the barbed wire fence and waited, but nothing happened and I lay down and rolled under the fence, coating myself in mud and tearing my shorts. I walked towards the river.

Although it was daylight my memory tells me it was dusk. There was something on the bank. I could not make it out. Was it a haversack? I am sure it was not there earlier. Is it a dog? There is no dog of that shape and it is not moving.

Then I got it – the shape was Jess. She was covered in blood and holding out a front leg, and her paw and wrist dropped from it, held only by skin. Blood dripped from it. It was like a scene from a horror film.

I caught her in my arms. She was silent. I tried to carry her but she was solid muscle – too heavy to make more than ten yards and I was a mile from the boat. I tried to roll under the barbed wire and caught my clothes and caught her leg and she cried out.

I was covered in blood and sobbing and Jim was barking and barking and running around tangling us in his lead and trying to mount Jess. This is his way of showing concern and affection but it doesn't help, Jim, really it doesn't.

I closed my eyes and tried to slip across into a parallel universe where this was not happening but when I opened them I was still lying under the fence, bloody, helpless, with two dogs struggling on top of me.

Linda and Gordon Gray were walking up the towpath. Linda ran back to the *PM2* to fetch Monica and Gordon helped us to Barry James's farmhouse.

The kindness of strangers.

She's got a strong heart, said the pet ambulance driver, holding her against his ample tummy, his bare forearms covered with wounds from an earlier customer.

It's a bad break, said the vet. And it's so near the wristbone we haven't got much room to put in our steel pins. We have her on a morphine drip.

We went home and I washed the blood off Jim and myself. I could not imagine how such a wound could ever be healed.

I hope I never see another sight like that. Nor could I imagine how Jess injured herself – when she went over the bank, travelling so fast, lured by the duck, she must have somehow caught her paw in something awful – perhaps an old car rotting under the bank, a harrow thrown in by a farmer, oil drums, an old fence.

I went back to the bank the next day. It was just a riverbank – there was not even a tree. A ten-foot drop down a muddy bank into the river.

The valiant duck had left with her brood.

# CHAPTER ELEVEN

# DEWSBURY

## *Demonic Love*

*And hear their strange sad cries*

*The Queen was not seeking me out – You will get murdered
for your briefcase – The loyal staff, the bastards – Put up your
prices and answer the phones – Keep changing, reverse the
dominance – Waiting with a revolver – I saw a sign – Bandit
country – Rudd and Chubb and Tench – The dance of the
kingfishers – A long time since a dragon ate anyone – The
essence of the class system is exclusion – A dog that had
appeared to go mad – Deadly Ernest – Trying to shag his auntie – We'll be pulled down and eaten – Mr Palmer is not going
to die – Last night I dreamt of Manderley again – This one
will sell in six figures*

The Queen wore yellow. I suppose she wore yellow so
she would stand out among these soldiers, churchmen,
lawyers, court officials, mayors, butlers and frog foot-
men; all in uniform, purples and scarlets, some with
chains, and lots of civilians including the head of a
market research firm in a sharpish grey suit and his best
green spotted tie and his wife in a broad white hat, help-
ful in the hammering sun. I took another cucumber
sandwich from the silver tray and Monica had another
iced tea.

At the ticket office at Stafford station the gentleman behind the glass had asked if we were going to the garden party, as everyone else in Staffordshire was.

The Department of Industry had arranged our invitation. Research Associates was doing well with government work and indeed generally. The break-through had come ten years ago when Monica had come into the business as my partner and I could relax knowing that we wanted the same things from our efforts. Quite soon Monica and I hired some wonderful staff.

Such as Dan Park, who went behind the Iron Curtain to carry out a study into oil and gas in the Soviet Union. This sort of work was forbidden by the Russians, but Dan's fluent Russian and his courage and determination paid off. We published the study and woke up famous. General Motors followed with a job in six countries, and the Scottish Development Agency sent us round the world. Downing Street asked us to carry out the study about barriers to business. Airbus bought a study in ten countries and IBM a study in the USA. The *Economist* magazine hired us to do the research into its own activities. We became accepted as a big-league firm, though we were not twenty people. The Radfords was full and we were doing 10 per cent of UK industry's overseas research and turning over a million pounds a year.

The Queen was not seeking me out so Monica and I looked for some shade. There was not much in this part of the garden. The lavatories in the tents are so clean, I said to Monica. It is a privilege to piss in them. Another cucumber sandwich?

This must be the best day of my life, I thought, chosen to come to Buckingham Palace. I was running, I was fit, barely fifty, independent, successful. My lovely wife at my side, my lovely kids at home, my house with thirty rooms, my two retrievers, my BMW. Good afternoon, Wing Commander – still quite close isn't it?

The Department of Industry had said I was just the sort of chap the Queen would like to meet. But that was fantasy – I don't suppose the Queen saw me at all. If she had she would perhaps have looked behind the sharpish suit and the Church's shoes and the Rolex and looked into my eyes and seen that I was completely and totally knackered.

Six months later I was in the doctor's surgery.

What seems to be the trouble?

Someone comes along in the night and siphons all the blood out of my veins and replaces it with cold piss, Doc.

He told me I had something called ME and would feel like this for twelve months. He was right in his diagnosis but wrong in his prognosis as I had the disease for four years. It was pretty obvious how it happened – I was running a business and marathoning and earlier in the year had had to go to France to complete the job of one of my executives who had gone mad in the Grand Hotel de L'Arc de Triomphe, and I had taken on too much for too long.

Fortunately as I worked for myself I was able to keep going on two cylinders until I got better. I feel so sorry for those poor people who have ME really badly, and angry when some prat announces without any evidence that it is all in the mind.

Lord King, the chairman of British Airways, came out of his head office and walked towards his taxi and the Research Associates executive was on him like a beast of prey. Lord King, have you a moment – I would like to ask you a few questions about your choice of aeroplane for British Airways.

Go and see Colin – Colin buys the planes.

And my daring and resourceful executive went to see Colin Marshall, the Managing Director, to explore why British Airways bought its planes from Boeing in Seattle. After all Airbus, the French and British enterprise, was gagging to make him some planes in Toulouse.

We did quite a few jobs for Airbus.

Less daring and resourceful was the executive whom I accompanied to Lagos on a job about screws. Nigerian corruption was legendary but I had decided with my low church background that however dirty Lagos proved to be I would stand above it, milk-white and shining. I would give no bribes and accept no favours. Nothing would tempt or move me. Nigerian society was lucky indeed to have such a man moving among them for a week.

The plane swept in across the dust and scrub of the Ivory Coast and arrived at Lagos as night fell, very quickly. The foyer in the Airport Hotel was full of people shoving and shouting. I got to the desk. Fifty pounds said the clerk, but we are full. I can find you a room but you will have to give me thirty pounds for myself. Otherwise you can sleep in the bush where you will get murdered for your briefcase.

As I walked the damp corridors towards my room a waiter came towards me. In the Airport Hotel, Lagos, it is the guest who steps aside.

My room was damp, no – wet. Water was running down the walls. The only way sleep would come would be with the help of alcohol.

We had plenty of help in the next few nights. Although it is the worst hotel in the world the Airport Hotel, Lagos, has the best music. In its yard in the equator night a band playing Highlife music, music to make your blood run fast and your heart thump and your mind fill with joy. We danced with the local girls, who were not at all the colour or shape of girls as I knew them.

The music played on – a couple more beers and I will turn in. I enjoyed the curried snails in the dining room tonight (the Nigerian snail is the size of a baseball) and the fieldwork is going well and I am beginning to appreciate Nigeria.

In the morning my executive looked a bit drawn. I have to confess, sire, I have landed in the shite.

He had become involved with a black girl, or refused to become involved – anyway he had been attacked by her large black friends and spent the night under a bush, with the friends looking for him. Most of his money had been in his socks and he still had his passport, but he had lost a hundred pounds and had a bruise where he had been hit over the head. I had been tempted to hit him over the head a number of times myself since I hired him a year ago but I was sorry he had had such a bad time. They had snails again that night and that cheered him up and he went to bed early and watched the water running down the walls.

At the airport going home I forgot to bribe the luggage clerk and the bastard sent my bags to Helsinki.

*What is it like running a market research firm?*

Like running any sort of firm, I guess. The patches of plain sailing, the warm feeling when a big contract arrives. Economic downturns, with the misery of laying off staff. The loyal staff, the bastards; the knowledge that if no work comes in, there, six weeks ahead, is the abyss.

*What were the best bits?*

A good report – a happy client.

The overseas fieldwork – the respondents who give you all the help they can, even if they are competitors of your client.

And the fun – running round Central Park in New York at five o'clock in the morning and melting the ice off my beard in the washbasin. Drinking with Dan in Arturo's in Houston Street New York, with Margot at the bar. The day the nice man from the KGB came to The Radfords to check us out. Discovering the Galleria and the Duomo in Milan. Realizing in Norway that I could understand a few words because I had studied Anglo-Saxon. Running round the Imperial Palace in Tokyo. Racing the local jocks in Victoria Park Hong Kong.

*And the worst?*

Laying off staff in the recessions. And once or twice when work had dried up and I thought I was done for – clutching my head – My God I am ruined! I can really understand those chaps who kill themselves when they go bust – you feel so ashamed – but you shouldn't – you have had a go after all. It is the loss of status and self-esteem that does it. I always appreciate that bit of Shakespeare – *men have died from time to time, and worms have eaten them, but not for love.*

*Who were your best customers?*

Hairy-arsed managing directors who are responsible for a payroll. Tough, straight people who can use our work properly – nature's gentlemen. You can divide the human race into men and women and people who have had to meet a payroll and people who have not. These guys had to meet a payroll and we were there to help them do it.

*And your worst?*

We did a lot of public sector work but I was never at ease with it.

I never worked out what anyone did in the Department of Trade and Industry but I am sure at least 50 per cent of the officials we met did not need to be there. Sometimes I wondered if all they were doing was hanging round us making sure that we were not going to comment unfavourably on the department in our reports. Trying to establish some intellectual basis for one of their lunatic and interventionist schemes, I asked them once how many firms there were in England by broad size sector. They did not know.

We did two very large programmes of research for the European Commission. At our first meeting I was shocked to have to spend the first half-hour sitting around with a dozen senior officials as they filled in their expenses forms. I was shocked when the official who came to Stone made sure his first call was into our local bank.

What matters to the Commission officials is their corner office. They will drag you across Europe to see their corner office, with its views on two sides of the leafy avenues of Brussels.

The Scottish Development Agency, now defunct, was another lulu. Not a force for good, said dear old Jim Francis.

This benighted bunch was set up to spend money allocated by Edward Heath to keep Scotland quiet. We did a worldwide study for them. It took them a year to commission it, they changed the brief three times, and they interfered remorselessly with the programme.

After this shambles they called us to Scotland to prepare a costly proposal on how they could transform the Scottish economy by developing the bus station opposite their offices.

*How good were you as a businessman?*

Not particularly good – I panicked too easily and did not care enough about profit. Too much of an arteest perhaps. What interested me was the research – trying to do it better than anyone else. I was weak with the staff and almost incapable of laying people off – before I would do that I would pursue absurd strategies like my two attempts to open an office in New York.

I had some strengths – I was able to see to the heart of a problem quickly and I was not afraid to tell the truth to a client. I worked hard. I was good at writing reports. I valued clear conclusions and scorned consultancy-speak. I did not proposition my female staff.

People trusted me. I remember one client saying at a presentation – We liked Dr Boyd and trusted Mr Darlington!

*How did Research Associates do overall?*

When we retired Monica and I were well off. We had the pleasure of working with our three kids at one of the most interesting jobs in the world. We ran the firm for thirty years and Lucy and her husband Richard took it over when we left and are running it better than we did.

There were times (I thought you knew) when we bit off more than we could chew but we came through those and most of all we were able to do it our way.

What do I conclude from our studies all over the world? What universal truths emerged? Did the tens of thousands of customers we interviewed and the thousands of suppliers reveal some underlying business trends or principles, or did I just slave away with my nose at the coal face, understanding nothing?

Well, here are a couple of ideas, to put alongside my tips for boaters as revealed in earlier books – I mean things like Always pick up string from the beach as you never know when you will have a loose fender, and the advice about *Droppus Droppus Deddus*, the mushroom – an important one, that.

Company after company would spend twenty thousand pounds and report after report would come back with the same conclusions. And here they are, for you, free of charge and obligation – Darlington's Universal Research Report Recommendations.

1. *Your promising new markets are half the size you think they are so forget it*

When an executive brought me a report to edit I would normally look at the estimates of market size and halve them. Markets are like fish – they look bigger in the water. Beware of reverse accounting – setting your sales estimates high enough to cover your expenses. Most of the new ideas we reviewed were stiffs, and it would have made so much more sense to concentrate on the existing business.

2. *Put up your prices and answer the phones*

Businesses are so often frightened of charging enough to cover service. If you don't believe me and you are a businessman ring your business and try to buy something, or get someone to put in a complaint and see what happens. Customers want more than the naked product on the mat. They want a little love, and they will pay for it.

Oh, and don't forget to wear your sunglasses for a couple of days and take them off as you sail into the tunnel.

★ ★ ★

We pulled up outside a small house towards the end of an endless terrace in Pembroke Dock looking out over

Milford Haven towards Neyland. Bloody hell, I said, I thought Charlie would be in a mansion.

Charlie had been my best friend when I was nine, ten, eleven. He was a bit older than me but in the same class, where he always came first. I would always come third or fourth, where no one would notice me. We would do what boys do in the country – make dens, play in haystacks, run away from bulls, go to Cub Scouts, nearly drown ourselves in the Mill Pond.

When Pembroke Castle was built the stone was quarried at Pennar Gut and the quays and little canal cuts were still there from the sixteenth century and we would swim in them. We wrestled a lot in an endless play of establishing dominance. Charlie was a big chap and he always won.

He opened the door and seemed almost pleased to see us. His wife seemed almost pleased to see us too. We sat down and had one of those strange conversations. I think I knew what would happen and Monica got the idea early on and we managed to fill a couple of hours – *don't say we live in a big house, don't say we have our own business, don't say we have another two cars, don't for God's sake say I went to Oxford. Ask them lots of questions but tell them only what they want to know.*

Of course Charlie knows I went to Oxford. Of course Charlie knows we are doing well and any dominance has been reversed but he does not want to discuss it and I know that he is deeply sorry we looked him up and he will never want to see or hear from us again.

I have been spared much in life – despite driving sports cars for forty years, sometimes at great speed, God forgive me I have not had a serious motor accident. My children grew up healthy and I have been able to pay my bills. My wife is wonderful and my illnesses have gone away except for the shingles and this will go one day.

My griefs have mainly been related to the loss of friends who have decided that they want no more of me. My childhood friends like Charlie and my best friends from Oxford cut the ties that bound us and it hurts like hell.

My fault was to keep growing, keep changing, to reverse the dominance, buy a big house.

It was a funny empty time after I retired and before I took up writing. I would walk with Jim and sort and weed my private papers so things were tidy when I died.

My father had left a number of small diaries filled with the day-to-day news of the last fifteen years of his life. There was not much news – *Got up, went for a walk, put in a row of marigolds, went for a walk, went to church.* And there was a chest full of photographs of the thirties, pictures of my dad in India and the lovely young couples who were my relations long ago.

There was one big picture of an Indian lady.

One day my father said Son you are fifty now and I feel I can talk frankly to you about sexual matters. I shall tell you something about my time in India, as a young airman.

Dad's mother was part Burmese – that was one reason why he was so handsome, and he sunburned very brown. In Karachi he would dress as a local and go out into the bazaars.

One day, he said, I met a lady. An Indian lady. I was twenty-two and she was twenty-nine. She was married but could not have any children. It was great for some time and then it was time for me to go home. Unfortunately as I thought at the time, I missed the train on Karachi station. But it was a bit of luck in fact as her husband was waiting for me on the platform with a revolver. If I had been in time for that train I would probably not be here and neither would you.

After Dad died I mentioned the lady to my mother. I think Dad had a girl in India before he came back and married you.

I knew nothing of her – if I had I would never have married him.

But she knew damn well – I marvelled at the way her generation could hold on to two realities at once. Many an illegitimate child was accepted into a family and everyone knew but no one knew. Where there is no money around you just have to get on with it.

I put all the photos back in the chest.


My next retirement project was to grow a ponytail, just like Willie Nelson.

Willie Nelson looks great in a ponytail but he has a neat and narrow head and I don't. As my hair grew over my collar I just looked degenerate. I was in the Star one day when Maurice Hamer the publican God rest him said Terry I don't want you to take offence but although I am proud to count you among my friends I may not be talking with you much in future – if I am seen talking to a tramp it might encourage low trade to come into my pub.

So I wandered round Stone with Jim, an old man with nothing to do, a vagrant and a threat. Sometimes I would drop into the pub and talk to the old chaps and it could be good but all too often it would get awkward because I lived in The Radfords and had big cars and in their terms I was rich and how could I ever fit into their groups, their hierarchies?

Along the towpath – My God they are pulling down the Rising Sun! They can't pull down the Rising Sun! Piles of bricks and rubbish! You are pulling down my town, my memories. This is the pub opposite the Stone Master Marathoners' clubhouse! What is going on? And what is that on that pile of rubbish? It's the sign – the lovely swinging sign of the sun rising over the canal – two oil paintings back to back!

I found the dominant male, the owner – It had to go, he said, losing money.

Look, can I have this sign? I think you were throwing it out. I don't have any money on me but I can go home and get some.

Just give me what you have in your pocket.

I had seventy-five pence.

I carried the sign over to the clubhouse. Monica was inside with her middle-class friends playing bridge. I propped the sign against our camper-van and went in.

I walked up the stairs to the room where fifty people were arranged at tables being dummies or redoubling their spades or winking or pressing each other's feet under the table or whatever they do in bridge clubs.

I went in, my grey hair sticking out under my cap, my coat covered in dust and rubble. The room fell silent. Somebody said Can we help you?

I saw Monica in the far corner. There was a sign, I shouted, I saw a sign, I saw a sign!

★   ★   ★

When Jess was injured we boated on for a few miles and tied up in a little marina on the outskirts of Dewsbury, not far from the vet.

Bandit country, said one of my friends in an email, but it suited us fine. A pub, a canalside walk. A lot of tattoos, but we have tattoos ourselves.

Each evening for three weeks we would leave Jim in the boat and walk to the vet. The nurse brought Jess out to a little room where we would all lie on the floor and she would crawl over us and lick us. Her leg was heavily bandaged – a different colour each day. When first we visited she was very quiet and then she started to get more cheerful. We would bring her some Spam Lite. I think she looked forward to the visits and they made it easier for her.

On the way home we would pass through a part of the town where there were many families from Pakistan. One evening there seemed to be a party some-where because there were a lot of young girls in pyjamas in vibrating green or pink walking along in the sun.

Monica liked to call at the supermarket, where there were racks of vegetables we had not seen before and shelves of curry sauces. One day I went along the vegetables and picked out those that we did not know – mainly things that looked like small cucumbers. We took them home and Monica cooked them and they were awful.

But Monica made a curry with vegetables we knew and it was smashing and we have it every week now.

The gentleman behind the till was dressed like a bandit chief in an old film. He had a menacing face and a grey beard and a turban and probably a scimitar under his robe. He fancied Monica rotten and would smile and smile for her and make jokes which we did not understand and then he would smile some more and I think he let her have one or two of the little cucumbers on the house.

Off down the towpath with Jim.

A freckled boy on a bike. Are you digging for worms?

No, the trowel is to clean up after my dog.

Cute dog – a greyhound?

No, a whippet – they are smaller. School is over today?

I don't go – I'm seventeen tomorrow. I'm going for an interview about the army in September. Is that your boat? Very nice. I've been talking to the fishermen. I like fishing.

What do you fish for?

Jack Pike.

What is a Jack Pike?

A Jack Pike is a female Pike, and the male Pike are just Pike. Jack Pike are smaller.

Oh. What are all those fish we have in the marina under our boat?

They will be Rudd and Chubb and Tench and Bream and Roach. I catch Carp as well as Pike, usually under a boat. The bottom of your boat is growing plants and stuff and the fish eat it and when a new boat arrives the Carp say Great and hurry to get the new plants first. See the way the canal is moving now – very slowly that way? Eighty per cent of the fish always swim with the flow and 20 per cent against it Goodbye.

Goodbye. Nice to meet you. Good luck in September.

So 80 per cent of the fish always swim with the flow, and 20 per cent against it. Bit like people really.

★   ★   ★

After we retired we still lived in The Radfords and so did the business and we needed from time to time to escape. Stone is central to the UK waterway system and we set about getting to know the world of boating.

We realized that buying a boat for leisure alone would be folly. We would have to live on a narrowboat for four months a year to get any value. That was fine by us.

So there we are looking round marinas at boats. Dreadful boats full of plywood partitions, ugly boats, rather nice boats but rather expensive, and we came upon *Sinnita*. I shall not tell of her virtues, her sweeping shape, her open-plan layout, her windows each of which could hold a cloud. Or of her vices – the rubbish engine, the dead batteries. I try not to think of her too much as I get upset.

I had just lost my beloved mother Phyllis May – my beloved father George Jubb had gone eight years before. The beautiful couple from Pembroke Dock were together again. I bet my mother is sending Dad up the highest crags in heaven to pick a spray of valerian. He was watching Peter Davison as Albert Campion in some detective story about a chalice, when death released him from it.

We had a mooring at Hoo Mill nine miles south of Stone, where we could watch the sun set over the fields. We would sail to Brewood and back and up to Stone.

Sunset with the fish rising, the swan looking into our bedroom window, cruising at night by our tunnel light, the snow muffling the morning on the Shropshire Union, new curtains of gypsy's lace, the dance of the kingfishers, the goldfinches on a thistle, the perfumes of Arabia from the cut grass and the may, the waterbirds the waterfish the waterplants, the lilies and their yellow flags and the marigolds, the fruit on the bushes and trees.

One day we were moored and I looked out of the window and cried out Mon, a fox!

The fox came partially out of the bushes on the other side of the cut and I rushed for my camera. I won't get him, I'll miss him, it always happens.

The fox revealed himself and walked about a little bit and I shot a roll of film. He sat back and waved his front legs in the air. I shot another roll. He rolled on his back and I rushed to my film drawer.

Now the fox seemed to be doing some sort of tango – perhaps it is a mating dance, I thought.

He was still there two hours later, grinning at me. My film drawer was empty.

The dragon flicked out a black tongue so he could catch my smell before he attacked. He was ten feet long. These dragons, you know, do not run at you and nip your ankles like a dog – they get up on their back legs and hold out their arms and stare at you and give you the upright rush and overwhelm you and then chomp you.

The guide explained that it was a long time since a Komodo dragon had eaten anyone. The last person had been a Swedish lecturer.

When Monica and I handed over Research Associates we decided to have an expensive holiday, and among the more expensive available was a tour in a small cruise ship round Indonesia. Although I had knocked about a bit I was not quite sure where Indonesia was, or indeed what it was. It turned out to be a massive archipelago – a pattern of islands along the Equator, stretching east as far as you can go before you hit the Pacific.

We sailed from Singapore. Not my kind of place really. If they catch you throwing away a gum wrapper they take away all your clothes and brand you on the bum and send you home in a tramp steamer. I don't chew gum but there must have been many other things for which you get branded on the bum and I didn't know what they were.

The outdoor food market was superb, and we went to the Raffles Hotel. I love old hotels – they are often not the most expensive if you can put up with a bit of running down. My favourite was the Waldorf in London – tea dances in the Palm Court. Then the Pera Palace in Istanbul, the Château Frontenac in Quebec, the Adelphi in Liverpool, the Royal in Leamington Spa, the Paul Revere Motel in Boston (I'm joking).

We don't usually do what one is supposed to do but we had gin slings in the bar in the Raffles Hotel. Noël Coward did it or something. Then we had dinner. That was fine but the staff kept coming out of the kitchen and hiding behind pillars and looking at us and scream- ing behind their hands. Aren't they used to English people here? It's a famous international hotel, after all.

We checked around to see if anything else was exercising them, and I checked my flies under the table, but all was well as they ran in and out of the kitchen and made moaning noises.

They think you are James Bond, explained the waiter. You are going bald like Sean Connery and you are tall and you have a round face and the whiskers just like him.

Well, tell them they all look the same to me too.

The ship was smallish – none of your towering halls. It had been a factory boat for a fishing fleet before it was poshed up. We booked late and had the worst cabin – it had a porthole but it was small and most of the time there was an oriental gentleman under the bed groaning and knocking with his spanner at some piece of equip- ment that was central to our voyage.

The ship set forth, our oriental friend still slaving

under the bed, into the blue equatorial seas under a blasting sun, and soon we arrived at an island.

The island was the size of a football field. The sand so white and the water so clear and the warm wind rolling the surf. It was more Eastmancolor than Technicolor – you remember, the film stock that made things look bluer than they were – and the projectionist had put in his brightest bulb.

A hill with cliffs and about a hundred inhabitants lived in sheds below it. We moved among them as if they were animals in a zoo. One was a lad who wore a black leather jacket and held a guitar. He looked at us proudly – keen that we should notice him – the local rebel, the James Dean of his tiny island forty hours from land.

In the afternoon an expedition set off from the ship in rubber boats to see whales and stuff and I said Bugger that and stayed on the ship and wandered round and dozed in the library. I was delighted when they all came back and said they had seen nothing. In the evening there was a long presentation by our expedition staff of the adventures we had had during the day, because we were not just a bunch of rich farts living high and patronizing the locals, we were intrepid – we went out in rubber boats!

We saw many wonderful sights. Borobudur was a monument deep in the jungle showing the Buddha's life in stone as you walked up and round it. It is up there with Stonehenge, St Paul's, *Paradise Lost*.

We saw the fruit bats flying out to sea on their leather wings to feed on far islands – a thousand thousand in the dusk throwing an early night over the ship. I thought of my very own fruit bat in London Zoo. Stone Master Marathoners paid for his keep and the zoo authorities put his name with ours on the plaque outside his aviary or battery. We called him Ernest. There were many fruit bats in the battery but you could tell Ernest the mascot of Stone Master Marathoners – he was the one with the biggest dick.

We stood by the captain on the bridge as he came into harbour. The pilot didn't speak English and that did not help and we were almost at the quay and the ship was not straight. The captain asked for a rope from the bow to that bollard on the shore and *Spring her in!* – that means rev up and put the tiller hard over and she will ease herself sideways until she is right. Exactly the manoeuvre that I had learned with the *Phyllis May* – we sailors have our tricks.

Among the curiosities of our trip were the tour buses that took the intrepid travellers out to the tourist sites. The machines usually had air conditioning, though never enough. They went very fast on spent suspension, with the guide bellowing into a mike and speakers rebellowing back to our seats. The language used was unknown to science. After a while I realized it was supposed to be English.

On the ship the voyagers were getting organized. As they were English they were doing this by dividing into social classes. In America they would have divided by money, in France by knowledge of food and wine, in Wales by artistic or sporting talent, but these were English so they divided by social class.

First were the aristocracy. We didn't have much

aristocracy on the ship but we had a countess. She had a retinue including an assistant and one or two of the highest among the passengers attended her, including the ex-head of the RAF and his wife. This party did not speak to anyone else, but once the intrepid birdman threw me a smile that was so warm and full of meaning that I blushed and turned away.

Then the money. There were half a dozen guys who were obviously extremely rich. They didn't go round saying Look I am extremely rich – you just knew it. The main indicator was their hundred-mile stares, as if they were on some drug that took them away to somewhere rather nice where You can't come sorry. They all knew each other and knew all the other extremely rich people in the world, and didn't speak to anyone else.

The county set – the people who live near you but you never see because they go to different schools and belong to different clubs and speak loudly in a way ordinary people find difficult to understand. They live in those houses behind trees, on the edge of town. There are lots of them in Staffordshire, so my daughter Lucy tells me, because she has a county friend and goes to a dance at a private preparatory school once a year and says the county set are loud and a bit stupid and most of the ladies seem to have had cosmetic surgery. On the ship they stuck together on corner tables, shouting. They were not interested in anyone else.

The business people. People who had made it with their own business to the extent they could afford to come on the voyage. I thought of this group as We. It was pointless trying to break into any other scene. I had learned at Oxford that the essence of the English class system is exclusion.

The rest. Unclassifieds like the ship's doctor, the lecturers, the shy chap on his own, the funny couple who kept trying to make friends but whom no one liked. There was a university professor whom we had to have surgically removed when we got to Bali. The expedition staff did not count as they were the serving class.

I could see on the ship the cliques, the rejections, the pacts, the closing up. I suffered from these things and I could see other people getting hurt. On the last night we had our own little group and organized our table in advance and were sitting down when the shy chap on his own came down the room. He was terrified but had plucked up courage – Can I join your group for dinner?

It was the last night but he was still friendless, bereft. But there was no room at our table.

Was his hurt and embarrassment our fault? Were we a clique just like the rest? Could we not have found another chair or something? Were we guilty of not looking out, not responding, of selfishness and carelessness for others?

But enough – despite the class divides, the heat, the language unknown to science, the oriental gentleman under the bed, we had a grand holiday.

How many of us have had the chance to travel with a flock of rich English, and as the sun sets over the Java Sea, listen to their strange sad cries?

★  ★  ★

We don't want to let you have her back, said the nurse. Everybody loves her.

She put Jess on the floor and Monica got down and Jess licked her and then she came to me and threw her front legs round my neck. Her bandage was blue today.

Today we were all going back home to the boat basin. The vet loaded us with medicines and instructions and Monica paid the bill and we were off, Jess trotting cheerfully to the taxi.

It cost almost as much as when I was ill in America, I said.

No it didn't said Monica, and in any case you weren't in hospital for three weeks.

I never thought they could save that leg, I said. I knew there were lots of three-legged dogs and they do very well and we would love her just as much and she would still be Jess but Goodness I wanted that leg to be saved.

Jess was meant to be a friend for Jim and we had been so disappointed when he hated her. He didn't attack her but would leave the room when she came in. If he was on the bed with Monica and Jess arrived he would jump down and stalk out. The worst bit was the way he would lie in the corner and look at me.

Then he seemed to be accepting her, especially in the spring, when he would sometimes lick her behind the ears, and sometimes he almost seemed to be running with her and chasing and playing, as I had imagined him to do.

When we brought Jess back Jim was just inside the

boat door, staring through the glass, and when Jess came down inside he screamed and huffed and whined and screamed and gasped and flung himself on her and burrowed his head under her chin and pushed and mounted her and staggered and screamed and there was no controlling him in his passion. So there was I holding Jess on the lead, and Monica wrestling with Jim, who is strong and determined and possessed of a demonic love and the furniture was going over and For God's sake he'll break her leg again!

So we had one dog who was injured and one that appeared to have gone mad.

Three days later Jim had calmed down.

He went sort of quiet when she left for the vet's, said Monica. And twice he tried to pull me down the towpath back to where the accident happened, but I thought he didn't miss her and might even have been glad because he is the only child again. But although we have had him ten years we don't really understand him. I mean he must have such deep feelings.

Jess was unattended on the other side of the saloon and Jim hurled himself across the boat to love her some more, screaming and knocking her down.

★   ★   ★

Shortly after we retired I was sitting in the sun outside the boat at Hoo Mill when my son Clifford rang. Dad sorry to ring you on the boat but have you heard of Ernest Saunders?

You mean Deadly Ernest, of the Guinness scandal?

Yes – we are going down to see Charles Dunstone at the Carphone Warehouse and they rang to say his special consultant Mr Saunders would be there. Can you come with me? I feel a bit nervous about him. He's a famous criminal and I've never met any famous criminals and he might not be very nice.

I thought he had Alzheimer's so they let him out of jail.

No, he recovered. He is the only person ever to recover from Alzheimer's.

I always enjoyed working with my son Clifford. Apart from the fact that he is a good businessman he makes me laugh.

What were the offices like of the firm you saw today, Cliff?

The hanging gardens of John Lewis, said Cliff.

Then there was that meeting in the City, high over the Thames, with a dozen heavy hitters round the table. Far below one or two boats worked up and down the river. Soon we will be doing that, I thought. Those boats look so small and the water like rippled metal.

One of the heavy hitters was looking at us in a funny way. Would you gentlemen by any chance be related?

Never seen him before in my life, said Clifford.

At Carphone Warehouse the chief executive Charles Dunstone and I were working on his customer satisfaction scheme. Research Associates' consumer work relies on organization of comments and no one else does it the same way. As I finished explaining each point Charles Dunstone was there first, waiting for me. It was almost as if he could read my mind.

You can say what you like about the reasons for success in business – hard work, courage, determination, luck – they all help but it certainly does no harm if you are bloody brilliant.

The door creaked open and Deadly Ernest came in. He looked just like he did in the pictures outside the courthouse in London.

He was charming.

When we got back to The Radfords Lucy's husband Richard told us he was sitting in his office looking on to the garden when a fox walked across the lawn in broad daylight.

Was it a fox, Richard, or a vixen?

I don't know.

What do you mean, you don't know? Did it have any balls, man, did it have any balls?

Well it walked across the lawn in broad daylight.

We have bought a boat, I said, and now it is time to get me a dog. Every retired man should have a dog. Every old man should have a dog. If he drops dead out walking the dog will stay by his corpse whining. If he goes blind the dog will take him for a walk. If he becomes destitute the dog will sit by him on the pavement next to his tin can. I have decided on my dog. I will have a pug. They have little flat faces and are cuddly and won't need walking all the time.

But you are going to France on your boat, said our friend who knows about dogs. A pug is not a good breather and he will choke in the heat.

I went back to the book and read all the breeds in

alphabetical order – when I got to W it said A Whippet is an easy dog, the ideal family pet. And there was a picture of a whippet with that great chest and lungs – looks like a good breather, I thought.

In Grimsby there was barking and scratching and as the door opened six whippets came at us shoulder-high, each with a teddy bear in its mouth. We struggled in and sat down. There were kennels in the garden and whippets everywhere. There were beautiful mature whippets, puppies, nursing whippets, and in the corner a very old grandma whippet – comfortable, waiting to die. The whippets were all a soft fawn colour.

These over here are the ones that are for sale, said the lady. Eight weeks old.

The puppies were fighting and growling and rolling around. You can have a dog or a bitch, said the lady. The bitches are more popular, and more expensive. A bitch is more affectionate – she gives more and asks more. But some say a dog gives you more love, because he has deeper feelings.

One little dog had an ear that stuck up and the other was broken and lay over his forehead and somehow made you think of a flat cap. He was trying to shag his auntie – that seemed to me to be a mark of vigour.

Jim's first act in our ownership was to escape from the car before we set off and try to run back to his front door. Then he settled in Monica's arms, and threw up only once.

At home he loved to race around the halls and rooms and lawns of The Radfords, and would sleep on my chest in the afternoons.

Daddy's Little Moon-mouse. I had not had a dog of my own before.

So Jim trained with me as I prepared for the Late Show – a fourteen-mile hill race in Lanzarote when I was sixty-five. Over the mountains and down to the sea.

The usual coarse remarks in the locker room – Lost a bit of weight at last, Terry – must be nice for you to see your dick again!

The announcements of race results in the clubroom – there are a lot of results. Jim starts to howl. I think he is disappointed with some of the times, I explain.

Out with the pack. Jim running happily on a slack lead.

Until the pack splits – Look, those guys have gone the other way! We had a lovely big pack, all safe and strong. Now we are only a few. We'll be attacked and pulled down and eaten. This is bloody stupid!

It's OK, Jim, don't fret, steady old chap. We'll see them again soon enough. Come on we are going up this hill by Moddershall – from the top I can see the Wrekin! Then we'll go back to the club and you can wrestle with Roger's Jack Russell he keeps in his inside pocket.

I had a really good run in Lanzarote – I think I was fourth in my age group. There weren't many in my age group but there were more than four. Between you and me I felt a bit rough afterwards – worse than I remembered when I was younger. It needed a couple of pints of San Miguel to reboot the system.

I heard the other day a chap over seventy has run a marathon in under three hours.

★

Derek Palmer was always a bit of a rival to me in the marathon club. Of course all the chaps were rivals all the time, and any change in the hierarchy of speed would cause much grief, hilarity, and comment.

Derek is thinner than Jim, and older than me, but faster. He's a lovely bloke but every time I meet him I feel inferior.

One day Derek was out training and he was taken short and he slipped behind a bush for a while and came out and ran hard to catch up.

He tripped and fell and hit his head and lay by the side of the lane unconscious.

The pack came back for him and sent for a car and took him to hospital.

Please relax, ladies and gentlemen, said the nurse. I know how worried you have all been but I am pleased to tell you Mr Palmer is not going to die. In fact he is going to be all right. He's got concussion, but he'll be out in a day or two. He is very fit, and his heart rate and blood pressure are that of a man thirty years younger. The consultant was astonished. There was just one question he raised – why has Mr Palmer got grass growing out of his arse?

Research Associates, now managed by Lucy and her husband Richard, moved out of The Radfords, leaving its thirty rooms to two pensioners and a whippet.

There we are, I said, our career is over, our house and offices are to be sold. The race is run, the bets paid out, the scores added up. It's all over bar the twilight years in

NARROW DOG TO WIGAN PIER

the back bars of Stone. We have brought up a family; been valiant for business efficiency and poetry and sport. I know I have not achieved the thing I wanted most – to be a writer. You could say my life has been a failure, a desert of shame. But not many people have done everything they wanted to do.

The day we put The Radfords on the market was the day of the Twin Towers atrocity, and selling it was not easy. In the end we fled south on the boat and left the great house in Lucy's hands. She sold it for thirty times what we had paid for it and started smoking again.

*Last night I dreamt I went to Manderley again.*

I dreamt about Manderley sorry Westfields sorry The Radfords every night for six months and then every other night for another six months and now I don't dream about it much at all.

Our new house is down the road nearer the centre of Stone. It is a narrowhouse, just twice as wide as the *PM2*. We bought it from Georgia our daughter, who had converted it from an old shoe workshop. It has three storeys and a cellar and you live upstairs. It has an alley on the side and looks out over a pub car park and a square. The garden is like one of those little walled ones at the Chelsea Flower Show.

Within a hundred yards there is a convenience store, a Chinese takeaway, a pub, a church, a flower park, a chip shop, an Indian restaurant and a tattoo parlour. Everything you need, really.

My studio is in the roof and I have a big window and

a high ash for my window tree and a spire across the square and lots of shelves and two copiers and a big desk. Jim and Jess lie under my feet.

It's great.

Last night I dreamt I went to Manderley again.


The day we set out to sail round the UK the *Phyllis May* sank at its moorings because of a loose stern gland and the canals were closed because of Foot and Mouth.

We waited at home and waited and waited and watched the cattle burning on the telly until the canals were freed and we sailed south.

Down the Grand Union, past the Houses of Parliament, across the West Country to Bristol and up the Severn Estuary. We loved travelling with Jim, though he hated the boat, and everybody loved our skinny little puppy with the heartbreak eyes. I began to write little joke passages about him, and sent them to friends so they would know where we were on the cut and that we were still alive.

Andrew Davies, the television writer, is an old school-friend. This stuff is good, he said. You are not wasting a word. Keep sending me this stuff. You should write a little book about whippets and flowers.

No, I said, if I am to write I want to be a real WRITOR like you, and write a real book.

First I chose a title – *Narrow Dog to Carcassonne*.

Then I bought a lot of travel books.

Then I bought twenty books on how to write, and read them and took notes. I preferred the American books – hard-arse, practical.

I wrote the first two chapters and rewrote and rewrote. I sent them to Andrew who sent them back with lots of comments, most of them critical. He was afraid I would be offended, but I wasn't. I had lost my way and now I was back on track. I rewrote again.

Then I sent the chapters to the Literary Consultancy, a firm in London, together with some money and heard back from Alan Wilkinson. He said I had a Voice, and that was a Good Thing, and the stuff was promising, but do this, do that – this is your opening sentence, you can develop Monica's character.

I did exactly what he said.

Then I emailed the chapters to Annette Green Authors' Agency. We were moored opposite Windsor Castle.

David Smith rang in a few hours. This one will sell six figures.

It hammered with rain and then the sun came out and the swifts threw themselves around like anything.

CHAPTER TWELVE

# THE PENNINES

## *The Ghost Train*

*My dog died of grief in Gdansk*

*The incredible leaping producer – The citadel of Carcassonne is beautiful and startling – I did not say a word, just dribbled lightly – Thirty tons of shit and an actor – They were starting to get worried about the esses – Let's hear it for the guys in special effects – I like to ambush and frustrate the reader – Rivers run down your neck – Water is necessary to the whole activity – How the nation dealt with Jive Bunny – My pockets full of water – Personally I prefer sexual reproduction – Destruction to your boat*

In Ramsgate the sun is shining, the lines tapping on the masts of the yachts. No narrowboats apart from us. Narrowboats can't get to Ramsgate unless they are prepared to spend seventeen hours sailing from London round the North Foreland. If you try that you will die, many an old salt and bearded narrowboater told us.

We had tried and we had not died and now we were setting out on the afternoon tide for Calais.

We had done what we could to reduce the risks. Monica had learned to swim and we had attended a ship-to-shore radio course. We were jogging three miles a day to keep fit. The bow of the *Phyllis May* had been enclosed and the front windows sealed. Grab rails were installed all along the roof. Jackstays – straps – ran down the side of the boat and a safety harness to clip on to them. Life jackets of course and one for Jim and emergency flares and an anchor. We had a pilot on board and an escort vessel.

It didn't stop us being scared.

Monica was on the tiller when we sailed out into the choppy blue tide, which swept us past the Goodwin Sands towards Dover. We tried to turn left to cross the twenty-mile stream and the tiller snatched and heaved. Terry, I can't hold her!

But once we had made the turn into deep water it was easier.

Our pilot on the *Phyllis May* had decided we were going to make it and was asleep below with Jim on his lap. Keith Wootton, the producer of the ITV canal series *Waterworld*, was on the pilot vessel with his cameraman.

In the middle of the Channel the vessel came near and Keith leapt on to our roof. The jump was extra-ordinary, but to carry a great camera on his shoulder at the same time! The Incredible Leaping Producer got some excellent footage, particularly of us crossing the six-foot wake of a ferry as we approached Calais, and he won a prize for it.

It's all in *Narrow Dog to Carcassonne*, of course, except for the new bits and here is another new bit. Before leaving Stone I had rung a leading canal magazine and said I was going to France and writing a book. Are you sailing across the Channel? asked the editor.

Yes, I said.

I think that is stupid, he said, and launched into his reasons as I hung up on him.

In Calais I rang another canal magazine and offered an article about the crossing to France. My readers are not interested in that sort of thing, said the editor. It is not the sort of thing they do themselves.

So no climber is interested in an account of climbing Everest because they are not likely to do it themselves? I asked.

He printed a picture the size of a postage stamp showing our boat in the Channel and a long letter from a chap who gave firm and detailed explanations about crossing the Channel, advising against it. He had not done it himself.

These were our first contacts with the dark side of adventure and fame. We learned that if you accomplish something most people will appreciate you, but some feel threatened or jealous. It is all about the territory people feel they occupy. The negative editors moved on, the magazines became our friends, and there is much more interest these days in river and estuary cruising and France.

We seem to polarize opinion – some people stop us in the street to shake our hands and call us brave and others write blogs calling us idiots. Three-quarters of Amazon comments on *Narrow Dog to Carcassonne* give the book five stars and the rest one star. The positive guys say the kindest things, but the negative chaps get really worked up – *festering, he's on drugs*. It is hard to believe they are reading the same book.

★

Was it brave to sail a narrowboat over the Channel? Sometimes I look back and it seems easy, and other times I begin to sweat. But remember a large number of people have crossed the Channel in no boat at all, though as far as I know no one has done it since in a narrowboat. Perhaps they saw the footage of us crossing the wake of the ferry.

A long break in Calais to come to terms with the fact we had done the crossing, then away through Belgium, into Paris, down the Burgundy Canal, down the Rhône to the Camargue and the Mediterranean, into the Canal du Midi and so to Carcassonne. Coming from Wales, we had already seen a few castles, but the citadel of Carcassonne is beautiful and startling.

In Carcassonne we gave someone a lot of money and he came with a big lorry and on a separate lorry a mobile crane. The crane was yellow and like *Thunderbirds*, and the driver was tall and handsome and wore a white uniform. When he arrived he spent an hour polishing the crane. Then he put lifting wires round the *Phyllis May* and set her seventeen tons swinging in mid-air and she fell out and dropped into the basin. Then he hoisted her up again and gave me a rope and suggested I control her and knocked the concrete ball off the marina gatepost.

*Narrow Dog to Carcassonne* went into the publisher and came back out as proofs.

Hand me my first copy of one of my books and I will smile, but send me proofs and my heart sings. I love working with the copy editor, the little final choices, the last flick of the polishing brush.

I love the arcane signs of the proofing alphabet. I love pushing the omelette of language by choosing unfamiliar words like *dove* instead of dived, *spitten* instead of spitting. I love using words like *omelette* when I shouldn't. I love the sense of power when I override a publisher's suggestion – *stet* – let it stand. Amid all the frustrations and humiliations of a writer's life is the moment when you are reminded that without you there is no money for the printer, for the bookseller, the publisher, no pleasure for the reader. This is your baby and you choose the ribbons for its hair.

I set about getting as much publicity as I could for my book. My publisher's marketing people advised me not to trouble myself with such activity as I was an arteest. But I see the writing and the marketing of a book as part of the same process.

On our return from France the local paper welcomed us home and the serious papers picked up the story and soon we were, as they say, everywhere. Nine seven-minute spots on *Waterworld*, produced by the Incredible Leaping Producer, ensured that in the Midlands we would be stopped in the street ten years later. Then the publisher put its weight to the lock beam and we found ourselves on breakfast telly and chat shows without number.

Whippets are people, said Kate Silverton on *Breakfast*, and Dermot Murnaghan smiled as if we had already made his day. A dab with a powder puff and we were pushed out in front of a sleepy nation. I was more frightened than I had been while crossing the Channel, but we managed to answer a few questions and have a laugh.

Whyever did you do it? asked Libby Purves on *Midweek*.

So I could boast about it in public houses, I explained.

How far did you actually go out into the Mediterranean?

Oh, I don't know – twenty, thirty yards.

Interviewers always ask why we did it. When Sandi Toksvig asked I quoted from *Narrow Dog to Indian River* –

*Our feelings surprised us both – this longing to sail out into the dawn, this ache to try our courage, to extend our range, to know what we did not know, to be who we were meant to be.*

We met Joanna Lumley – more of a visitation than a meeting. I don't think we were introduced and I did not say a word, just dribbled lightly. She came across the room, immensely tall. She did not walk – she sort of slid. She came and stood right before me, blotting out the scene. Just those eyes, the golden hair. She took my little face in her hands and rubbed my beard. You lovely lovely man, she said.

Either she had read *Carcassonne* or she had been overwhelmed by my aquiline good looks or the cut of the only suit I could still get into. Anyway now when the shadows gather and all forsake me and the wind is like a knife and the beer is sour and they are sending back my manuscripts and Jim has thrown up on the hearthrug and Monica is saying she has had a bloody nuff I can always say to myself – Joanna stroked my beard.

★

One evening about half past ten we found ourselves in a dim studio and at the mike on the other end of a long table was Henry Kelly, a thin Irishman. Oh goodness, we cried, we remember you in that TV show.

Where are you from?

We told him.

Ah, Stafford! Do you know Lord Stafford? Lord Stafford, dear Staffie, what fun we have had. He is a member of the aristocracy, you know, a senior member of the aristocracy, and as it happens a dear friend of mine. So many evenings in laughter and chat, so many dew-drenched rides round Swynnerton. Soon we will meet again and I shall feel his firm handshake, see that brow wrinkle with laughter . . .

We expected Lord Stafford to creep into the studio at any moment and come up behind Henry Kelly and plant a kiss on the top of his head.

Then Henry Kelly decided to tell us a joke. We had heard it before, but perhaps you have not –

*An actor trying to get to London from the Midlands could not afford the rail fare so he went down to the canal to try his luck. Soon he came across a seventy-foot barge loaded with horse manure.*

*My dear man, can I trouble you for a ride on your barge? I am going to London and I am temporarily short of funds and it would oblige me considerably. I will make a modest payment and do my best to assist you in small ways as we travel.*

*The bargee was a good soul. Make yourself comfortable on top of the load, old darling. You can help at the locks.*

*Off they went, the horses plodding steadily – they knew*

*what they were doing and the actor dozed as they slipped down the long pounds.*

*They came to a loading office. The official shouted What are you carrying?*

*Thirty tons of shit and an actor! cried the bargee.*

*On towards the south down the long pounds to another loading office.*

*What are you carrying?*

*Thirty tons of shit and an actor!*

*The actor stepped off on to the towpath and walked back to the stern where the bargee stood at the tiller. I wonder if I could have a word?*

*A word?*

*Yes, I'd like to have a word about the billing.*

A few days after the paperback launch of *Carcassonne* we set out for the USA to begin our *Narrow Dog to Indian River* voyage.

We called at three bookshops in Heathrow but *Narrow Dog to Carcassonne* had sold out. It appeared in the *Sunday Times* top ten and sold the best part of two hundred thousand copies and is still selling. It was short-listed for the Saga Award for Wit and in the USA won the Audie for the best non-fiction audiobook of the year. The judges said they could not face another historical biography and canals and a whippet suited them just fine.

The book was translated into German and into Polish. I did not get on with the Poles, who wrote to me asking if they could put the punctuation back in and proposed a cover which would have suited a book called

*My Dog Died of Grief in Gdansk.*

*Narrow Dog to Indian River* was also a *Sunday Times* bestseller and a travel bestseller in the US though it did not reach the heights of *Carcassonne.* When you think of it – not many people go to the south-east coast of the USA.

But our nine months in Virginia, the Carolinas and Florida and our thousand-mile voyage gave us the most treasured memories of our lives. The shining sounds, crossing Moon River, the ocean on our left and on our right the Marshes of Glynn, the dolphins, the pelicans, the alligators even, and most of all the Yanks, with their overflowing hospitality.

All our stories are in the book, except how the boat got back. It was craned out from Owl Creek near Fort Myers and driven back across the continent to Portsmouth, Virginia, then into a container ship and to Liverpool and Stone. Not a cup was broken.

We developed a website, and fan letters arrived from all over the world – thousands of them, full of stories and pictures. Monica took over and we answered them all. We like fan letters and we like fans – they are like gongoozlers but better. Gongoozlers do nothing but stare and perhaps ask a daft question. Fans have at least written a letter. Most are enthusiastic about how I write but a few ask Why don't I use inverted commas to indicate speech? Nearly everyone else does after all.

It is time to tell the truth. My publisher, Transworld, a model of efficiency in so many ways, but not all, emailed me and explained that Bill Bryson had used up all the inverted commas and perhaps I could think of a way to do without them, and while I was at it could I go easy on the aitches?

Well, what can you do? I wanted my book out there, so I worked out a sort of stream-of-consciousness way of writing which left out the inverted commas. I told everyone it was a modern way to write and used a lot in the States by advanced arteests.

When Transworld came back and said they were now starting to get worried about the shortage of esses I told them Bugger off – have a word with Andy McNab.

Early on the requests for talks started to arrive. Monica took these on too and I came along to the big ones. A full hall at a public school – the kids thrilled with the dogs. A theatre at Ilkley, a church at Redditch, two hundred people in Stafford.

At Saul Junction on the Gloucester and Sharpness Canal Monica gave a talk about our US adventure, in the belly of an old barge.

I was reading extracts –

*Cascades of water were coming into the front deck, and against the front window like a rainstorm from hell. Slap, spray, the air full of waterfalls. Outside the windows a maelstrom of blue waves and sunlight and foam. Would the front deck drain, or fill and sink us?*

There was a crashing of water as a wave fell down from the ceiling and drenched us both. It was raining and the canvas covering the old boat had split.

Let's hear it for the guys in special effects, I said.

I quite often look on the web for the latest postings about *Narrow Dog to Carcassonne* and *Narrow Dog to Indian River* and indeed about me and Monica and the *Phyllis May* and Jim and Jess. It is extraordinary how much stuff there is, and always something new. If I forget what I am doing I can always look myself up.

One US site *Wellreadhostess* posted a long review of *Carcassonne*, and the lady who wrote it seemed to know more about my writing style than I did. She had a lot of trouble deciding whether she loved or hated the book, but came down on the right side in the end.

*Dear Wellreadhostess*

*On 24th July you posted a piece about* Narrow Dog to Carcassonne, *written by Terry Darlington. I was that Terry Darlington, and indeed I still am. I enjoyed your comments, and if they erred it was on the side of generosity.*

*You enquire about Shakin' Stevens. In the UK he is slightly less well known than Father Christmas. He looks and sings like a caponized Elvis.*

*You point out that I use 'epic and deadly personification' – for example – 'Villeneuve had swept its stone quay and turned its pansies to the sun and checked that its electricity was pure sine wave.' I was quite unaware of this – in my flawed mind things often appear as other things or people and I seem to tip over into fantasy without realizing it.*

*I shall not attempt to defend my style of writing, except to say that when I realized some people did not like it I cried all the way to the bestseller lists. But in explanation – I find*

*conversation marks make an ugly page and follow some of the
US modern writers (Sontag, Doctorow) in leaving them out. I
love riddles and running gags and see no reason why every
reader should enjoy every sentence as long as he is involved
with the flow. I like to ambush and frustrate and surprise the
reader and make him work. I suppose in that way I am
the last of the modernists.*

★  ★  ★

We are going under the Pennines, said Monica. See
there they are on the map, the backbone of England, all
the way down to the last flicker in Stone. To get up the
Pennines we have to do forty-two locks in eight miles
and then the biggest canal tunnel in the UK. It's THE
STANDEDGE TUNNEL.

She paused, so I could hear the blast of music that
followed her words, just like the Dr Morelle thriller on
the radio last night, when Ernest put the trumpets in
behind his most dramatic moments.

But I have been through the Harecastle Tunnel, I said,
where the walls come at you crashing, and rivers run
down your neck. You can't scare me.

The Standedge Tunnel is much worse, said Monica.
You have to book in advance and a British Waterways
guy is on the back with you and it is too low and narrow
for the boat and it keeps changing its size and direction
and you have to wear a hard hat because it bashes you
around and it takes two hours to go through.

I've been three times through the Harecastle, I said.
Nothing is worse than the Harecastle – how can it be?

★

The Huddersfield Narrow Canal is the same gauge as the Midlands canals, but the locks are deeper and the lock paddles are not to be lifted by mortal arms.

Under a bridge and at once we were stretched out on the mud like a beached whale. You can deal with many sorts of trouble from a narrowboat but you really do need water. In fact I would venture that water is necessary to the whole activity of boating. The water in the pound came up an inch and then went down again.

A British Waterways chap appeared. These excellent fellows in their green overalls sleep behind the bushes on the locksides and when they sense trouble they wake up and stretch and grab a spanner and a windlass and come out and help you. I'll let some water in from up ahead, said the chap.

He went up and round the corner to the next lock and worked the paddles and a very small amount of water ran down to us. I started the engine and the *PM2* dragged herself along the mud like a wounded snake. Now and then her prop cracked on rocks. This was a new sort of boating – navigating a small pond in the middle of the cut, with mudbanks around you, trying to guess where the deepest inches lay under the muddy water. I was quite good at it, but I didn't enjoy it, and it was deadly slow.

There were other hills to climb. We have two windlasses with which we wind the lock paddles up and down – one is shiny and neat and light for normal use. The other is heavy with a longer handle. At one lock Monica could not wind up the paddles even with the heavy windlass so I got out of the boat to help. I put all my weight on the shaft and it started to bend. I was afraid I would break the windlass, which in turn would break my wrist and fly up and spoil my looks. I changed my angle and at last the paddle began to shift.

I want to do some locks, I said. I need the exercise.

I walked up ahead swinging the windlass, the dogs trotting in front on their leads. We cannot let Jess run free for another ten days in case she breaks her leg again. She is trotting freely on her bandaged leg – perhaps just throwing that broken paw a fraction. What a miracle that paw is, so soft and flexible but strong enough to take the shock of a turn at forty miles an hour. What skill to mend it when it was broken off –

> And what shoulder and what art
> Could twist the sinews of thy heart?

Oh dear I'm at the wrong end of the lock. Now which way does this windlass turn? These steps make me feel dizzy.

Monica is shouting – You have left a paddle up.

I must be tired and it's the shingles medication – I get sleepy and confused. If I carry on like this I'll finish up in the bottom of a lock.

If you carry on like this, shouted Monica, you'll finish up in the bottom of a lock.

It rained like the end of the world.

The next day we had another ten locks to do and that is a lot of locks when the paddles are stiff and even if you get through you might not have any water on the other side. We were closing on a town called Slaithwaite. It is one of those places pronounced different to how it is spelt. It is spelt Slaithwaite but pronounced St Petersburg or something.

Pretending a problem isn't there, however monstrous, even when it is staring you in the face, is one of the most common and effective strategies in life. That is how the nation dealt with Jive Bunny, and John Prescott. But the strategy never works on a boat. Ignore a rattle and a piece of your boat will tear itself off and fall into the cut. Ignore a whippet whining at night and heaven knows what will face you in the morning. Get something on the prop and it will stall you in a cross-current as the trip boat is coming for you.

I looked behind me – *look behind you!* There was no clean tunnel of prop-wash but a confused mess of foam. The tiller was rattling and I had slowed and my steering was off. We pulled in and I lifted the trap in the back counter and lowered myself until I was sitting in the engine. I reached down through the weed-hatch and felt round the propeller. One always fears something sharp, or something dead.

Once we pulled up through the weed-hatch a hundred yards of wire. Another time it was a duvet, and the boat filled with feathers. Then there was that rather nice sweater that I wore for a while. This time it was a sack, not made of sacking but a white fibre like steel. It had been thoroughly mashed but I got it up before lunch.

When we reached the mouth of the Standedge

Tunnel there was one of those information centres with no one in it and no information. The rain was pitiless. A British Waterways man appeared – You need to take the cratch cover off or it will get torn, and the navigation lights.

The navigation lights? But they are only pimples! My pretty little brass navigation lights? But they will help light our way through the mysterious caverns of your great tunnel!

I had never screwed or unscrewed anything into the steel of the boat before, but the lights came off easily. The British Waterways man fitted me with a white hard hat and stepped on the back counter with me. He was small and fair and muscular and white-hatted and yellow-jacketed and life-jacketed and had been doing this for ten years.

At least it was not raining in the tunnel, though from time to time streams came down from above. I don't see too well in the dark, and found it hard to separate the buttress ahead from the one behind it and chose the wrong one and ran bang into the rock. Over and over again I ran into the rock. You didn't have inches to spare, you had fractions of inches, and sometimes you had nothing and the front corners of the boat were grinding into the stone. I tried letting the boat find the water – a trick that only a sophisticated boatman like me can pull off. You let the tiller go slack and a well-behaved boat like the *PM2* will seek the deeper part of the channel.

No good doing that, said the British Waterways man

– there is eight foot of water here so there is no pressure to keep her in the middle. She will just bang into the side.

She just banged into the side.

Then a mighty hand slapped me across the top of the head and hit me again and again as my hard hat thumped into the geology. I crouched until only my eyes were above the roof and the boat scratched through. A trout stream went down my neck.

An earthquake – a roar and a roar and the boat trembled in its channel and a smell I had not smelt since Pembroke Dock, when I stood with my mother on the station platform and the locomotive hissed and clanked and inside the upholstery smelt of smoke.

Heavens – a ghost train!

Steam and smoke poured into the tunnel and the roar reached a climax and slowly died and the canal stopped trembling.

A light ahead down on the left – how can there be a light down here?

I turned and looked down a passage which linked the tunnel to railway tunnels alongside. There was a bloke and he waved his lamp and my British Waterways man shouted to him. He turned to me – It's a safety check. He is following us in the railway tunnel.

Ahead a blank wall. Just a blank wall.

I considered my position – I could drive into it, or do an emergency reverse, or jump overboard. I could not reverse for shame as I had my pilot with me on the back so I kept going. It was the strangest feeling – all the evidence of my senses told me I was going to break a lot of crockery and probably bend the hull of my boat, but the rock wall slid aside like Open Sesame and we motored on, with a couple of minor collisions and the pockets of my coat full of water.

How was Monica below with the whippets? They hate noise and bumps scare them. We had held a board meeting in the morning and decided that one tranquillizer was too little and two too many so one and a half, mixed with Spam Lite. (Spam Lite is very nice, even without tranquillizers.)

Monica came up – My turn.

I wanted to explain that this was not women's work but my knees were so tired with crouching and my neck was sore with the cuffs across the head and I would kill for a sit-down so I swapped with her.

She started chatting with the Waterways man right away and she seemed to have brought the boat to a halt as the banging had stopped. But look carefully through the window – we are moving! It's just that she isn't hitting anything.

I sat down and stretched out. The best thing about boating is stopping boating.

The dogs were not whining but Jess was panting so two pills next time poor dears. She put her upper body on my lap in her special way and looked into my eyes – Don't let them hurt me, master, with the shaking and the bangs.

Jim lay tight against my chair with his head between his paws.

I dozed as we slid along – an occasional bump, and chatter and laughter coming from the back counter. As we came out of the tunnel a steam train barrelled by – it looked not in the least ghostly as it hissed and chuffed and thundered.

We moored up and the British Waterways man and Monica said Goodbye. You're a grand steerer, he said.

He wasn't friendly to me like that – he didn't seem to think I was a grand steerer at all, telling me what to do all the time. I looked at the new scratches on the boat. Good job we took those navigation lights off – they would have been swatted off the side of the boat like flies.

We have crossed the Pennines, said Monica. From underneath.

Tunnels allow water to be stored above them to charge the canal. They are always the highest point of a canal.

The Huddersfield Narrow Canal climbs to the Standedge Tunnel and then drops towards Manchester and the West Midlands. Going down, the locks were empty and we had to fill them before sailing in. So it was slow, but the canal pounds now had more water in them. Monica explained that we were bringing our water down with us and I think I understood her.

You reach an understanding with your partner when you are boating. A raised finger, a little wave, and you can convey all the information needed as the lock goes about its furious business. It is like your own language. For example look up at Mon now from the boat – you can tell what she is saying –

*There are three green beetles coming down through the woods. They are two and a half feet long. They have already eaten one of the dogs and if they get on to the roof of the boat we are done for.*

What the hell are you trying to say? I shouted. Monica shouted back –

*When the lock fills I want you to pass me my green coat and a blanket for the dogs to sit on.*

Like I said, your own language.

But it did not matter as we were in Paradise Garden. Greenery crowded round – the rich greens of high summer, leaves and ferns and flowers. Buddleia, rosebay willowherb, yellow loosestrife, meadowsweet, foxgloves, purple vetch – heaped over each other, searching for the light and space over the water.

And Himalayan balsam. In full purple flower with seed pods forming.

There are all sorts of seeds – seeds that fly, seeds that beg to be eaten, seeds that persuade animals to bury them, seeds that stick to you, seeds that float, seeds that give you a fruit if you will throw away the stone. There are seeds that tumble across the set in cowboy films.

The balsam seed pods are full of sap and get fuller and fuller and tighter and tighter until one day they are ready and then if they are touched the pods twist under the pressure of the sap like an explosion and the seeds fly out. It is a successful method of distribution – if you seek a monument, look around you.

Monica told me that in Tiffin Girls' School when she was teaching there one of the staff pinned to the notice-board an essay from a little girl in a lower form –

*There are many ways of reproduction in nature. However personally I prefer sexual reproduction.*

Stalybridge is defined by the canal, which goes straight up the high street, in its new concrete channel. We moored under a block of flats and in the evenings there were flashes all the time – people were taking pictures.

Each morning I went to Tesco for a paper and outside was a big chap who looked like a murderer – fat and fully tattooed, with slitty eyes. He would sit and hold the dogs until I came out. He said he was sorry we were going and Jim licked his tattoos.

As we left the couple in the flat nearest to us leaned out of the window and wished us well.

We stood on the back of the boat.

What do you make of the Huddersfield Narrow Canal? asked Monica. It was opened after we started boating fifteen years ago. People worked very hard on it and it is a jewel in the crown of the canal restoration movement.

The bloody thing in unnavigable, I said, like the restored Kennet and Avon with its swing bridges. It is a snare for poor boaters who have to struggle through locks that don't work and pounds with no water. And no one goes along the Huddersfield Narrow Canal – how many boats did we see? It was all for us – very flattering but consider the amount of the national wealth that is being wasted on this useless facility.

Will you remember the journey?

I will never forget the green valleys, the trees and flowers, the mills, the mills. Every quarter of a mile a mill – usually derelict, usually elephantine, but always beautiful. The soft grey stone with black shading, the rows of windows always in proportion. However big a mill might be, it looks in balance, comfortable. The chimneys confirm the shape, give the mills a vigour, a finish. To hell with the fancy architects in London – they should come up here if they want to learn about style.

It wasn't much fun getting stuck, was it?

You could find a bank with enough water to moor but before you had started to put your pins in the level would drop. And then when you found some water the bank would turn out to be solid stone. You would wake up with the boat listing and you were stuck for hours. It was awful.

What about the Standedge Tunnel?

Like the rest of it, unnavigable. Destruction to your boat, hell and banging and thumping and no sense in it.

So what is the final verdict on the Huddersfield Narrow?

Great – I shall never forget it.

# CHAPTER THIRTEEN

# STONE

## In a Somer Seson, Whan Softe Was the Sonne

*Now it is ending – ten years of adventure*

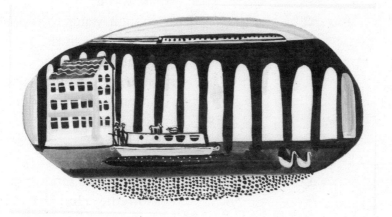

*Big small dogs – Doing dreadful things to his maggots – I could have lost Mon and Jim and the* Phyllis May *– The Pain in the Arse – The sky had leaked on to the distant fields – Those waves are still coming in – I bet they lay rusty eggs – The mermaid winked at me and her bosom heaved – You work your side of the street and I'll work mine – When Ulysses arrived at Ithaca he felt like a bloody good sit-down*

Are Jim and Jess small dogs or big dogs? asked Monica.

Small dogs.

But they are tall, and they are all muscle.

But look at them alongside a big dog, like a Newfoundland. Or a greyhound or even a retriever.

Well, they are certainly not small small dogs.

They are big small dogs.

Yes – big small dogs.

It was getting dark as we moored. A ghost train raved and thumped and shrieked over the viaduct above us, invisible, furious. A narrowboat came by and the geezer shouted Are you going up tonight?

We were not going up. The Marple Flight was sixteen

locks and if you don't do it in one go you will cause an obstruction and you will be disgraced and British Waterways will find out you are the chap who buggered up a stretch of waterway because you were too much of a weakling to go up the Marple Flight in one and he will issue it in an email and people will not say hello any more as you pass in your boat.

You have to say hello to everyone you pass on the cut or on the towpath, and to each dog and squirrel. The greeting should be set at just the right level. If one of you is raising a finger the other must raise a finger as well. *Morning, nice again now* must be met with four words of equal weight – *Hello, better than yesterday.*

It is not acceptable to ignore a greeting, unless of course you are a fisherman, who lives in a different world, and has drawn in his rod and is looking down and doing dreadful things to his maggots. I don't expect by right a reply from a fisherman but to be fair I usually get one, perhaps because our engine is quiet and does not disturb his fish. Our friend Pauline expects a reply from every fisherman and abuses them from the boat if they keep their peace.

Next morning out of bed at six thirty and away. It is cold and overcast. Past the geezer, who is moored at the bottom of the flight.

Monica has put the rain jackets on the dogs and I am carrying their foam beds as well as a lock key. The locks are so close together that there is no exercise for the whippets but if we leave them in the boat they suffer so much it breaks your heart. They call it separation anxiety in the colour supplements but it just means they want to be on the scene. I settle them down near the top of the lock and they snuggle down in their beds and look out over the top and everyone who passes says Aaaah.

Let's walk up to the edge of the lock and look in. My God it is deep and I get the vertigo. But at least it's empty – the *PM2* can sail in when I have opened the bottom gates. Heave ho my darlings and Monica will push open the other gate with the boat.

Now back to the top of the lock – there are steps and verges and steps some shallow some steep and I have the vertigo with the depth of the lock and my pills make me dizzy just be careful – it doesn't matter how slow you are we'll get there but don't finish up dead in the bottom of a twenty-foot lock like that poor chap a few years ago and he was a canal expert who knew all about the history. Didn't do him much good in the end knowing all about the Jam 'Ole Run.

Now fit the key on to the paddle gear and turn Oh damn it's one of those – put your full weight behind it and get a click of the ratchet, now another click, now three. Now pause and then give it some wellie – look at that water flooding up under the boat and just under my feet a hole puffing and gasping as the air comes out from somewhere and goes somewhere else.

Look down – Mon OK? I hope she doesn't start making signs to boss me about. This is my lock and I am setting the pace. I won't rush her don't worry. I shall never forget that fool girl on a trip boat who rushed all the paddles up one day on the Grand Union and there was so much water coming in that the *Phyllis May* went out of control and could have filled and sunk. Just think that girl was working on a hotel boat with a dozen guests. I am afraid I shouted and was coarse but if I hadn't stopped her I could have lost Mon and Jim and the *Phyllis May*.

Now the gate paddles – Heavens what a rush – keep the boat back Mon, well done. The water pushing up the walls.

Walk over and pet the dogs – you are comfortable now, darlings, because your master loves you and brought your beds. Your master is a very fine fellow and most attentive to his ungrateful hounds.

Push on the gate – no, too soon.

Now here we go. A nice smile from Mon as she comes out of the lock. Now close the gates and don't forget the dogs this time and on to the next lock, just fifty yards away round the corner.

When we looked into the next pound we could see that it was empty, a basin of mud. So I went ahead to open paddles and let some water through. You are not supposed to do that if you are not a British Waterways man and I am not and I didn't know what I was doing but working from first principles it seemed to me if I opened one or two paddles up ahead I could flush some water down and perhaps even float the boat again. I did this and Monica slithered across the pound and shuddered into the lock, her prop banging on the bottom with a noise like the death of a machine.

The geezer who had passed us last night appeared, swinging his lock key. He was slim, half my age, bronzed, with hairy legs and white teeth. He was one of those chaps who do a lot of boating and it's his thing and he thinks everyone else is a civilian who should have stayed on dry land and he measures his own worth by how fast he can get through the locks. This sort of chap is known in the boating community as a Pain in the Arse.

He ran up to the lock. Running is not safe around locks.

What time did you start this morning? he asked, annoyed that we had slipped on to the flight before him, and now he would have to stay behind us for the whole flight and he would have to work our locks with us otherwise we will be here all bloody day.

He started rushing around and yelled incomprehensible instructions to me full of technical words for paddles and pounds and keys and went back down to his boat.

His boat was stuck solid and all his shouting from the bank would not move her and we carried on up the flight and the shouting died and that was the last we saw of him. Perhaps he is still there.

On the Macclesfield Canal we were five hundred feet above sea level, with the Pennines on our left and the plains of Cheshire on our right. It was early evening.

> In a somer seson, whan softe was the sonne,
> I shoop me into shroudes as I a shepe were,
> In habite as an heremite unholy of werkes,
> Wente wide in this worlde wondres to here.

I wasn't dressed like a shepherd, unless shepherds wear T-shirts these days with slogans on them saying I'm the Biggest Bitch on the Beach, and it was not necessary to wear shawls on this lovely evening.

On the left green beyond green, and the fields seemed to vibrate and sing. And before the fields swaying grasses along the towpath, and flowers red and purple and yellow and trees like a statement that all this had been here for a while, was here when Piers Plowman wandered into the world wonders to here seven hundred years ago, and he felt just the way we do and don't let any bugger think they can take it away.

On the right the land of lost content! Away over the plains of Cheshire the eye reaches towards the horizon and meets a blue as if the sky had leaked on to the distant fields.

What is this Macclesfield Canal? This upstart water-way, this route home of which I expected nothing. It is more beautiful than the Camargue, more luscious than Georgia, more green than the Burgundy Canal, and (*Write it!*) more beautiful than my own Trent and Mersey at Aston. I have wandered far in the world on my little boats, and seen many wonders, but today let's hear it for the Macclesfield Canal.

We moored where we could see the blue horizon and settled down to a chaste dinner of Diet Coke and pollock. I hate Diet Coke and don't ask me why I drink it. Pollock is my favourite fish because I used to catch them in Milford Haven when I was a boy. They taste of nothing, but to me they taste of Milford Haven.

Outside the boat a terrible commotion. Honking and

screaming and splashing and quacking. I knew it was a fight because when I was in the Coronation School and a fight would start it was the same cruel and joyful shouting as the circle gathered together, with the fighters in the middle.

Five hundred Canada geese in a crowd in the middle of the cut. In the middle of the crowd were two large specimens. One got the other in a Canadian Stranglehold and held his head under the water, then the other countered with a Flying Wingbash and thumped him six feet across the cut and followed him and got him by the throat feathers. The crowd were shouting and waving their wings – Come on, kill the bugger, hey hey hey, honk honk honk!

The fighters rolled over and over and lay in a bed of foam for a moment and then set on each other again. Slowly one was winning. How any of the geese knew which one was winning I cannot tell, because Canada geese are so alike they must forget which one they are themselves.

The fight wound down into hissing and crouching but one was hissing and crouching better than the other and the loser slunk away.

The chap on the next boat explained – It was a struggle to choose the dominant male. Must have been some sort of change of government.

My God, I said, it was worse than a Stone Master Marathoners committee meeting.

Remember Jim in Calais? asked Monica.

You mean when he pissed against the mattress in the

market stall and the big brown chap got threatening?

No, on the beach.

My word he was marvellous, wasn't he? He can fly and he was flying then, in great circles in the sun. I measured his pawmarks and he hit the sand every ten feet.

And we walked right down to the water and watched the ferries. They were so big, and seemed to stand in the water rather than float, and I could not believe there was enough water for them.

There is a channel dredged I guess.

And you could see England, said Monica, but it did not look near – the Channel was huge and the waves and you could feel the currents and I thought of how we sailed it and I was amazed.

I couldn't believe it either. Fancy messing with the Channel, with all that power, all that depth. In our little *Phyllis May*. I would say we must have been mad but that's a corny thing to say. The only time the Channel did not scare me stiff was when we were on it.

Jim remembered the Channel-beach, said Monica, when we took him to Freshwater West in Pembrokeshire last year. He pulled us down the dunes with Jess and could not wait to reach the sand and they ran almost but not quite as if they were together. They ran and ran – I don't know why sand suits them so well – they weren't bred to it.

But think of when we were in training – grass is soft and slows you down, and the roads are hard but sand is true and forgiving.

The day we took Jim and Jess to Freshwater West

there had been a strong wind and the waves were coming from America like rows of terrace houses. The sun was bright and the wind was shouting and tearing off the crests and throwing them to the side, along the line of the waves, in crystal and white fire. The waves rushed towards us and one by one fell crashing and then they spread and turned to glass and died at our feet.

The beach had been empty but here is a man in a black rubber suit, fussing with some ropes on the sand. He had a red face and big shoulders like a farm labourer. Jim and Jess greeted him and he patted them absently.

He walked down to the surf and threw a kite into the air and leapt up after it, flying along the waves, twenty, thirty feet up. What strength to pull himself up, what stamina to control the flight for so long. We stood and clapped but he could not have heard us in the thundering or seen us as air and water fought around him.

Remember, every day whatever we are doing those waves are still coming in. Sometimes they are quiet, sometimes driven by a hurricane. They are breaking now as I write – see how that crest rolls over and the foam, the foam.


Our mooring on the Macclesfield Canal is among the finest ever seen. I know I keep saying things like that but I guess I just like canals. Anyway we are on a viaduct hundreds of feet above a river valley so you have one valley crossing another and Christ how green and soft is the sun.

I go for a walk back up the flight of locks with Jim and Jess. There are half a dozen boats coming down and five of them greet Jim and me by name and come and say hello to Jess. One of them is reading *Carcassonne* on a Kindle – I had never seen a Kindle and it seemed a strange little machine. Soon they will invent something to replace the dog. You will be able to have a different breed each day. You will switch it on and it will eat the zip off your best jacket.

On the boat Monica is mixing up the Spam Lite with the dogs' tranquillizers, ready for the Harecastle Tunnel. Hey, leave some for my lunch!

Two tablets each this time because when we went through the Standedge Tunnel they were not happy.

The canal water is turning orange – iron ore in the tunnel. The ducks don't seem to mind – I bet they lay rusty eggs, and God knows what colour the fish are round here. No waiting today – the British Waterways gentleman waves Monica into the Harecastle.

Monica is moving along and not hitting anything. It is an advantage to be small if you are going through a tunnel – you are less likely to be bashed on the head. I went down from the back counter and Jess was waiting for me. I turned on all the lights in the boat with Jess glued to me all the time. Now Monica can see the sides of the tunnel. Jim and Jess took up their emergency positions on and around me but they were not distressed this time. Steady, darlings, we'll be there soon.

Only forty minutes and the world reappears in grey and green and a bright white sky. We always have a glass of rum after a tunnel, for the nerves and to warm us up – tunnels are cold.

Oh yes, I will, thanks Mon, just to keep you company. What was it like after the Standedge?

Like driving up the M6.

Past pretty Westport Lake with its coots. Coots make a noise like a pebble being dropped into a bucket. In fact if you look closely under the bank you can sometimes see the little black chaps dropping pebbles into a bucket.

Now past Longport basin, where the *PM2* was built. The owner who designed her was not in but there was a mermaid. We roped up for some diesel.

The mermaid lay up the arm and shoulder of the big chap on the next boat. He bent his arm and she waved her tail invitingly. He had other tattoos but the mermaid was best. You have cost me a fortune, he said.

*Moi?*

Yes, I read your book and sold my house and bought this fifty-footer. Very expensive boat. Many times I have blamed you for being an influence when I couldn't really afford it but I'm glad now.

The mermaid winked at me and her bosom heaved.

Onward to the south. When we bought the *Phyllis May* fifteen years ago we sailed her right through the heart of the Shelton steelworks, through the blasting and clanging, but now the lone and level sands stretch far away.

Etruria, to moor in the Festival Park. We can go to the pictures. Last time we saw a picture about Australia with Nicole Kidman, who looked as if she needed a cup of tea and a lie-down. Hugh Jackman was in it too, looking so handsome I almost fancied him myself.

Tomorrow Dave is coming to help us down the locks into Aston.

Dave was captain of Stone Master Marathoners before Monica. He is a young chap, ten years younger than me, and a devil with a lock key. He slung his bike under the cratch and in no time we were through the steep locks of Stoke.

Poor derelict Stoke, so ill served by management and government. When I was teaching there, new council offices were built, looming over the five towns from high ground, ugly and arrogant. I called the building the castle of Mordor. Five years ago it was pulled down – it was never safe.

Lovely, bonkers people. One day Monica and I were having a drink in a pub in Stoke when a chap sitting near us commented on her watch – the Rolex I had bought her when we became business partners. He showed us his watch, which was rather smart and curious and then rolled up his sleeve. He had watches all up his arm.

Now we are alongside the great incinerator. The weak sun struck its corrugated walls and roof green and cream, as if newly washed. Blunt arches like a Norman castle, a fat chimney. Stoke's beautiful dustbin.

Barlaston and the Plume of Feathers. We had to have a pint after all that – I mean we always do – Come on Mon, be a sport – I know we never drink in the middle of the day but this is the Plume, the last stop before our destination.

Jack Bissex used to run this pub, Dave. He was a

jogger forty years ago – grand chap – older than us, probably dead now. If you are out there, Jack, do get in touch. But if you are dead it's probably best if you work your side of the street and I work mine.

Past the Star and on to Aston Lock. It all began at Aston Lock, where you can look out on the fields and spires. And now it is ending – ten years of adventure – France, America, England.

On a summer evening in Stone any time not spent drinking beer by a canal is time wasted. We sat in one of those little cabins on the side of Aston Marina with Dave and Rose. Rose won many marathons as a veteran runner, some in less than three hours.

The dogs were at our feet and there were bottles on the table and bags of scratchings.

Jim is changing colour, said Rose. He's going all white from the end of his nose – it's almost reached his ears.

Yes, I said, whippets go white slowly from the nose and when the white reaches their tail they die.

How is Jess's leg? asked Rose.

Sometimes it seems stronger, then she stops using it again. It's been months. We don't know, we don't know.

She seems cheerful about it, said Rose.

She breaks my heart, I said.

What are you two doing next, Mon? asked Dave.

In February we are going to Hong Kong and then up across Australia from Adelaide to Darwin on a train. It's to celebrate our golden wedding. It'll be lovely – I can let someone else do the organizing and the driving. A lady who is visiting Stone is going to live in our house and look after Jim and Jess.

And when you get back, more crazy expeditions on your narrowboat?

I don't know, I said. It's too soon to say. I am still on painkillers and there is poor Jess. But the main thing is I really can't think of anything I want now out of life that I haven't got or haven't done, including adventures. I know it's a negative view and arrogant even and I haven't done that much really and the world is a big and marvellous place and maybe it's the shingles and there is so much out there but at the moment I am saying to myself I'm seventy-five and I have had my share.

Why did you do your adventuring?

We wanted to show that old guys can have adventures, same as when we all proved that you could become an athlete in your forties or even your seventies. We wanted to push the omelette and change the way people think. In the process we had the best and most successful years of our lives, and I hope we showed some others the way.

But what's next?

Dave, I bet when Ulysses arrived at Ithaca he felt he would just like a bloody good sit-down.

He went off again, said Monica, with his old mates.

> *Death closes all: but something ere the end,*
> *Some work of noble note, may yet be done,*
> *Not unbecoming men who strove with Gods.*

We didn't strive with Gods, I said.

No, but we strove with the Thames, and the Severn, and the Channel, and the Rhône, and the Albemarle Sound, and Lake Okeechobee. I bet those places would have had Gods in the old days.

The Severn has got a God, said Rose. She is called Sabrina. I saw her statue in Shrewsbury.

When I was in business, I said, I thought it would be marvellous if our telephonist could say – *Mr Darlington cannot speak to you today, he is navigating the drains.*

The Norfolk drains, said Monica. Yes there are quite a few places even in the UK that we have not navigated yet.

You have written a Narrow Dog Trilogy, said Rose. Every writer should have an ilogy, and you've got an ilogy. Terry and his ilogy.

That may be enough, I said. Terry and his ilogy.

There should be something ere the end, said Monica – some work of noble note.

The dogs look so happy, said Dave. They know what they want – they are home and that's fine and they don't want you to go anywhere.

On the floor Jim and Jess were trying to push both their bodies into the same bag of scratchings.

Jim looked up and grinned and Jess farted.

*News of the* PM2 *and its crew can be found at www.narrowdog.com.*

# NOTES

A reader with nothing worthwhile to do could seek entertainment in some of the sources mentioned. (The poem by Lord John Wilmot is rude, so you won't want to bother with that one.)

Some of these notes may appear obvious, but bear in mind that the book will be read in savage lands, where people may not have heard of Kathy Kirby.

## Chapter One – Stone

*Jim Francis is Dead* – poem by Terry Darlington.

*Parable of the talents* – Matthew 25. All biblical references are to the King James Version, and I should think so too.

*Horseman, pass by.* Inscription on gravestone of W. B. Yeats.

*I fled Him, down the labyrinthine ways/ Of my own mind* – poem by Francis Thompson, 'The Hound of Heaven'.

*Ancient person of my heart* – poem by Lord John Wilmot, 'A Song of a Young Lady to Her Ancient Lover'.

*Consummatum est* – John 24.

*Go, litel bok* – poem by Geoffrey Chaucer, *Troilus and Criseyde*, V.

*Othello's occupation's gone* – *Othello*, IV. iii.

*Wreck upon the sand . . . one thing worse* – song by Alfred Williams, 'A Man Without A Woman (Silver Dollar)'.

*Young Hearts Run Free* – song by Candi Staton.

*What spires, what farms?* – poem by A. E. Housman, 'Into My Heart an Air that Kills'.

*The Grimpen Mire* – deadly bog in *The Hound of the Baskervilles* by Arthur Conan Doyle.

*Creature from the Black Lagoon* – film directed by Jack Arnold, written by Arthur A. Ross and Harry Essex.

*They fle from me that sometyme did me seke* – poem by Sir Thomas Wyatt.

*To every thing there is a season* – Ecclesiastes 3.

*To die, to sleep* – *Hamlet*, III. i.

*Nothing left remarkable* – *Antony and Cleopatra*, IV. xv.

*All her bright golden hair* – poem by Oscar Wilde, 'Requiescat'.

*Moving finger* – poem by Edward FitzGerald, 'The Rubáiyát of Omar Khayyám'.

*Gone with the Wind* country – Margaret Mitchell's novel is set in South Carolina.

# Chapter Two – The Mersey and Liverpool

*I never loved the* Phyllis May – sentiments by Jim the Whippet, words by Terry Darlington.

*Russell Newbery* – engines developed in the twenties and thirties.

*Jam 'Ole Run* – until 1970 pairs of narrowboats would travel from Atherstone to Brentford carrying coal for the Kearley and Tonge jam factory. The trade ceased when two crew members and a journalist died of boredom while talking about it.

*May there be no moaning* – poem by Alfred Lord Tennyson, 'Crossing the Bar'.

*Tits Magee* – see *Narrow Dog to Indian River*.

*Cutty wrens* – *cutty* is a corruption of *petit* and is Pembrokeshire dialect (like *elligug* for guillemot and *laverack* for mole).

*Drowsed with the fume of poppies* – poem by John Keats, 'Ode to Autumn'.

*Divinely formed and fair* – poem by Cecil Day Lewis, 'The Unwanted'.

*Zounds* – the oath is more than five hundred years old, as is Odds Boddikins (God's little body).

*There rain'd a ghastly dew* – poem by Alfred Lord Tennyson, 'Locksley Hall'. (Blood falling from fighting airships.)

*Inferno 1940* – paperback by Vernon Scott. Western Telegraph publications.

*Strange images of death* – Macbeth, I. iii.

*Have you got your shorts on the right way round?* – *Narrow Dog to Indian River*.

*Over the mirrors* – poem by Thomas Hardy, 'The Convergence of the Twain'.

*Yours* – song by Gonzalo Roig and Jack Sherr.

*The White Cliffs Of Dover* – song by Walter Kent and Nat Burton.

*Jane* – *Daily Mirror* strip cartoon.

*Big Eggo, Corky the Cat* – front-page characters in *Beano* and *Dandy* comics. (Big Eggo was an ostrich.)

*Of paradise, so late their happy seat* – Milton, *Paradise Lost*, VII.

# Chapter Three – Liverpool and the Rufford Branch

*The kingdom of the mad* – poem by Robert Lowell, 'Man and Wife'.

*Dr Morelle* – I made this extract up.

*Dear dead days* – song by James Lynam Molloy, 'Love's Old Sweet Song'.

*'Tis all a Chequer-board of Nights and Days* – poem by Edward FitzGerald, 'The Rubáiyát of Omar Khayyám'.

*I saw Eternity the other night* – poem by Henry Vaughan, 'The World'.

*Blood on the leaves* – from 'Strange Fruit', poem about Southern lynchings by Abel Meeropol, music by Sonny White with Billie Holiday. 'A prime piece of musical propaganda' – attack by *Time* magazine, 1939. 'Song of the century' – *Time*, 1999.

*O how amiable* – Psalm 84.

*Roger* – if you are out there do get in touch. Tony and I would love to see you again and I might be able to fix a gig at a harvest festival in Penkridge.

*Yukkers* – Pembrokeshire schoolboy slang for unfledged birds.

*Lord, send me some comfort*; *Gulls' wings*; *I hang from a rope of light* – verses by Terry Darlington.

*Roswell High* – US television series, 1999–2002.

*A placeman* – from Ben Pimlott's biography *Hugh Dalton* – 'The County Durham educational system was highly politicised, with key appointments in the hands of the Labour party machine . . . when you saw a teacher in the party you should beware. He was there until he got his headship, and then that was all you ever saw of him.'

*State scholarship* – national award based on papers outside A-level syllabus – carried a rather bigger grant. Monica got one too. In the fifties few went to university and it was normal to have a grant which covered nearly all the cost.

*Heidi* – 1880 novel for children by Johanna Spyri. BBC Wales was strong in drama; attracted large audiences.

*When I go mad* – translation by Terry Darlington.

Jack Nicholson and Nurse Ratched – in the film *One Flew Over the Cuckoo's Nest,* Jack Nicholson played Randle McMurphy, a mental patient, and Louise Fletcher the power-hungry ward sister.

*Post-War Credits* – refunds of wartime taxation finally repaid in 1973.

*Deep insulin treatment* – now discredited.

*Between my teeth* – verse by Terry Darlington.

*Electro-convulsive therapy* – still widely used.

*Co-op dividend* – traditional source of funds as last resort. Our fund held twelve pounds.

*Wide World* – adventure magazine, published from 1898 to 1965.

# Chapter Four – The Ribble and the Lancaster Canal

*A-wop-bop-a-loo-bop* – 'Tutti Frutti', song by Little Richard.

*Patrick Garland* – actor, writer, director.

*Anthony Page* – stage and film director.

*I could not get the ring/I coupled with your mate* – *The Changeling*, play by Thomas Middleton and William Rowley, III. iv and V. iii.

*Isis* – the university magazine.

*Newdigate Prize, Hawthornden Prize* – winners Stuart Evans and Dom Moraes.

*Professor Tolkien* – J. R. R. Tolkien, author of *The Lord of the Rings*.

*Allen Ginsberg* – poet, leader of the beat movement.

*W. H. Auden* – leading poet of the thirties.

*Henry Hall* – famous mid-century UK bandleader. His introductory catchphrase was 'This *is* Henry Hall speaking.'

*Anne Rogers* – actress, singer. Original lead in *The Boy Friend*.

*Mike Hall* – actor, sometime MC at the Players Theatre, Charing Cross.

*Clemence Dane* – Winifred Ashton, playwright and novelist. *A Bill of Divorcement*, screenplay for *Anna Karenina*.

*Let me count the ways?* – poem by Elizabeth Barrett Browning, *Sonnets from the Portuguese*, No. 43.

*Through a glass, darkly* – 1 Corinthians XIII.

*Battalions* – *Hamlet*, IV. v. 'When sorrows come, they come not single spies,/ But in battalions'.

*Smokehouse* – Port of Lancaster Smokehouse, Glasson Dock.

*If I could snare* – poem by Terry Darlington, after Edmund Waller's 'Go, Lovely Rose'.

*Allen key* or hex key – one of those thin L-shaped things that you stick into the end of a special screw and turn.

*In a nook* – poem by J. M. Synge, 'In May'.

*Charles Baudelaire* – I attracted Monica's attention the night I met her by talking about the nineteenth-century poet – she was about to take her finals.

## Chapter Five – The Lancaster Canal

*The smylere with the knyf* – Chaucer, 'The Knight's Tale'.

*While meeting in the sales office* – poem by Terry Darlington.

*The Dam Busters* – 1954 film with Michael Redgrave as Barnes Wallis, the inventor of the bouncing bomb.

*Gentlemen, the Board is most concerned* – poem by Terry Darlington.

*Miss Joan Hunter Dunn* – poem by John Betjeman, 'A Subaltern's Love Song'.

*Surly bonds of earth* – poem by John Gillespie Magee, 'High Flight'.

*Pamela Tiffin* – film star – *Harper, Viva Max!*

*Robin Douglas-Home* – socialite.

*Petula Clark* – pop singer – 'Downtown', 'Don't Sleep in the Subway'.

*Kathy Kirby* – pop singer – 'Secret Love', 'Let Me Go, Lover'.

*Janette Scott* – film star – *School for Scoundrels, The Day of the Triffids.*

*Claudia Cardinale* – film star – *The Pink Panther, Fitzcarraldo.*

*Ghosts on the sand* – Nick Broomfield's TV film *Ghosts* tells the story of the death of twenty-three Chinese picking cockles in Morecambe Bay. Abuse of workers from overseas was evident for years, and government regulatory agencies failed to act.

*Eric Gill* – sculptor, typeface designer.

## Chapter Six – The Leeds and Liverpool

*Little Dutch liner* – 15,000 tons. The modern Holland America *Ryndam* is 55,000 tons.

*Mad July gale* – poem by John Masefield, 'Cargoes'.

*Off-peak Off-beat* – article in *Punch* by Terry Darlington under the name Ian George, 1965.

*It is a truth* – opening of *Pride and Prejudice* by Jane Austen.

*Moon River* – song by Henry Mancini.

*When the Good Lord made the Canadian woods* – poem by Terry Darlington.

*CFRB* – Toronto's oldest broadcaster.

*It was a face which darkness could kill* – poem by Lawrence Ferlinghetti from *Pictures of the Gone World*, in the collection *A Coney Island of the Mind*. The latter has a million copies in print.

*Beat poets and novelists* – Jack Kerouac, *On the Road*; William Burroughs, *The Naked Lunch*; Ken Kesey, *One Flew Over the Cuckoo's Nest*; Allen Ginsberg, 'Howl'.

*Super Region Four*, Fall 1965 – editor David Morton.

*OZ* – psychedelic hippy magazine, London, 1967–73. Subject of obscenity trial.

*Scott McKenzie* – song 'San Francisco (Be Sure To Wear Some Flowers In Your Hair)' by John Phillips.

*Broken Arrow* – fifties western with James Stewart.

*Esther Williams* autobiography – *Million Dollar Mermaid*.

*Many mansions* – 'in my Father's house are many mansions', John 24.

*It Happened In Monterey* – song by Mabel Wayne and Billy Rose.

*Howard Marks* – 'Mr Nice'. Seven years in American prison for smuggling cannabis. Rector of Glasgow Caledonian University.

*Simon Rodia/Funny little guy* – poem by Terry Darlington.

*The Watts Towers* – built over thirty years by Simon Rodia (d. 1965). Local authorities and neighbours tried to destroy them. Now a National Historic Monument.

## Chapter Seven – Aston

*Why, this is hell* – Christopher Marlowe, *Doctor Faustus,* I. iii.

*Old Joe Guyer* – a harmless old man. Children would sing this song.

*A seed floats through* – verse by Terry Darlington.

*Flights of angels* – *Hamlet*, V. ii.

*Book about cocktails* – *Classic 1000 Cocktail Recipes* by Robert Cross.

*Brought forth a mouse* – Horace, *parturient montes, nascetur ridiculus mus.*

*Beaker full of the warm south* – poem by John Keats, 'Ode to a Nightingale'.

*But I was desolate* – poem by Ernest Dowson, 'Cynara'.

*I am a fish/I am a rook* – poems by Terry Darlington.

*How I surfed the fields lady* – poem by Terry Darlington.

*Remember with advantages* – *Henry V*, IV iii.

## Chapter Eight – Willington

*A little academe* – *Love's Labour's Lost*, I. i.

*These two emparadised* – Milton, *Paradise Lost*, IV.

*Vanity of vanities* – Ecclesiastes 1.

*Stafford Hospital* – 'a gross and terrible breach of trust' – Sir Bruce Keogh, medical director of the NHS, 17 March 2009.

*Dans le vieux parc* – poem by Paul Verlaine, 'Colloque Sentimentale'. 'In the old park lonely and frozen, two shapes have just passed'. I changed park to station.

*Plan B* arts society organized monthly readings 1972–6. Poets included Patricia Beer, Martin Booth, Edwin Brock, Pete Brown, David Calcutt, David Chaloner, Jeni Couzyn, Carol Ann Duffy, Paul Gater, Lee Harwood, Philip Higson, John Hind, Libby Houston, Enos Lovatt, Norman MacCaig, Barry MacSweeney, Edwin Morgan, Peter Philpott, Tom Pickard, Peter Porter, Omar Pound, Bill Symondson, Charles Tomlinson, W. Price Turner, Nigel Walker, and others mentioned in text.

*Roger McGough* – member of pop group The Scaffold as well as a poet.

*Three great twentieth-century poets* – he was referring to William Butler Yeats, Dylan Thomas and himself.

*His little son dying* – poem by Jon Silkin, 'Death of a Son'.

*Carol Ann Duffy* – Poet Laureate, 2009.

*The Bells Of Rhymney* – poem by Idris Davies, music by Pete Seeger.

*Plaisir d'Amour* – song by Jean Paul Égide Martini, 1780.


# Chapter Nine – Shardlow to the Tidal Trent

*Vegemite* – Australian Marmite.

*Shangri-La* – lost city of the Himalayas. I thought I was going to Tibet.

*John of Gaunt* – *Richard II*, II. i.

*Stewed in corruption* – *Hamlet*, III. iv.

*I fled Him, down the nights* – poem by Francis Thompson, 'The Hound of Heaven'.

*Leslie Watson* – Now a physiotherapist. Ran 206 marathons and won 68.

*Ninja* – Japanese spies and assassins.

*Two hours and fifty-eight minutes* – in 1896 I would have won the Olympic Marathon, but this was 1978.

## Chapter Ten – North to York

*No Name restaurant* – I have seen mixed reviews now.

*Bill Rodgers* – 58 marathons at the highest international level, won 22, many long-distance records.

*Stone Master Marathoners* – founded 1978 by Terry Darlington, Bill Couldrey and Tom Chitty: www.stonemm.co.uk.

*Weave a circle* – poem by Samuel Taylor Coleridge, 'Kubla Khan'.

*Chris Brasher* – Olympic Gold Medal steeplechaser, later director of the London Marathon.

*Rosetta Stone* – ancient Egyptian stone carved in three languages allowing deciphering of hieroglyphics.

*A book about it all* – *Run for Your Life*, Columbus Books, 1985.

*Music dwells lingering* – poem by William Wordsworth, 'Inside of King's College Chapel, Cambridge'.

*Mama Cass, Michelle Phillips* – the US vocal quartet The Mamas and the Papas.

*Calder and Hebble handspike* – shaped wooden stake to open locks on the Calder and Hebble Canal.


## Chapter Eleven – Dewsbury

*Oil and Gas in the Soviet Union* – Dr J. Daniel Park, Research Associates, 1978.

*Lord King* – chairman, British Airways, 1981–93.

*Colin* – Colin Marshall, managing director, British Airways, 1983–2004.

*Highlife* – fusion of African and American sounds.

*Nigerian snail* – delicacy, widely farmed.

*Arturo's* – Houston Street, New York. The restaurant lives on.

*Galleria, Duomo* – the great arcades and the cathedral.

*Men have died from time to time* – *As You Like It*, IV. i.

*Scottish Development Agency* – 1975–91. Aimed to encourage Scottish industry.

*A worldwide study* – *Opportunities for the Scottish Wool Textiles and Knitwear Industries* – published by Scottish Development Agency, 1980.

*Willie Nelson* – country singer and songwriter – 'Crazy', 'Funny How Time Slips Away'.

*James Dean* – film star – *East of Eden, Rebel Without a Cause*.

*Borobudur* – demonstrates in stone the route to perfection.

*The Guinness Scandal* – chief executive Ernest Saunders was sentenced to five years in 1990 for false accounting, conspiracy and theft, for inflating the Guinness share price to allow the takeover of Distillers. Sentence reduced on appeal.

*Charles Dunstone* – founder and chief executive of Carphone Warehouse.

*Last night I dreamt I went to Manderley again* – first sentence of *Rebecca*, novel by Daphne du Maurier.

*Flower park* – Stonefield Park – two acres very near our home, maintained by Stafford Council.

*Andrew Davies* – prolific adapter of classics for TV. Best known for *Pride and Prejudice*, 1995.

*Books on how to write* – My favourites are *The First Five Pages*, by Noah Lukeman, and *How to Tell a Story*, by Peter Rubie and Gary Provost.

*The Literary Consultancy* – editorial advice, particularly for new writers.

*Annette Green Authors' Agency* – my agents, recommended by the Literary Consultancy. David Smith suggested this book, combining travel with memoirs.

## Chapter Twelve – The Pennines

*ITV Waterworld* – a half-hour weekly prime-time programme in the Midlands in the noughties, reaching audiences of over a million.

*Carcassonne* was featured in 9 episodes in 2004–5. There was later a seven-minute feature on *Indian River*.

*He won a prize* – best feature programme of the year in ITV annual awards.

*Thunderbirds* – mid-sixties marionette series by Gerry and Sylvia Anderson.

*Kate Silverton and Dermot Murnaghan* – broadcasters, presenters of BBC show *Breakfast*.

*Libby Purves* – broadcaster, presenter of Radio 4's *Midweek*, author of *One Summer's Grace*, the story of sailing round the UK with her family.

*Sandi Toksvig* – broadcaster, presenter of Radio 4's travel programme *Excess Baggage*.

*Joanna Lumley* – actress, comedienne, beauty, campaigner.

*Website* – *www.narrowdog.com*.

*Bill Bryson* – travel writer published by Transworld.

*Andy McNab* – military writer published by Transworld.

*Standedge Tunnel* – opened 1811. Reopened 2001. Longest (5000 metres) canal tunnel in UK, and deepest underground (200 metres) and highest above sea level (600 metres).

*Harecastle Tunnel* – opened 1777. 2700 metres long.

*And what shoulder and what art* – poem by William Blake, 'The Tyger'.

*Jive Bunny* – an estate agent in Rotherham who added drum and bass to well-known music in the eighties and sold it to people whose understanding was impaired.

*John Prescott* – British Deputy Prime Minister, 1997–2007.

*If you seek a monument – si monumentum requiris, circumspice* – inscription on the tomb of Christopher Wren in St Paul's.

*Kennet and Avon Canal* – 87 miles, 100 locks, reopened 1990.

## Chapter Thirteen – Stone

*In a somer seson* – poem by William Langland, 'Piers Plowman'.

*The land of lost content* – poem by A. E. Housman, 'Into My Heart an Air That Kills'.

*(Write it!)* – poem by Elizabeth Bishop, 'One Art'.

*The lone and level sands* – poem by Percy Bysshe Shelley, 'Ozymandias'.

*Australia* – film by Baz Luhrmann.

*The castle of Mordor* – *The Lord of the Rings* by J. R. R. Tolkien.

*You work your side of the street* – Steve McQueen to Robert Vaughn in the film *Bullitt*.

*She breaks my heart* – Jess lost her leg two months later. She is happy and active and Monica and I are expected to recover over time.

*Death closes all* – poem by Tennyson, 'Ulysses'.

**Terry Darlington** was an athlete and a businessman before becoming a writer. Like many Welshmen, he is ill at ease with practical matters and known to linger in public houses. He likes boating, but is not very good at it.

**Monica Darlington** was beauty queen of Brecon and Radnor, has a first-class degree, has run thirty marathons, and leaps tall buildings with a single bound. She quite likes boating.

**Jim** is sprung from a long line of whippets with ridiculous names. He is cowardly, thieving and disrespectful, and hates boating.

**Jess** is a rescue whippet. She is affectionate but three parts wild. She really really hates boating.